LOT VIEWING
Heritage Auction Galleries, 17th Floor
3500 Maple Avenue • Dallas, Texas 75219

Wednesday, July 14 – Thursday, July 15, 2010
by appointment

View Lots Online at HA.com/7025

LIVE FLOOR BIDDING
Bid in person during the floor sessions.

LIVE TELEPHONE BIDDING *(floor sessions only)*
Phone bidding must be arranged on or before
Thursday, July 15, 2010, by 12:00 PM CT.
Client Service: 866-835-3243.

HERITAGE Live!™ BIDDING
Bid live from your location, anywhere in the world,
during the Auction using our HERITAGE Live!™ program
at HA.com/Live

INTERNET BIDDING
Internet absentee bidding ends at 10:00 PM CT
the evening before each session. HA.com/7025

FAX BIDDING
Fax bids must be received on or before Thursday,
July 15, 2010, by 12:00 PM CT. Fax: 214-409-1425

MAIL BIDDING
Mail bids must be received on or before
Thursday, July 15, 2010.

*Please see "Choose Your Bidding Method" in the back of this
catalog for specific details about each of these bidding methods.*

LIVE AUCTION
SIGNATURE® FLOOR SESSIONS 1-3
(Floor, Telephone, HERITAGE Live!,™ Internet, Fax, and Mail)

Heritage Auction Galleries, 1st Floor Auction Room
3500 Maple Avenue • Dallas, Texas 75219

SESSION 1
Friday, July 16, 2010 • 1:00 PM CT • Lots 83001–83339

SESSION 2
Friday, July 16, 2010 • 5:00 PM CT • Lots 83340–83718

SESSION 3
Saturday, July 17, 2010 • 11:00 AM CT • Lots 83719–84026

NON FLOOR/NON PHONE BIDDING SESSION 4
(HERITAGE Live!,™ Internet, Fax, and Mail only)

SESSION 4
Saturday, July 17, 2010 • 3:00 PM CT • Lots 84027-84380

AUCTION RESULTS
Immediately available at HA.com/7025

LOT SETTLEMENT AND PICK-UP
Available immediately following each floor session or
weekdays 9:00 AM – 5:00 PM CT by appointment only.

Extended Payment Terms available. See details in the back of this catalog.

*Lots are sold at an approximate rate of 100 lots per hour, but it
is not uncommon to sell 125 lots or 150 lots in any given hour.*

This auction is subject to a 19.5% Buyer's Premium.

THIS AUCTION IS PRESENTED AND CATALOGED BY HERITAGE AUCTIONS, INC.

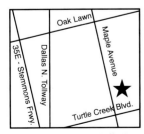

Heritage Auction Galleries

HERITAGE HA.com
Auction Galleries

3500 Maple Avenue, 17th Floor • Dallas, TX 75219
Design District Annex • 1518 Slocum Street • Dallas, TX 75207
Beverly Hills Office • 9478 W. Olympic Blvd., First Floor • Beverly Hills, CA 90212
214.528.3500 | 800.872.6467 | 214.409.1425 (fax)
Direct Client Service Line: Toll Free 1.866.835.3243 • Email: Bid@HA.com

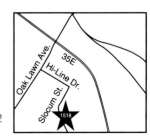

Heritage Design District Annex

TX Auctioneer licenses: Samuel Foose 11727; Robert Korver 13754; Scott Peterson 13256; Bob Merrill 13408; Mike Sadler 16129; Andrea Voss 16406; Jacob Walker 16413; Charlie
Mead 16418; Eric Thomas 16421; Shaunda Fry 16448; Marsha Dixey 16493; Tim Rigdon 16519; Cori Mikeals 16582; Stewart Huckaby 16590; Wayne Shoemaker 16600; Chris
Dykstra 16601; Teia Baber 16624; Peter Wiggins 16635. Associates under sponsorship of Andrea Voss 16406: Leo Frese 7985; Paul Minshull 16591; Ed Beardsley 16632.

DIRECTORY FOR DEPARTMENT SPECIALISTS AND SERVICES

COINS & CURRENCY

COINS – UNITED STATES
HA.com/Coins

Leo Frese, Ext. 1294
Leo@HA.com
David Mayfield, Ext. 1277
DavidM@HA.com
Jessica Aylmer, Ext. 1706
JessicaA@HA.com
Diedre Buchmoyer, Ext. 1794
DiedreB@HA.com
Win Callender, Ext. 1415
WinC@HA.com
Katherine Crippe, Ext. 1389
KK@HA.com
Chris Dykstra, Ext. 1380
ChrisD@HA.com
Sam Foose, Ext. 1227
SamF@HA.com
Jason Friedman, Ext. 1582
JasonF@HA.com
Shaunda Fry, Ext. 1159
ShaundaF@HA.com
Jim Jelinski, Ext. 1257
JimJ@HA.com
Bob Marino, Ext. 1374
BobMarino@HA.com
Mike Sadler, Ext. 1332
MikeS@HA.com
Beau Streicher, Ext. 1645
BeauS@HA.com

RARE CURRENCY
HA.com/Currency

Len Glazer, Ext. 1390
Len@HA.com
Allen Mincho, Ext. 1327
Allen@HA.com
Dustin Johnston, Ext. 1302
Dustin@HA.com
Michael Moczalla, Ext. 1481
MichaelM@HA.com
Jason Friedman, Ext. 1582
JasonF@HA.com

WORLD & ANCIENT COINS
HA.com/WorldCoins

Cristiano Bierrenbach, Ext. 1661
CrisB@HA.com
Warren Tucker, Ext. 1287
WTucker@HA.com
David Michaels, Ext. 1606
DMichaels@HA.com
Scott Cordry, Ext. 1369
ScottC@HA.com

COMICS & COMIC ART
HA.com/Comics

Ed Jaster, Ext. 1288
EdJ@HA.com
Lon Allen, Ext. 1261
LonA@HA.com
Barry Sandoval, Ext. 1377
BarryS@HA.com
Todd Hignite, Ext. 1790
ToddH@HA.com

FINE ART

AMERICAN & EUROPEAN PAINTINGS & SCULPTURE
HA.com/FineArt

Ed Jaster, Ext. 1288
EdJ@HA.com
Marianne Berardi, Ph.D., Ext. 1506
MarianneB@HA.com
Ariana Hartsock, Ext. 1283
ArianaH@HA.com

ART OF THE AMERICAN WEST
HA.com/WesternArt

Michael Duty, Ext. 1712
MichaelD@HA.com

FURNITURE & DECORATIVE ART
HA.com/Decorative

Tim Rigdon, Ext. 1119
TimR@HA.com
Karen Rigdon, Ext. 1723
KarenR@HA.com
Nicholas Dawes, Ext. 1605
NickD@HA.com

ILLUSTRATION ART
HA.com/Illustration
Ed Jaster, Ext. 1288
EdJ@HA.com
Todd Hignite, Ext. 1790
ToddH@HA.com

MODERN & CONTEMPORARY ART
HA.com/Modern
Frank Hettig, Ext. 1157
FrankH@HA.com

SILVER & VERTU
HA.com/Silver
Tim Rigdon, Ext. 1119
TimR@HA.com
Karen Rigdon, Ext. 1723
KarenR@HA.com

TEXAS ART
HA.com/TexasArt
Atlee Phillips, Ext. 1786
AtleeP@HA.com

20TH-CENTURY DESIGN
HA.com/Design
Tim Rigdon, Ext. 1119
TimR@HA.com
Karen Rigdon, Ext. 1723
KarenR@HA.com
Nicholas Dawes, Ext. 1605
NickD@HA.com

VINTAGE & CONTEMPORARY PHOTOGRAPHY
HA.com/ArtPhotography
Ed Jaster, Ext. 1288
EdJ@HA.com
Kelly Jones, Ext. 1166
KellyJ@HA.com

HISTORICAL

AMERICAN INDIAN ART
HA.com/AmericanIndian
Delia Sullivan, Ext. 1343
DeliaS@HA.com

AMERICANA & POLITICAL
HA.com/Historical
Tom Slater, Ext. 1441
TomS@HA.com
John Hickey, Ext. 1264
JohnH@HA.com
Michael Riley, Ext. 1467
MichaelR@HA.com

CIVIL WAR AND ARMS & MILITARIA
HA.com/CivilWar
Dennis Lowe, Ext. 1182
DennisL@HA.com

HISTORICAL MANUSCRIPTS
HA.com/Manuscripts
Sandra Palomino, Ext. 1107
SandraP@HA.com

RARE BOOKS
HA.com/Books
James Gannon, Ext. 1609
JamesG@HA.com
Joe Fay, Ext. 1544
JoeF@HA.com

SPACE EXPLORATION
HA.com/Space
John Hickey, Ext. 1264
JohnH@HA.com
Michael Riley, Ext. 1467
MichaelR@HA.com

TEXANA
HA.com/Historical
Sandra Palomino, Ext. 1107
SandraP@HA.com

JEWELRY & TIMEPIECES

FINE JEWELRY
HA.com/Jewelry
Jill Burgum, Ext. 1697
JillB@HA.com

WATCHES & FINE TIMEPIECES
HA.com/Timepieces
Jim Wolf, Ext. 1659
JWolf@HA.com

MUSIC & ENTERTAINMENT MEMORABILIA
HA.com/Entertainment
Doug Norwine, Ext. 1452
DougN@HA.com
John Hickey, Ext. 1264
JohnH@HA.com
Garry Shrum, Ext. 1585
GarryS@HA.com

NATURAL HISTORY
HA.com/NaturalHistory
David Herskowitz, Ext. 1610
DavidH@HA.com

RARE STAMPS
HA.com/Stamps
Steven Crippe, Ext. 1777
StevenC@HA.com

SPORTS COLLECTIBLES
HA.com/Sports

Chris Ivy, Ext. 1319
CIvy@HA.com
Peter Calderon, Ext. 1789
PeterC@HA.com
Mike Gutierrez, Ext. 1183
MikeG@HA.com
Lee Iskowitz, Ext. 1601
LeeI@HA.com
Mark Jordan, Ext. 1187
MarkJ@HA.com
Chris Nerat, Ext. 1615
ChrisN@HA.com
Jonathan Scheier, Ext. 1314
JonathanS@HA.com

VINTAGE MOVIE POSTERS
HA.com/MoviePosters

Grey Smith, Ext. 1367
GreySm@HA.com
Bruce Carteron, Ext. 1551
BruceC@HA.com

TRUSTS & ESTATES & APPRAISAL SERVICES
HA.com/Estates
Mark Prendergast, Ext. 1632
MPrendergast@HA.com
HA.com/Appraisals
Meredith Meuwly, Ext. 1631
MeredithM@HA.com

CORPORATE & INSTITUTIONAL COLLECTIONS/VENTURES
Jared Green, Ext. 1279
Jared@HA.com

CREDIT DEPARTMENT
Marti Korver, Ext. 1248
Marti@HA.com
Eric Thomas, Ext. 1241
EricT@HA.com

MEDIA & PUBLIC RELATIONS
Noah Fleisher, Ext. 1143
NoahF@HA.com

BEVERLY HILLS OFFICE
9478 W. Olympic Blvd., First Floor
Beverly Hills, CA 90212

Leo Frese, Ext. 1294
Leo@HA.com
Michael Moline, Ext. 1361
MMoline@HA.com
Shaunda Fry, Ext. 1159
ShaundaF@HA.com
Carolyn Mani , Ext. 1677
CarolynM@HA.com

HOUSTON OFFICE
Mark Prendergast, Ext. 1632
MPrendergast@HA.com

NEW YORK OFFICE
Tiffany Dubin, Ext. 1673
TiffanyD@HA.com
Nick Dawes, Ext. 1605
NickD@HA.com

CORPORATE OFFICERS
R. Steven Ivy, Co-Chairman
James L. Halperin, Co-Chairman
Gregory J. Rohan, President
Paul Minshull, Chief Operating Officer
Todd Imhof, Executive Vice President
Leo Frese, Managing Director, Beverly Hills

Dear Fellow Collectors,

Let me start by thanking all of the bidders, buyers and consignors to our last auction for making it such an outstanding success. I hope you like our newest selection and that many items tempt your collecting interests.

We have a strong selection here and hope you will look through the great offering of early sound posters which include *Bulldog Drummond* (1929), *Anna Christie* (1930), *The 13th Chair* (1929), *Welcome Danger* (1930), *Hollywood Revue*, *Dynamite* and many more from those transition years of silent cinema to sound.

Also included are some wonderful Golden Age one sheets which include Bette Davis in *Golden Arrow*, Errol Flynn in *Adventures of Robin Hood*, James Cagney and Dick Powell in *Footlight Parade*, Clara Bow in *Hula*, William Powell in *Private Detective 62*, Tyrone Power in *Jesse James*, Charles Laughton in *Rembrandt*, Gary Cooper in *Beau Geste*, William Boyd in the very rare *Hop-A-Long Cassidy* and many, many more.

Check out our extraordinary offering in horror and science fiction. So many titles and so many different formats are offered! There is a beautiful insert to *The Bride of Frankenstein* and a gorgeous copy of the one sheet to Val Lewton's *Cat People*? Take a look at the rare and beautiful 40" X 60" poster to *It Came From Outer Space* or the beautiful Swedish poster to *Things to Come*.

Other highlights include a poster to one of the rarest of Hitchcock films, an Australian daybill to *Blackmail* (1929) and many other treasured Hitchcock posters, a wonderful selection of early Disney one sheets, a group of rare and early John Wayne lobby cards and one sheets, and many more.

There is also a new development underway in the hobby you might not yet be aware of: CGC or Certified Guaranty Company has undertaken the grading of lobby cards (11"X14") and Midget or Mini Window Cards (8"X14"). We believe this to be a great advancement for the hobby as it will take the owner out of the grading equation and will bring more objective information to the potential buyer of these wonderful cards. After similar certification was introduced to coins, sports cards, comics and currency, new collectors rushed in and prices for those collectibles in high grade skyrocketed. We are offering a nice selection of graded cards in this catalog and I hope you will look them over carefully.

So enough with the introduction; now please feast your eyes upon the treasures that await you!

Happy bidding.

Grey Smith
Director of Vintage Movie Poster Auctions
Heritage Auction Galleries

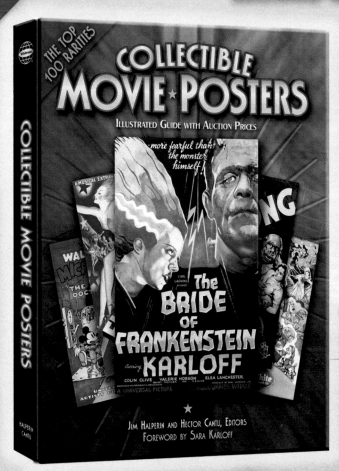

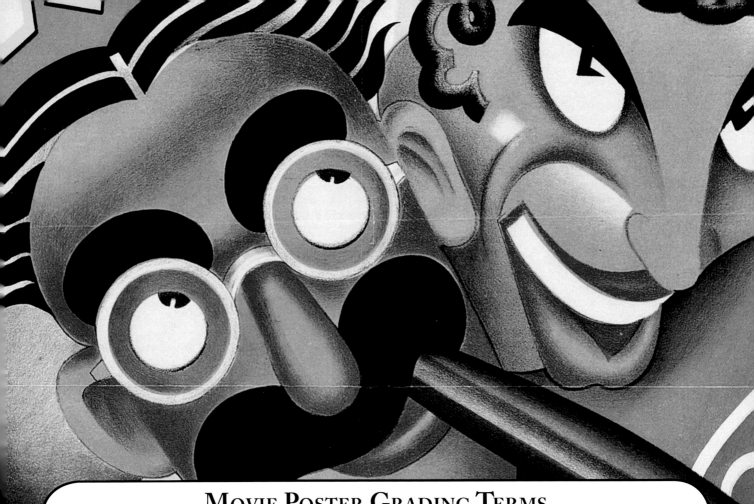

Movie Poster Grading Terms

The following condition terminology is used in this catalog and relates to the conditions of the lots. The Grading is a qualified statement of opinion and subject to Heritage Movie Poster Auctions and Conditions of Sale.

ALL GRADES WITHIN THE CATALOG ARE REPORTED TO BE PRE-RESTORATION GRADES.

MINT…A poster that has never been used or displayed. May show the most minor signs of age. On folded posters may show the most minimal signs of age to the exterior of the poster due to storage. The poster should have no holes nor tears.

NEAR MINT… A very lightly used poster with fresh, saturated colors. In folded posters, may show the most minimal wear at the folds. The poster should have no holes, no tears, and no paper loss.

VERY FINE…A poster with bright color and a clean overall appearance. It may have general signs of use such as slight fold separation and fold wear. It may have pinholes or very minor tears. The poster may be restored and put on linen or paper.

FINE…A poster with good color and, overall, still very presentable appearance. It may have tears, slight paper loss and minor stains. It may have some fold separation. It may have restoration.

VERY GOOD…The poster may be slightly brittle due to age, or it may have some paper loss or staining. The poster may have writing in an unobtrusive place. The poster may have some very slight fading to colors. The poster may have major or minor restoration.

GOOD…An average poster which may have tears, paper loss and general age wear. It may have some color fading, stains, tape or tape stains, and be in need of restoration. It may have significant restoration.

FAIR…Poster may have faded colors, and /or brittle paper, showing significant signs of use. May have tears and paper loss. May have tape, writing, stains in the image area. In great need of restoration.

POOR…A poster that is worn, torn and/or badly damaged. May have staining or dry rot. May be heavily soiled, and/or large pieces missing, and may be cracked or brittle. It would be in dire need of restoration.

VINTAGE MOVIE POSTERS

SESSION ONE

Floor, Telephone, HERITAGE Live!™, Internet, Fax, and Mail Auction #7025
Friday, July 16, 2010 • 1:00 PM CT • Lots 83001-83339

A 19.5% Buyer's Premium Will Be Added To All Lots.

To view full descriptions, enlargeable images and bid online, visit HA.com/7025

83001 **Walt Disney's Academy Award Revue (United Artists, 1937).** One Sheet (27" X 41"). This rare poster was for a compilation of five Academy Award-winning cartoon shorts that were released to coincide with the premiere of Disney's *Snow White and the Seven Dwarfs*. The cartoons included were: *Three Orphan Kittens, The Country Cousin, Flowers and Trees, Three Little Pigs*, and *The Tortoise and the Hare*. Prior to restoration, there were pinholes in the corners, minor border tears, and a stain on the right border. Fine/Very Fine on Linen.
Estimate: $6,000-up Starting Bid: $4,500

83002 Silly Symphony "Bugs in Love" (United Artists, 1932). One Sheet (27" X 41"). Walt Disney made seventy-five Silly Symphony animated shorts during the decade between 1929-1939, including this sweet seven minute tale of partying insects. The two Love Bugs of the group are harassed by a crow, but when the male bug escapes, he gathers the troops of fellow bugs for war. Although this was the last of the Silly Symphonies to be filmed in black and white, this stunning stone litho poster is in glorious color. It has been professionally restored to address fold wear, crossfold separations, a tiny chip in the left border, and one in the right. For all the legions of Disney fans, this very early and rare poster is a highly desirable item. Very Fine- on Linen.
Estimate: $6,000-up Starting Bid: $4,500

83003 The Bears and Bees (United Artists, 1932). One Sheet (27" X 41"). One of the early and most delightful Silly Symphony cartoons. It featured what collectors like to call "The Mickey Bears" in their first starring role. These were two cubs that shared the almost identical facial lines as our beloved mouse. The poster has been laid on paper with some touchup to address edge wear and staining in the borders, fold wear, and a chip in the top right corner. There was also a chip to the left of the bear. Fine on Linen.
Estimate: $6,000-up Starting Bid: $4,500

83004   Pluto's Dream House (RKO, 1940). One Sheet (27" X 41"). Lee Millar voices Pluto and Walt Disney himself portrays Mickey Mouse in this classic Technicolor domestic adventure. When Pluto digs up a magic lamp in the backyard, Mickey is granted three wishes. The first wish is a new doghouse for his faithful pet, which magically gets built by invisible hands working the tools. His next wish is for a bath for Pluto, which turns out to be far more complicated when a radio is broken and the lamp interprets a recipe on a cooking show to be directions from Mickey. Poor Pluto is rolled, and frozen in aspic rather than bathed. Millar was a regular as Pluto's voice until his death in 1941, when Pinto Colvig took over for the next twenty years. Prior to professional restoration, this fun one sheet had tears in the borders, a large chip in the top border, and chips in the bottom corners. It now displays very well and will be a highlight to any early Disney collection. Fine on Linen.
Estimate: $5,000-up Starting Bid: $3,750

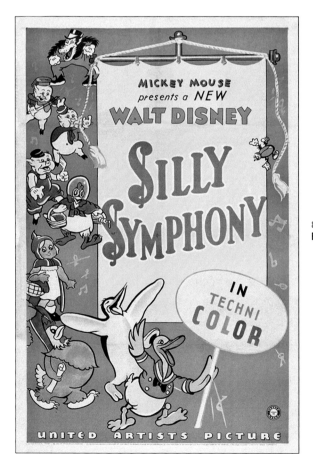

83005   Silly Symphony (United Artists, 1934). Stock One Sheet (27" X 41"). Fine- on Linen.
Estimate: $4,000-up Starting Bid: $2,000

83006   Donald's Cousin Gus (RKO, 1939). One Sheet (27" X 41"). This cartoon was one of Donald Duck's early starring shorts, his eleventh to be exact, and featured what was to be the only appearance of Gustave Goose. The gag of this short has Cousin Gus(Gustave) arriving at Donald's house with a note from Gus' mother advising him not to eat too much! Needless to say, he begins eating poor Donald out of house and home. This is a very rare one sheet and has had the top border restored. There was a slight quarter inch trim to the bottom border too but otherwise the poster was in great condition with the image area completely intact and with strong colors. Fine+ on Linen.
Estimate: $8,000-up Starting Bid: $6,000

83007   Golden Eggs (RKO, 1941). One Sheet (27" X 41"). One of the best Donald Duck shorts of the 1940's, due to great animation and some superb writing by Carl Barks, the most widely read comic book artist of all time. It was Barks that expanded Donald's character to encompass every human emotion possible. This totally fun poster has Donald sneaking into the hen house to steal eggs due to the prices going up because of the war. He's ridiculously costumed with a glove on his head, a feather duster for chicken tail plumage, and a dowdy chicken suit with patches. But it initially fools the Rooster on duty, who falls for this exotic new "hen". One of the best parts of the cartoon was the brilliance of Clarence "Ducky" Nash being able to actually "chicken cluck" in Donald's voice! There were few original issues with only slight foldwear and some small chips in the top horizontal fold and in the top border. Top linenbacking and minimal touchup has this one looking egg-ceptional. Very Fine- on Linen.
Estimate: $5,000-up Starting Bid: $3,750

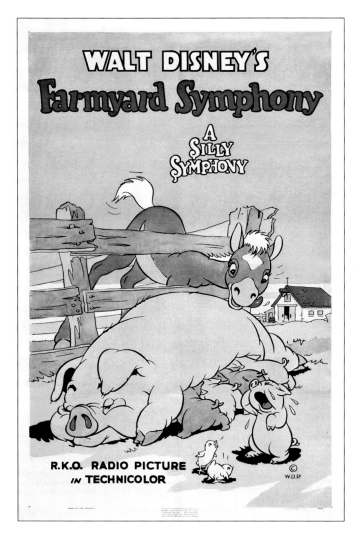

83008   Farmyard Symphony (RKO, 1938). One Sheet (27" X 41"). Fine/Very Fine on Linen.
Estimate: $5,000-up Starting Bid: $3,750

83009   **The Practical Pig (RKO, 1939)** One Sheet (27" X 41"). This was the only Three Little Pigs Silly Symphony credited as a "Three Little Pigs Cartoon". In this outing, "Fifer" and "Fiddler", featured on the poster, are captured by the Big Bad Wolf, while they are out swimming. That's him in the blonde wig playing the harp. It's up to their clever brother, "Practical" (the one who lives in the brick house) to rescue the two little oinkers before they're cooked in pork pie by the three little wolves. There were chips in the three corners, several small holes in the image, and a chip in the right horizontal foldline. The overall poster had a bit of color fade. The poster has been professionally restored, greatly minimizing many of these defects. Very Good/Fine on Linen.
Estimate: $4,000-up Starting Bid: $3,000

83010 **The Three Little Pigs (RKO, R-1947).** One Sheet (27" X 41"). Very Fine on Linen.
Estimate: $1,500-up Starting Bid: $500

83012 **Cat Nap Pluto (RKO, 1948).** One Sheet (27" X 41"). Fine/Very Fine on Linen.
Estimate: $1,500-up Starting Bid: $750

83014 **Melody (RKO, 1953).** One Sheet (27" X 41"). *From the collection of Wade Williams.* Very Fine+.
Estimate: $500-up Starting Bid: $250

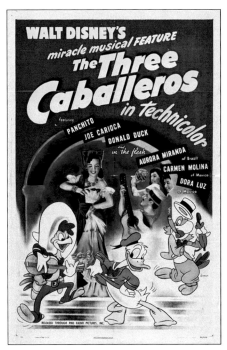

83011 **The Three Caballeros (RKO, 1945).** One Sheet (27" X 41"). Fine/Very Fine.
Estimate: $500-up Starting Bid: $250

83013 **El Gaucho Goofy (RKO, R-1955).** One Sheet (27" X 41"). *From the collection of Wade Williams.* Folded, Very Fine.
Estimate: $500-up Starting Bid: $250

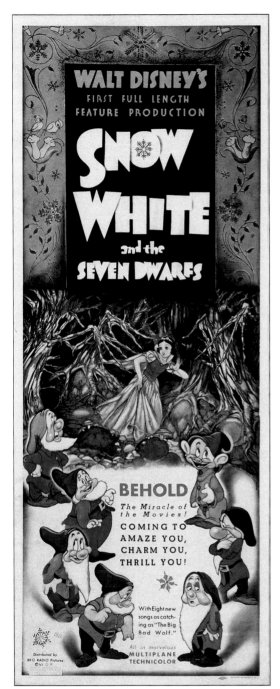

83015   Snow White and the Seven Dwarfs (RKO, 1937). Insert (14" X 36"). We cannot emphasize enough the scarcity of "rolled" posters for top titles of Hollywood's Golden Age. Posters in the common sizes used by theatres were by necessity folded in order to ship, transport, and exhibit. So we are thrilled to offer a poster in this grade for one of the greatest animation triumphs in film history. Disney's gamble of mortgaging his own home against the arguments of his own family to pay production costs has paid off handsomely since the day it was released. His successful producing skills and ability to collect talented artisans would revolutionize the process of animation itself with this film. The beautiful insert offered here features for its center image the famous "Forest Scene" with the art of Disney legend Gustaf Tenggren. His imaginative drawing of Snow White running through the trees with their lifelike animation has thrilled generation after generation. There is a small light stain in the left border, a minor dust shadow in the right border, and a small corner bend on the bottom left. There are light creases in the top credits on the right and in the bottom right corner. If you haven't begun your animation collection yet, here's a rare opportunity to start at the top! Rolled, Very Fine.
Estimate: $6,000-up Starting Bid: $3,000

83016   Snow White and the Seven Dwarfs (RKO, 1937). One Sheet (27" X 41") Style B. Good/Very Good on Linen.
Estimate: $8,000-up Starting Bid: $6,000

83017   Snow White and the Seven Dwarfs (RKO, 1937). French Affiche (23.5" X 31.5"). Fine+ on Linen.
Estimate: $2,000-up Starting Bid: $1,600

83019   Fantasia (RKO, 1940). British Mazda Tabletop Standee (16.5" X 11.25"). Very Fine-.
Estimate: $600-up Starting Bid: $300

83020   Bambi (RKO, R-1948). One Sheet (27" X 41"). Fine/Very Fine.
Estimate: $600-up
Starting Bid: $300

83018   Pinocchio (RKO, 1940). Insert (14" X 36"). Good+ on Paper.
Estimate: $2,500-up Starting Bid: $2,000

83021   Dumbo (RKO, 1947). Post-War Belgian (14" X 19.75"). Folded, Fine.
Estimate: $500-up
Starting Bid: $250

83022 Song of the South (RKO, 1946). Three Sheet (41" X 81"). Very Fine-.
Estimate: $600-up Starting Bid: $300

83024 Alice in Wonderland (RKO, 1951). Belgian (14" X 20"). Folded, Fine+.
Estimate: $500-up Starting Bid: $250

83026 Hatch Up Your Troubles (MGM, 1949). One Sheet (27" X 41"). Very Good+ on Linen.
Estimate: $1,200-up Starting Bid: $1,000

83023 Alice in Wonderland (RKO, 1951). Insert (14" X 36"). Rolled, Very Fine.
Estimate: $600-up Starting Bid: $300

83025 Peter Pan (RKO, 1953). One Sheet (27" X 41"). Very Fine- on Linen.
Estimate: $800-up Starting Bid: $400

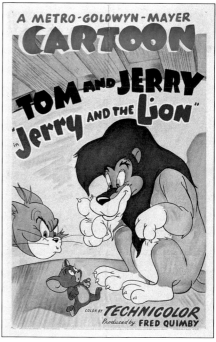

83027 Jerry and the Lion (MGM, 1949). One Sheet (27" X 41"). Fine/Very Fine.
Estimate: $1,200-up Starting Bid: $1,000

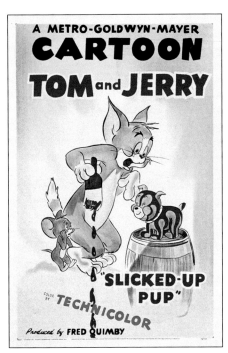

83028   Slicked-Up Pup (MGM, 1950). One Sheet (27" X 41"). Fine/Very Fine on Linen.
Estimate: $800-up Starting Bid: $700

83030   Puttin' On The Dog (MGM, R-1951). One Sheet (27" X 41"). Fine+.
Estimate: $900-up Starting Bid: $800

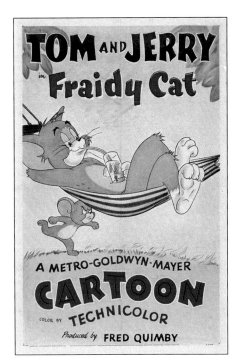

83029   Fraidy Cat (MGM, R-1951). One Sheet (27" X 41"). Fine+.
Estimate: $900-up Starting Bid: $800

83031   The Flying Cat (MGM, 1952). One Sheet (27" X 41"). There is an apocryphal story that instead of the slight cartoon mayhem we see sweetly drawn in this cute poster, that the animators wanted to use the violent gag where a plummeting Tom shears a 100-foot-tall tree in half with his crotch. Producer Fred Quimby said "NO!" We're glad, because with this piece, you get not one but all three of the central characters in the cartoon. The image of the tiny canary huffing and puffing to fly away, carrying Jerry, to escape Tom, is a really funny sight gag. And the ever merry pranksters Hanna and Barbera had Chopin playing underneath the action the whole time Tom was flapping his wings. An excellent copy to begin with, showing only slight fold wear, the poster has been expertly linen-backed to maintain the poster for all time. Very Fine on Linen.
Estimate: $2,700-up
Starting Bid: $2,500

83032　**Cruise Cat** (MGM, 1952). One Sheet (27" X 41"). Very Fine.
Estimate: $1,000-up Starting Bid: $500

83034　**Droopy's Good Deed** (MGM, 1951). One Sheet (27" X 41"). Fine.
Estimate: $1,500-up Starting Bid: $750

83036　**Krazy Kat** (Columbia, 1936). Stock One Sheet (27" X 41"). Fine.
Estimate: $1,200-up Starting Bid: $600

83033　**Jerky Turkey** (MGM, 1945). One Sheet (27" X 41"). Very Fine-.
Estimate: $1,200-up Starting Bid: $600

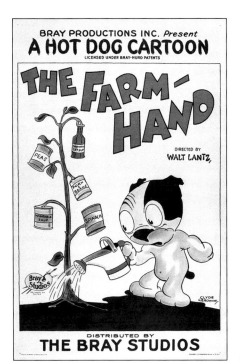

83035　**The Farm-Hand** (Bray Studios, 1927). One Sheet (27" X 41"). Fine/Very Fine on Linen.
Estimate: $1,500-up Starting Bid: $1,000

83037　**Popeye in "King of the Mardi Gras"** (Paramount, 1935). Swedish One Sheet (23.5" X 35"). Very Fine+ on Linen.
Estimate: $500-up Starting Bid: $250

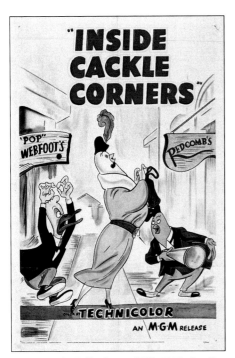

83038　Inside Cackle Corners (MGM, 1951). One Sheet (27"X 41"). Very Fine-.
Estimate: $600-up Starting Bid: $500

83040　Warner Brothers Cartoon Stock (Warner Brothers, 1946). One Sheet (27"X 41"). Fine on Linen.
Estimate: $600-up Starting Bid: $400

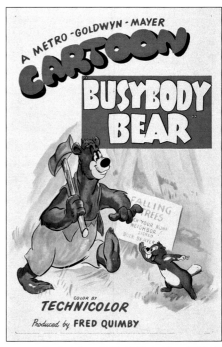

83042　Busybody Bear (MGM, 1952). One Sheet (27"X 41"). Very Fine+.
Estimate: $500-up Starting Bid: $400

83039　Looney Tune Cartoon Stock Poster (Warner Brothers, 1940). One Sheet (27"X 41"). Fine/Very Fine on Linen.
Estimate: $1,000-up Starting Bid: $800

83041　Warner Brothers Cartoon Stock (Warner Brothers, 1948). One Sheet (27"X 41"). Fine-.
Estimate: $500-up Starting Bid: $250

83044 **Bulldog Drummond (United Artists, 1929).** Title Lobby Card (11" X 14"). One of the earliest films in the popular Bulldog Drummond series, this sophisticated entry stars the impeccable Ronald Colman as the war veteran turned sleuth. Paper from this important title is hard to come by, as this is perhaps the best film in the series, and Colman's first talking role, not to mention Bennett's first starring role. With all that pedigree and the beautiful and brilliant color of the artwork, this title card will always be a highly sought item. It has been professionally restored to address the minor issues of pinholes at the bottom, one in the right border, and a small tear in the right side of the image. Fine+.
Estimate: $2,000-up Starting Bid: $1,000

83043 **Bulldog Drummond (United Artists, 1929).** Insert (14" X 36"). One of the most popular of gentleman detectives, Bulldog Drummond was the creation of Herman Cyril McNeile and was featured in his series of novels from the 1920s through the 1950s as well as a string of successful films. The debonair Ronald Colman depicts the WWI veteran-turned detective to perfection, earning an Academy Award nomination and returning once more in 1934's *Bulldog Drummond Strikes Back*. In this early film, Colman comes to the rescue of Phyllis Benton (Joan Bennett) whose uncle is kept hostage at a sanitarium. Nearly dying at the hands of the evil Dr. Lakington (Lawrence Grant), Drummond comes through and defeats the doctor and his henchman Peterson (Montagu Love). This rare and desirable insert has been professionally restored to address pinholes in the corners of the artwork, small tears in the left and right borders, a tiny hole above Colman's name, and a diagonal crease in the lower left side. The poster was rolled but had a razor cut through the poster within Colman's name without any missing paper. In rich, gorgeous colors, this striking poster from a title of which so little paper has been found, will be a highlight to any top collection. Fine+ on Paper.
Estimate: $5,000-up Starting Bid: $2,500

83045 The 13th Chair (MGM, 1929). Rotogravure One Sheet (27" X 41"). Tod Browning's first foray into talking pictures also marks his earliest collaboration with Bela Lugosi, two years before the pair made the horror masterpiece *Dracula*. Inspector Delzante (Lugosi) is called to a British mansion in Calcutta to solve two murders, at first thought to have been committed by the young Helen O'Neill (Leila Hyams) who is the ward of medium Madame LaGrange (Margaret Wycherly). Delzante gets to the bottom of the crimes by re-creating a séance at the location of one murder, and scaring the killer into a confession. Holmes Herbert and Conrad Nagel co-star. Tod Browning had been directing films for sixteen years at this point, with several early successes such as *The Unknown* and *London After Midnight,* which often starred Lon Chaney. Browning creates a dark and moody atmosphere in this thriller and Lugosi is powerful as the mysterious detective. Paper from this early Lugosi picture is scarce and always in high demand, and this gorgeous rotogravure is just sensational. It has been professionally restored to address fold wear, a few minor tack holes in the field, a small chip in the left border, one in the lower left corner, and a tear in the top border. Now displaying beautifully, this one sheet is a must have for fans of the horror classics. Fine/Very Fine on Linen.
Estimate: $5,000-up Starting Bid: $2,500

83046   The 13th Chair (MGM, 1929). Lobby Cards (2) (11" X 14"). Very Fine-.
Estimate: $500-up Starting Bid: $250

83047   The Mysterious Dr. Fu Manchu (Paramount, 1929). Title Lobby Card (11" X 14"). Fine/Very Fine.
Estimate: $1,000-up Starting Bid: $500

83049   The Mysterious Dr. Fu Manchu (Paramount, 1929). Lobby Cards (3) (11" X 14"). Fine.
Estimate: $500-up Starting Bid: $250

83048   The Mysterious Dr. Fu Manchu (Paramount, 1929). Lobby Card (11" X 14"). Fine/Very Fine.
Estimate: $600-up Starting Bid: $300

83050　**The Canary Murder Case (Paramount, 1929).** Title Lobby Card (11" X 14"). Louise Brooks makes a smashing appearance as nightclub singer "The Canary" on this beautiful title card. William Powell as famed detective Philo Vance is called in to investigate her murder in this early "part-talkie" mystery film. The film proved to be Brooks' Hollywood undoing as she refused to return to voice her lines for the sound version. The card has been restored to repair a 1/2 inch trim on the bottom border and a small chip in the left border. The work is superb and the card now looks as good as the day it was printed. An iconic image from the early days of sound films. Fine.
Estimate: $4,000-up Starting Bid: $3,750

83051　**The Canary Murder Case (Paramount, 1929).** Lobby Card (11" X 14"). Fine.
Estimate: $2,400-up Starting Bid: $2,000

83052   The Shadow Strikes (Grand National, 1937). One Sheet (27"X 41"). Rod La Rocque stars in this fun mystery, which is the first feature film appearance of the The Shadow. While Lamont Granston, a lawyer/ investigator by day, The Shadow adopts his disguise at night to find the guilty and cloud their minds to remain hidden, laughing in the darkness. The character was a hit in both radio and pulp magazines of the 1930s. In this feature, The Shadow solves the murder of a wealthy scion, who had numerous enemies including his heirs. Lynn Anders, James Blakeley, and Walter McGrail co-star. Prior to professional restoration, this gorgeous stone litho one sheet had fold wear, crossfold separations, a small hole in the top right corner, a chip in the right border, and missing 1/2 inch along the bottom border. All has been restored, leaving the amazing pulp artwork to shine. Fine on Linen.
Estimate: $1,200-up Starting Bid: $1,000

83053   Charlie Chan at Monte Carlo (20th Century Fox, 1937). Insert (14"X 36"). Fine/Very Fine on Paper.
Estimate: $2,000-up
Starting Bid: $1,000

83054   Charlie Chan at the Circus (20th Century Fox, 1936). Window Card (14"X 22"). Fine-.
Estimate: $500-up
Starting Bid: $250

83055 **The Black Camel (Fox, 1931).** Lobby Card (11" X 14"). Very Fine.
Estimate: $2,000-up
Starting Bid: $1,000

83056 **The Woman in Green (Universal, 1945).** One Sheet (27" X 41"). Very Fine on Linen.
Estimate: $800-up Starting Bid: $400

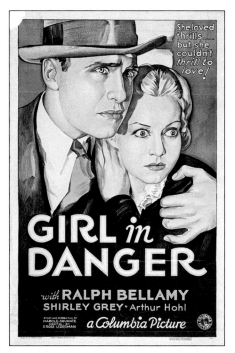

83058 **Girl in Danger (Columbia, 1934).** One Sheet (27" X 41"). Very Good+.
Estimate: $800-up Starting Bid: $400

83057 **The Night Club Queen (Olympic, 1934).** One Sheet (27" X 41"). Fine/Very Fine.
Estimate: $700-up Starting Bid: $350

83059 **Grand Exit (Columbia, 1935).** One Sheet (27" X 41"). Fine-.
Estimate: $800-up Starting Bid: $400

83060   Private Detective 62 (Warner Brothers, 1933). One Sheet (27" X 41"). Shortly before his huge success as gentleman detective Nick Charles in the *Thin Man* series of films, William Powell took on the role of PI Donald Free. Due to his lack of cases, Free becomes less than scrupulous and goes along with a scheme to blackmail heiress Janet Reynolds (Margaret Lindsey). Complications arise when he begins to fall for the intended victim. Always enjoyable and believable as a man of intrigue and morals, Powell once again gives a powerful performance, with direction from Michael Curtiz. Prior to professional restoration, this one sheet had a tear at the bottom that extended to the bottom of the title, a small tear below Powell's eye, a chip in the right border at the fold line, a small chip in the bottom border, and a one in the lower right corner. Showcasing a fantastic design, this is a hard to find one sheet. Fine/Very Fine on Linen.
Estimate: $8,000-up Starting Bid: $4,000

83061   After the Thin Man (MGM, 1936). Window Card (14" X 22"). Fine+.
Estimate: $600-up Starting Bid: $300

83063   Star of Midnight (RKO, 1935). Lobby Card Set of 8 (11" X 14"). Fine+.
Estimate: $600-up Starting Bid: $300

83062   Shadow of the Thin Man (MGM, 1941). Half Sheet (22" X 28"). Rolled, Very Fine-.
Estimate: $700-up Starting Bid: $350

83064   Sullivan's Travels (Paramount, 1941). Three Sheet (41" X 81"). Preston Sturges' classic comedy is well-represented with this rarely-seen three sheet featuring Veronica Lake in all her peek-a-boo blonde and beautiful glory. Joel McCrea stars as successful director John L. Sullivan, who wants to make a "serious" film after doing a series of fluff comedies. Hoping to see the "real" America, he dresses as a hobo and bums across the country, picking up actress Lake along the way. Comedy turns to tragedy and results in one of the finest films to come out of the Golden Age of Hollywood. Prior to restoration, there were pinholes in the corners, with minor fold wear and crossfold separations. Very Fine- on Linen.

Estimate: $10,000-up Starting Bid: $5,000

83065 **Sullivan's Travels (Paramount, 1941).** Lobby Card (11" X 14"). Very Fine-.
Estimate: $700-up Starting Bid: $350

83066 **I Married a Witch (United Artists, 1942).** Lobby Cards (2) (11" X 14"). Fine.
Estimate: $600-up Starting Bid: $300

83067 **The Glass Key (Paramount, 1942).** One Sheet (27" X 41"). Great dialogue, acting, plot, and action. It all came together in this timeless *film noir*. Luckily the one sheet matches the film, with its stylish highlighted "see-through" key motif with four collage scenes from the film inset, and a terrific oversize full color portrait of a luminous Veronica Lake with her famous draped-over-one-eye hair style. Looking at this piece, you can almost hear the scene stealing William Bendix rasping..."Wait a minute..you mean I don't get to smack Baby?" This highly sought poster had only small tears in the right and left borders into the background, pinholes in the borders and artwork, and two small tears to the left of the credits. There was a small chip in the left border. Top restoration has this poster ready to view. Fine on Linen.
Estimate: $6,000-up Starting Bid: $4,000

83068   The Glass Key (Paramount, 1942). Window Card (14" X 22"). Very Fine-.
Estimate: $1,200-up Starting Bid: $600

83070   The Glass Key (Paramount, 1948). First Post-War French Grande (47" X 63"). Fine/Very
Fine on Linen.
Estimate: $700-up Starting Bid: $350

83069   The Glass Key (Paramount, late 1940s). First Post-War Belgian (14.5" X 23"). Fine/Very
Fine on Linen.
Estimate: $600-up Starting Bid: $300

For full lot descriptions,
enlargeable images and
online bidding, visit
HA.com/7025

83071 **This Gun for Hire (Paramount, 1942).** One Sheet (27" X 41"). In their first film together, Veronica Lake and Alan Ladd created such chemistry they turned this crime drama, based on Graham Greene's novel *A Gun for Sale*, into a seminal *film noir* classic. Ladd was billed fourth, but after the immense success of this film, he received top billing on all of his following projects. Set in San Francisco during WWII, hit man Philip Raven (Ladd) is double-crossed by nightclub owner Willard Gates, played by Laird Cregar, one of the greatest "heavies" of all time. Raven enlists the aid of Ellen (Lake), not knowing she is a spy for the U.S. Government, as he outwits the police and finds the owner of the chemical company who is selling a formula for poison gas to America's enemies. Ladd gives a remarkable performance as the conflicted killer who learns to trust Ellen, in the end saving her fiancée's life and asking for redemption. This highly desirable one sheet had fold wear and crossfold separations. There were a few small chips in the right border and one in the bottom border, a tear on the right side of the horizontal fold, and a tear in Lake's forehead. This sheet has been professionally restored and these issues are not visible on this prized poster, which features remarkably strong color. One of the most sought after portraits of these icons, this poster is not to be missed. Fine+ on Linen.
Estimate: $20,000-up Starting Bid: $15,000

83072   This Gun for Hire (Paramount, 1947). Belgian (14" X 22"). Folded, Fine+.
Estimate: $800-up Starting Bid: $600

83073   This Gun for Hire (Paramount, 1942). Three Sheet (41" X 81"). Alan Ladd became a star with his portrayal of a disturbing killer in this perennial favorite. Director Frank
Tuttle had wanted to cast Robert Preston in the lead role, but later hunted for an unknown.
When Tuttle met Ladd, the director knew that the 28-year-old blond could make the cold-
blooded killer Phillip Raven a sympathetic character, which he thought was key to the film's
success. He was right. For his first of seven pairings with sultry Veronica Lake, Ladd would
receive only $300 a week! This cornerstone three sheet for the quintessential *film noir* is the
first original issue we've offered. It's great atmosphere art with a disinterested Ladd oozing
tough guy cool in trench coat and dangling "gat" receiving a kiss from Lake. Some paper loss
issues on the right side and small chips and tears in both credits have been professionally restored and the poster shows extremely well. There were pinholes, small chips in the crossfold
separations and some minor abrasions remain on the left side. Reward yourself with a true
piece of Hollywood greatness! Good/Very Good on Linen.
Estimate: $9,000-up Starting Bid: $4,500

83075   The Blue Dahlia (Paramount, 1946). Spanish Language Three Sheet (41" X 81"). Fine/Very Fine on Linen.
Estimate: $2,500-up Starting Bid: $1,250

83074   The Blue Dahlia (Paramount, 1946). One Sheet (27" X 41"). The third picture to feature the dynamic *film noir* team of Alan Ladd and Veronica Lake, this murder mystery centers around the shady happenings at the nightclub The Blue Dahlia. Ladd stars as Johnny Morrison, a returning veteran who discovers his wife (Doris Dowling) has been unfaithful and wants a divorce. She turns up dead shortly thereafter, and Johnny is suspect number one. It will take all his ingenuity, help from buddies William Bendix and Hugh Beaumont, and the estranged wife of the Dahlia's owner (Lake) to clear his name. With an original screenplay written by the great Raymond Chandler, this taut thriller never disappoints. This very desirable one sheet has pinholes with a few enlarged ones at the top, a small chip and tear in the top border, a corner crease, pinpoint cross fold separations, and a few small fold separations at the edges. There is a smudge under the title, a minor chip at the left edge, a small scratch at the top of the image and one in the title. The color images of a smoking Ladd, Lake and co-stars make for an unforgettable poster you do not want to miss. Fine+.
Estimate: $5,000-up Starting Bid: $2,500

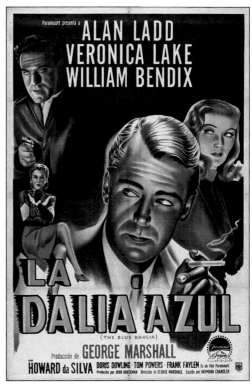

83076   The Blue Dahlia (Paramount, 1946). Argentinean Poster (29" X 43"). Fine/Very Fine on Linen.
Estimate: $1,000-up Starting Bid: $500

83077 **The Blue Dahlia (Paramount, 1946).** CGC Graded Lobby Card (11"X 14"). Very Fine.
Estimate: $300-up Starting Bid: $150

83080 **Double Indemnity (Paramount, 1946).** First Post War Belgian (14"X 21.5"). Very Fine on Linen.
Estimate: $800-up
Starting Bid: $400

83078 **Calcutta (Paramount, 1946).** One Sheet (27"X 41"). Very Fine- on Linen.
Estimate: $1,000-up Starting Bid: $500

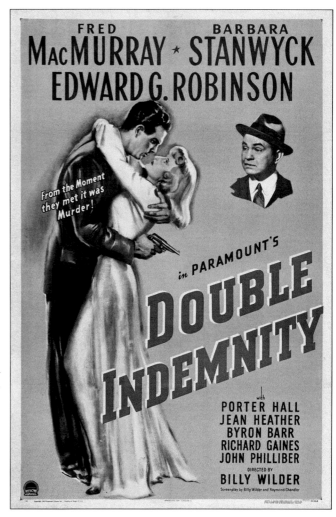

83079 **Double Indemnity (Paramount, 1944).** One Sheet (27"X 41"). Though reworked in 1981 as *Body Heat*, this hugely influential and entertaining *film noir* thriller rarely feels dated and moves at lightning speed with its Raymond Chandler dialogue and the deft hand of director Billy Wilder. Fred MacMurray plays the ultimate everyday guy, seduced by a *femme fatale* (Barbara Stanwyck) into committing murder for insurance money. Tension mounts as a near perfect crime unravels into a dark climax. This nice copy had slight fold wear and crossfold separation. There was a small piece missing from the center crossfold just below MacMurray's gun and minor border wear. The professional restoration was performed very well and the poster presents as near mint. Posters from the top *film noir* classics keep getting harder to find and this one is a very tough find. Fine/Very Fine on Linen.
Estimate: $4,000-up Starting Bid: $2,000

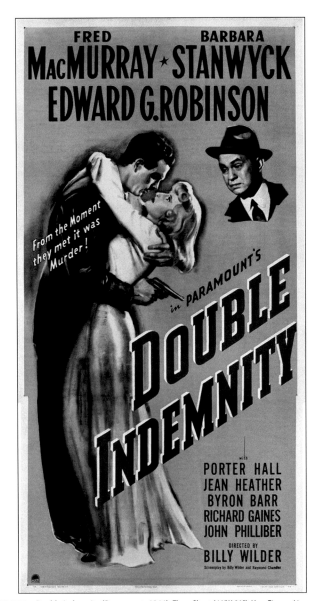

83081   Double Indemnity (Paramount, 1944). Three Sheet (41" X 81"). Very Fine on Linen.
Estimate: $7,500-up Starting Bid: $3,750

83083   Out of the Past (RKO, R-1953). One Sheet (27" X 41"). Very Fine-.
Estimate: $1,500-up Starting Bid: $750

83084   Out of the Past (RKO, 1947). Half Sheet (22" X 28") Style A. Folded, Fine+.
Estimate: $2,500-up Starting Bid: $1,250

83082   Double Indemnity (Paramount, 1944). Lobby Card (11" X 14"). Fine/Very Fine.
Estimate: $500-up Starting Bid: $250

83085   **Murder, My Sweet (RKO, 1944).** One Sheet (27" X 41"). Raymond Chandler's gritty crime novels adapted extremely well to the big screen and his screenplays became some of the best *film noir* pictures ever made, including *Double Indemnity*, *The Blue Dahlia*, *The Big Sleep*, and this Philip Marlowe classic based on Chandler's novel "Farewell My Lovely." Dick Powell stars as the disillusioned detective who is hired by the thug Moose Malloy (Mike Mazurki) to find a missing girlfriend. Claire Trevor gives a stunning performance as the femme fatale Velma Valento, and the unraveling of the lies and mystery makes for a very entertaining show. Otto Kruger and Anne Shirley co-star. This popular one sheet has been professionally restored to address pinholes in the corners, one in the title, small tears in the left border, fold wear, and crossfold separations. A striking image for one of the best *film noir* classics. Very Fine- on Linen.
Estimate: $4,000-up Starting Bid: $2,000

83086   The Postman Always Rings Twice (MGM, 1946). Three Sheet (41" X 81"). Very Good+ on Linen.
Estimate: $3,000-up Starting Bid: $1,500

83087   **The Postman Always Rings Twice (MGM, 1946).** CGC Graded Title Lobby Card (11" X 14"). Very Fine+.
Estimate: $600-up Starting Bid: $300

83088   The Postman Always Rings Twice (MGM, 1946). Insert (14" X 36"). Rolled, Very Fine+.
Estimate: $2,000-up Starting Bid: $1,000

83090   Laura (20th Century Fox, 1944). Half Sheet (22" X 28"). Fine/Very Fine on Linen.
Estimate: $1,500-up Starting Bid: $750

83089   Laura (20th Century Fox, 1944). Insert (14" X 36"). Folded, Fine+.
Estimate: $1,800-up Starting Bid: $900

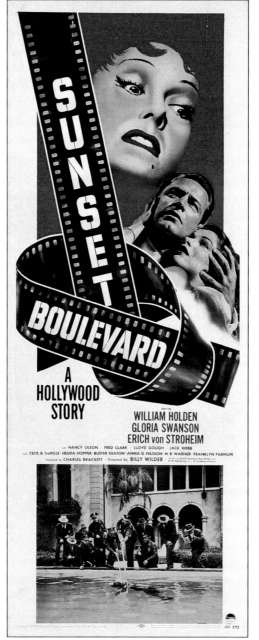

83091   Sunset Boulevard (Paramount, 1950). Insert (14" X 36"). Billy Wilder's masterful *film noir* begins with one of the darkest openings in all of cinema—with the lifeless body of the protagonist narrator Joe Gillis (William Holden) floating in a pool. This iconic scene is featured on this stunning insert, which always garners a lot of attention from serious collectors. The ultimate film about Hollywood, *Sunset* stars some of the era's cinematic royalty including: Gloria Swanson, Erich von Stroheim, Cecil B. DeMille, Buster Keaton, H.B. Warner, etc. And the atmosphere of decay, regret, doom, and nostalgia is exquisitely suffocating as Norma Desmond sinks deeper into her tragic final role. The poster shows two tears at the top and one at the left, with paper tape on the reverse. There are also some smudges on the left side. An iconic poster, this beauty will be a prized item for any collection. Rolled, Fine.
Estimate: $5,000-up Starting Bid: $3,000

83092   Sunset Boulevard (Paramount, 1950). Lobby Card Set of 8 (11"X 14"). Fine.
Estimate: $2,000-up Starting Bid: $1,000

83093   Lady in the Lake (MGM, 1947). One Sheet (27"X 41"). Very Fine on Linen.
Estimate: $500-up Starting Bid: $250

83094   Youth Runs Wild (RKO, 1944). One Sheet (27"X 41"). Very Fine.
Estimate: $450-up Starting Bid: $225

83095   Call Northside 777 (20th Century Fox, 1948). One Sheet (27"X 41"). Fine+ on Linen.
Estimate: $600-up Starting Bid: $300

83096   Night and the City (20th Century Fox, 1950). CGC Graded Lobby Card Set of 8 (11" X 14"). Near Mint/Mint.
Estimate: $500-up Starting Bid: $250

83098   The Big Heat (Columbia, 1953). One Sheet (27" X 41"). Very Fine- on Linen.
Estimate: $600-up
Starting Bid: $300

83099   Fury (MGM, 1936). Pre-War Belgian (23.75" X 30.5"). Very Fine- on Linen.
Estimate: $1,100-up
Starting Bid: $550

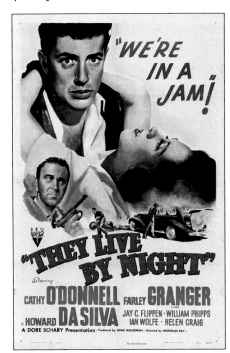

83097   They Live by Night (RKO, 1948). One Sheet (27" X 41"). Fine.
Estimate: $400-up Starting Bid: $200

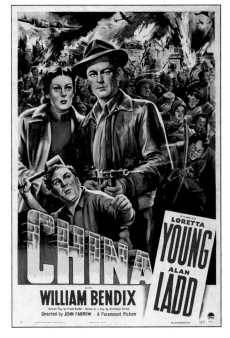

83100   China (Paramount, 1943). One Sheet (27" X 41"). Fine on Linen.
Estimate: $500-up
Starting Bid: $250

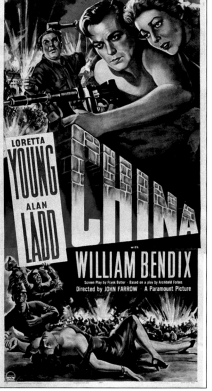

83101   China (Paramount, 1943). Three Sheet (41" X 81"). Fine+ on Linen.
Estimate: $600-up Starting Bid: $300

83103   The Night of the Hunter (United Artists, 1955). German A1 (24" X 33"). Folded, Very Fine-.
Estimate: $700-up Starting Bid: $600

83102   Kiss of Death (20th Century Fox, 1947). One Sheet (25" X 39.5"). Victor Mature is at his best as a father, husband and petty thief sentenced to 20 years for robbery. After his wife commits suicide, Mature agrees to turn stoolie in exchange for his freedom and a reunion with his two little girls. Richard Widmark (in his first feature role) is brilliant as a sadistic hit-man. This poster was the only black and white poster done in the *noir* genre and has gained a following due to its unusual design and full-bleed printing. The poster has been mounted on linen but not restored. Condition includes small tears in the bottom border and credits area, a smudge of paint in top left near the "K," and a tiny amount of surface paper loss in the bottom right corner. Very Fine- on Linen.
Estimate: $3,000-up
Starting Bid: $1,500

83104   The Stranger (RKO, 1946). Lobby Card Set of 8 (11" X 14"). Very Fine-.
Estimate: $500-up Starting Bid: $350

83105 Nightmare Alley (20th Century Fox, 1947). Lobby Card Set of 8 (11" X 14"). Fine+.
Estimate: $500-up Starting Bid: $250

83107 Leave Her to Heaven (20th Century Fox, 1945). Insert (14" X 36"). Folded, Fine+.
Estimate: $800-up Starting Bid: $400

83109 Crossfire (RKO, 1947). Three Sheet (41" X 81"). Very Fine-on Linen.
Estimate: $900-up Starting Bid: $450

83106 Mildred Pierce (Warner Brothers, 1945). Three Sheet (41" X 81"). Fine+ on Linen.
Estimate: $1,200-up Starting Bid: $600

83108 The Asphalt Jungle (MGM, 1950). Insert (14" X 36"). Rolled, Fine/Very Fine.
Estimate: $800-up Starting Bid: $400

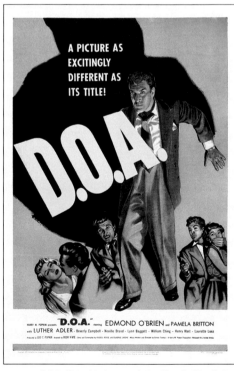

83110 D.O.A. (United Artists, 1950). One Sheet (27" X 41"). Fine on Linen.
Estimate: $800-up Starting Bid: $400

83111   The Great Gatsby (Paramount, 1949). Six Sheet (81" X 81"). Fine/Very Fine on Linen.
Estimate: $900-up Starting Bid: $450

83112   I Love Trouble (Columbia, 1948). One Sheet (27" X 41"). Very Fine- on Linen.
Estimate: $800-up Starting Bid: $400

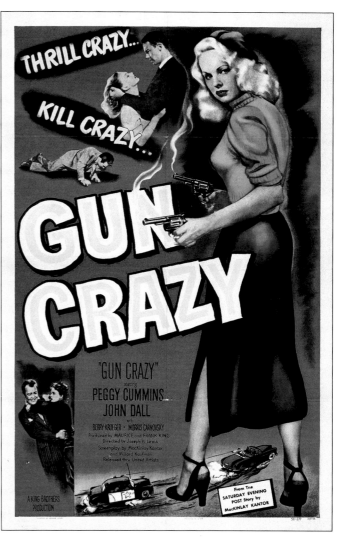

83113   Gun Crazy (United Artists, 1949). One Sheet (27" X 41"). "We go together, Annie. Maybe like guns and ammunition go together." Joseph H. Lewis directed this *Bonnie and Clyde*-style *film noir* about a disillusioned WWII vet (John Dall) and his carnival sharpshooter girlfriend (Peggy Cummins) who have a perverse fixation with guns. The two go on a psychotic shooting spree, as they travel on a cross-country string of daring robberies. Offered here is the luridly lush one sheet showcasing Cummins' considerable assets. The only condition issues on this terrific unrestored sheet are fold wear with some crossfold separations, and a minor ink mark in the background at lower left. You'd be "crazy" to miss out on this sweet poster. Very Fine+.
Estimate: $7,000-up Starting Bid: $3,500

83114   Crack-Up (20th Century Fox, 1936). Title Lobby Card (11" X 14"). Fine/Very Fine.
Estimate: $700-up Starting Bid: $350

83115 Touch Of Evil (Universal International, 1958). One Sheet (27" X 41"). Fine+.
Estimate: $1,200-up Starting Bid: $800

83116 Touch Of Evil (Universal International, 1958). Three Sheet (41" X 81"). Fine/Very Fine.
Estimate: $1,400-up Starting Bid: $700

83117 T-Men (CID, 1950). Italian 4 - Foglio (55" X 78"). Fine.
Estimate: $600-up Starting Bid: $300

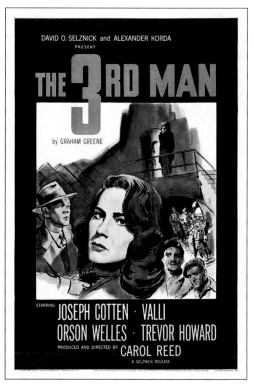

83118 The Third Man (Selznick, 1949). One Sheet (27" X 41"). Very Fine on Linen.
Estimate: $1,000-up Starting Bid: $500

83119 Dirty Harry (Warner Brothers, 1971). CGC Graded Lobby Card Set of 8 (11" X 14"). Near Mint-.
Estimate: $600-up Starting Bid: $300

83122 Bullitt (Warner Brothers, 1968). One Sheet (27" X 41"). Very Fine .
Estimate: $1,000-up Starting Bid: $500

83120 The Italian Job (Paramount, 1969). One Sheet (27" X 41"). Fine+.
Estimate: $600-up Starting Bid: $300

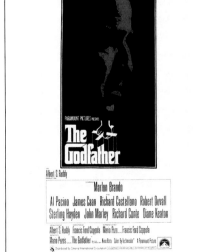

83121 The Godfather (Paramount, 1972). British One Sheet (27" X 40"). Very Fine- on Linen.
Estimate: $600-up Starting Bid: $300

83123 Mean Streets (Warner Brothers, 1973). Lobby Card Set of 8 (11" X 14"). Very Fine.
Estimate: $500-up Starting Bid: $250

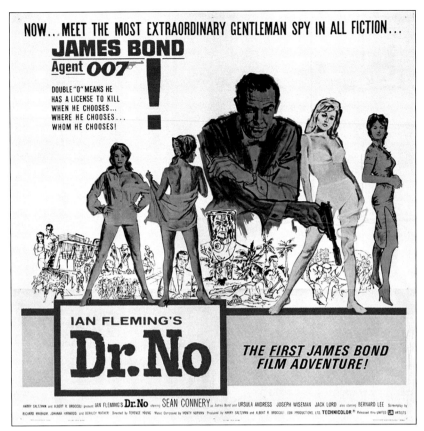

83124 **Dr. No (United Artists, 1962).** Six Sheet (81" X 81"). The first, and to many fans, the best James Bond spy adventure, this seminal adaptation of Ian Fleming's novel is directed by Terence Young, who would soon return to helm two more 007 films, *From Russia With Love* and *Thunderball*. Sean Connery will forever be remembered as 007, the role of a lifetime. The action packed plot, arch-enemy organization SPECTRE, guns and gadgets, and of course Ursula Andress as Honey Ryder, combined to make this into an iconic spy thriller, and model to all subsequent Bond pictures. This sensational and rarely seen large format poster has a minor dust shadow at the join of one of the bottom panels, light stains at the edges of the top panels, and corner creases in the bottom panels. Very Fine-.
Estimate: $2,000-up Starting Bid: $1,000

83125 **Dr. No (United Artists, 1962).**
Lobby Card Set of 8 (11" X 14"). Fine.
Estimate: $1,500-up Starting Bid: $750

83126 **Goldfinger (United Artists, 1964).** Poster (40" X 60"). Rolled, Fine/Very Fine.
Estimate: $1,400-up Starting Bid: $1,000

83127 **Goldfinger (United Artists, 1964).** Insert (14" X 36"). Rolled, Very Fine+.
Estimate: $800-up Starting Bid: $500

83128 Goldfinger (United Artists, 1964). Lobby Card Set of 8 (11"X 14"). Fine+.
Estimate: $1,500-up Starting Bid: $750

83130 From Russia with Love (United Artists, 1964). Insert (14" X 36"). Fine/Very Fine on Paper.
Estimate: $500-up Starting Bid: $300

83131 From Russia with Love (United Artists, 1964). Half Sheet (22"X 28"). Very Fine on Paper.
Estimate: $500-up Starting Bid: $250

83129 From Russia with Love (United Artists, 1964). British Quad (30" X 40"). A rare country-of-origin British quad with vastly superior artwork makes this the most desirable poster for this very popular title. Dominated by an iconic illustration of Sean Connery as Bond by Ranato Fratini and Eric Pulford, this poster was a harbinger of the great things to come. This piece required only minimal restoration to address slight fold wear with minimal crossfold separation, and the result is a gem that will be a prized addition to any Bond collection. Very Fine on Linen.
Estimate: $5,000-up Starting Bid: $2,500

83132 Dr. No (United Artists, 1962). One Sheet (27"X 41"). Very Fine-.
Estimate: $1,000-up Starting Bid: $500

83133   Dr. No (United Artists, 1962). Insert (14" X 36"). Very Fine on Paper.
Estimate: $600-up Starting Bid: $500

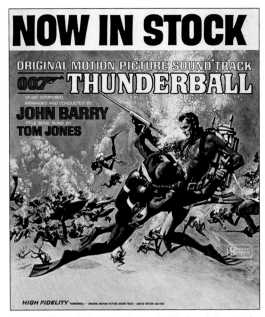

83135   Thunderball (United Artists, 1965). Record Store Display (12" X 14"). The art on this record store display is the same art used on the two sheet or subway poster. It's by one of the best of the Bond artists, Frank McCarthy. The soundtrack with John Barry's haunting string and wind arrangements, with two suites comprising 20+ minutes of the film's concluding underwater intrigue is illustrated beautifully on this very rare store display! A unique find for any Bond collection. There is only a slight wrinkling in the left and right sides. Rolled, Fine/Very Fine.
Estimate: $600-up Starting Bid: $300

83137   Thunderball (United Artists, 1965). Insert (14" X 36"). Very Fine on Paper.
Estimate: $600-up Starting Bid: $400

83134   Thunderball (United Artists, 1965). Subway (41" X 54"). Fine/Very Fine.
Estimate: $500-up Starting Bid: $250

83136   Thunderball (United Artists, 1965). One Sheet (27" X 41"). Fine/Very Fine.
Estimate: $600-up Starting Bid: $300

83138   You Only Live Twice (United Artists, 1967). Insert (14" X 36"). Rolled, Very Fine+.
Estimate: $500-up Starting Bid: $250

83139   You Only Live Twice (United Artists, 1967). One Sheet (27" X 41") Flat Folded Advance. Folded, Very Fine-.
Estimate: $500-up
Starting Bid: $250

83142   The Man With the Golden Gun (United Artists, 1974). One Sheet (27" X 41") Style B. Fine+.
Estimate: $600-up
Starting Bid: $400

83140   On Her Majesty's Secret Service (United Artists, 1970). Italian 2 - Foglio (39" X 55"). Very Fine+.
Estimate: $500-up
Starting Bid: $250

83143   The Man With the Golden Gun (United Artists, 1974). British Quad (30" X 40"). Folded, Near Mint/Mint.
Estimate: $400-up Starting Bid: $300

83141   Everybody Against James Bond (United Artists, 1972). Italian 4 - Foglio (55" X 78"). Near Mint.
Estimate: $600-up
Starting Bid: $300

83144   Octopussy (MGM/UA, 1983). Large Japanese (52" X 75.5"). Folded, Fine/Very Fine.
Estimate: $500-up
Starting Bid: $250

83145 **Just Imagine (Fox, 1930).** Lobby Card (11" X 14"). Fine.
Estimate: $500-up Starting Bid: $250

83146 **Things to Come (United Artists, 1936).** Swedish One Sheet (27.5" X 39.5"). Based on a tale by H. G. Wells, *Things to Come* opens prior to World War II and takes the viewer on a hundred-year time trip to 2036 A.D. when a man and a woman are rocketed to the moon. When it was first released in 1936, Benito Mussolini reputedly had every print of the film in Italy destroyed due to the extreme similarity between himself and Ralph Richardson's portrayal of "The Boss" of Everytown. This stunning and rare Swedish poster has had some restoration to address edge wear at the left and right, small stains in the right border, a tear at the top that just extends into the artwork, and a tear at the bottom that also extends well into the art. This is an amazing art deco design done by Swedish artist Moje Aslund for a classic of early science fiction cinema! Fine+ on Linen.
Estimate: $2,500-up Starting Bid: $2,000

83147 **It Came from Outer Space (Universal International, 1953).** Poster (40" X 60"). One of the very best of the 50's sci-fi offerings with a great cast, above average plot and story (Ray Bradbury), and a whole bunch of film firsts. Thanks to Mr. Bradbury, it was the first sci-fi movie to portray aliens as anything but psychopathic killers. It was Universal's first 3-D film. It was the first of the "desert" sci-fi's. It was certainly one of the first to use the theremin for the sci-fi electronic sound we all know and associate with the 50's genre. It was the first time the monster's perspective was used, letting us view through the cyclops eye. This is a format we seldom see. These oversize 40" X 60's were usually ordered by larger theatres and had much lower print runs than the other seven commonly used sizes. This art was used only in this format and features great shots of the cast reacting in fear to the eye. It carries the all important "3-Dimension" banner at the top. There has been some restoration touch up for pinholes, small chips in the "3-D", and edge wear with small chips and tears. There are minor creases throughout. Rolled, Very Fine-. .
Estimate: $3,000-up Starting Bid: $1,500

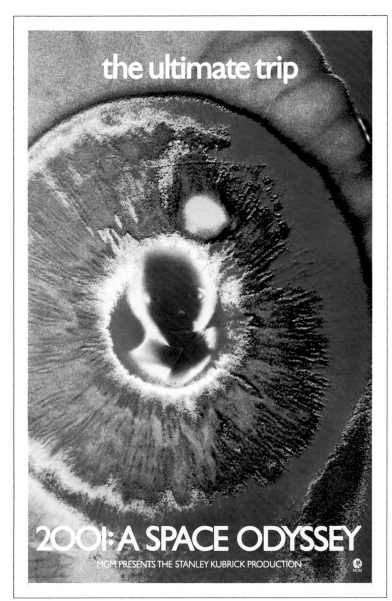

83148 2001: A Space Odyssey (MGM, 1969). One Sheet (27" X 41"). When MGM decided to revamp the advertising campaign for this blockbuster film in 1969 they chose the tagline "The Ultimate Trip." The EYE poster, as this poster is most often referred to, was conceived for the 1969, 70 mm relaunch in New York while the film was still playing around the country in its original 1968 standard 35 mm format. This poster was primarily used for wilding (i.e. posting on building sites, etc.). It was therefore printed in a smaller quantity than the STAR CHILD poster, the campaign's principal image. The STAR CHILD was retained for subsequent releases for the next decade. Some of the EYE posters were displayed at the Ziegfeld Theatre but as a secondary image, and never for newspaper ads, etc. It is therefore the rarest of all the U.S. one sheets for *2001: A Space Odyssey*. The original printing of the EYE and STAR CHILD posters have no NSS or other information in the bottom border, as they were created in rush time, not knowing if the campaign would take. After the successful New York opening, the campaign was adapted in other U.S. cities. This beautiful example is unrestored and unfolded, with only two very minor stains on the left edge of the poster. Rolled, Near Mint.
Estimate: $12,000-up Starting Bid: $8,000

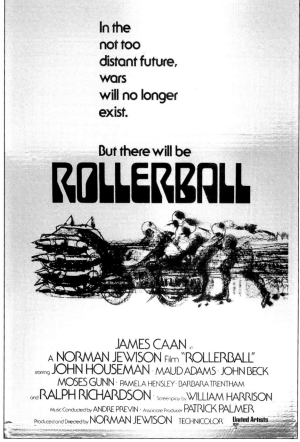

83149 Rollerball (United Artists, 1975). One Sheet (27" X 40") Mylar Advance. In the not-too-distant future, corporations rule the world and control the teeming masses through the ultra-violent sport of Rollerball, which graphically demonstrates the futility of individuality. Jonathan E. (James Caan), one of the greatest players of all time, learns to think for himself, however, much to the displeasure of his corporate masters. This is the very rare mylar advance poster with art by Bob Peak. In excellent condition, this shows only light wrinkles. Rolled, Very Fine/Near Mint.
Estimate: $700-up Starting Bid: $350

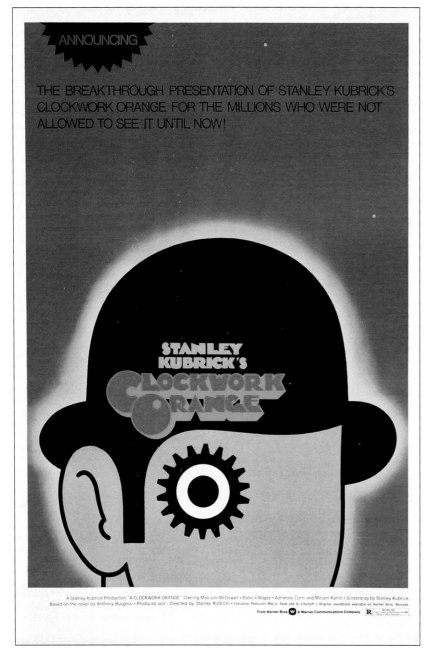

83150 A Clockwork Orange (Warner Brothers, 1971). One Sheet (27" X 41"). The original poster of this groundbreaking film with the Philip Castle artwork was used for the original X-rated release in all the major markets, beginning with the four-city premiere engagements in NY, LA, San Francisco and Toronto in December, 1971. The film, in its X-rated version continued playing for the next six months as it was released in all key North American cities, almost always establishing house records. When *Clockwork* was marginally altered to achieve an R-rating, Stanley Kubrick wanted to call attention to the rating with another image, as the Castle artwork had already become iconic and the film would now be available for viewing by a wider audience. He liked this design by David Pelham of the Canadian paperback edition of the Anthony Burgess novel and had it adapted as the new poster for an R-announcement release. It was used for a short time before the original Castle image was reinstituted. This poster had a limited press run and as it was directly tied to the American rating, it was only seen in North America, whereas the Castle design was used throughout the world. It is therefore the rarest of official *Clockwork Orange* posters. This copy has light wrinkling and light edge wear, and is a stunning prize for fans of the genius Kubrick. Rolled, Fine/Very Fine.
Estimate: $12,000-up Starting Bid: $6,000

83151 Alien (20th Century Fox, 1979). One Sheet (27" X 41") Advance. Near Mint-.
Estimate: $1,000-up Starting Bid: $500

83152 Blade Runner (Warner Brothers, 1982). Insert (14" X 36"). Rolled, Near Mint.
Estimate: $600-up Starting Bid: $300

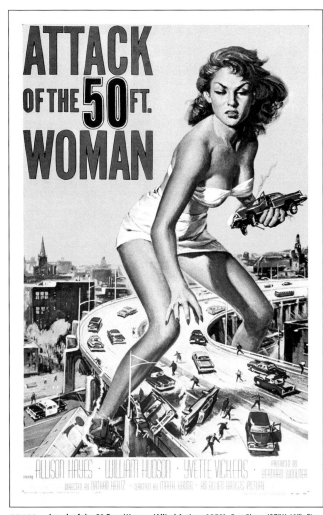

83153   **Attack of the 50 Foot Woman (Allied Artists, 1958).** One Sheet (27" X 41"). Fine+ on Linen.
Estimate: $8,000-up Starting Bid: $4,000

83154   **The Man from Planet X (United Artists, 1951).** One Sheet (27" X 41"). Fine on Linen.
Estimate: $6,000-up Starting Bid: $5,000

For full lot descriptions, enlargeable images and online bidding, visit HA.com/7025

83155   **The War of the Worlds (Paramount, 1953).** Three Sheet (41" X 81"). Very Fine- on Linen.
Estimate: $5,500-up Starting Bid: $2,750

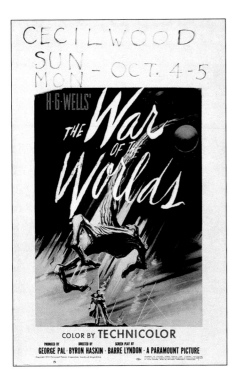

83156   The War of the Worlds (Paramount, 1953). Window Card (14" X 22"). Fine.
Estimate: $800-up Starting Bid: $400

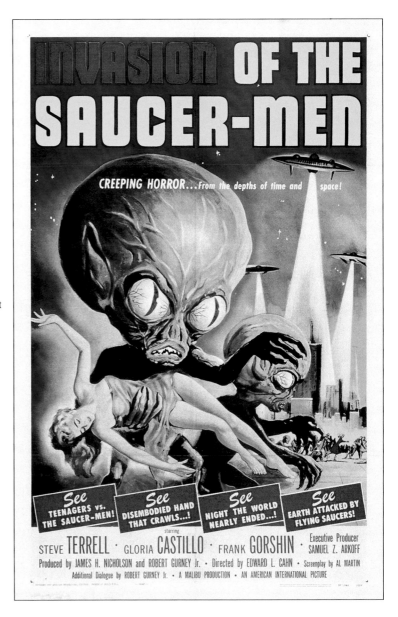

83157   Invasion of the Saucer-Men (American International, 1957). One Sheet
(27" X 41"). Very Fine-.
Estimate: $6,000-up Starting Bid: $3,000

83158   Tarantula (Universal International, 1955). Poster (40" X 60"). Rolled, Very Good/Fine.
Estimate: $500-up Starting Bid: $250

83159 Tarantula (Universal International, 1955). British Quad (30" X 40"). Very Fine+ on Linen.
Estimate: $1,800-up Starting Bid: $1,500

83160 The Blob (Paramount, 1958). British Quad (30" X 40"). Fine-.
Estimate: $600-up Starting Bid: $300

83161 The Thing From Another World (RKO, 1951). Half Sheet (22" X 28") Style A. Fine+ on Paper.
Estimate: $1,500-up Starting Bid: $750

83162   **Forbidden Planet (MGM, 1956).** One Sheet (27" X 41"). Very Fine on Linen.
Estimate: $7,000-up Starting Bid: $5,000

83164   **The Day the Earth Stood Still (20th Century Fox, 1951).** One Sheet (27" X 41"). Good+
on Linen.
Estimate: $8,000-up Starting Bid: $4,000

83163   **The Invisible Boy (MGM, 1957).** Poster (40" X 60"). Rolled, Fine-.
Estimate: $500-up Starting Bid: $250

83165   **The Day the Earth Stood Still (20th Century Fox, 1951).** Photos (9) (8.25" X 10"). *From
the collection of Wade Williams.* Very Fine+.
Estimate: $300-up Starting Bid: $150

83176 **Fantastic Voyage (20th Century Fox, 1966).** British Quad (30" X 40"). Very Fine+ on Linen.
Estimate: $800-up Starting Bid: $400

83177 **The Fly (20th Century Fox, 1958).** Insert (14" X 36"). Rolled, Very Fine+.
Estimate: $800-up Starting Bid: $400

83178 **The Fly / Return of the Fly (Grand National Pictures, R-1960's).** British Quad (30" X 40"). The producers made so much money with Vincent Price's first insect epic, they brought him back, used the same sets from the year before, and quickly put another one together. This is an reissue in the early 1960's from England, where they put a fun new campaign together for the combo showing of both films, "See Them Together...But Don't See Them Alone". Many think the artwork here is actually better than the original British quad. There's more blood and he's drawn in a larger perspective. You can compare all the quad's in Ron Borst's *Graven Images*. Only a few issues needed to be professionally restored when the poster was placed on linen. There were pinholes in the corners and background, a "color" snipe in the lower right, and a small tear in the top border. Very Fine- on Linen.
Estimate: $1,200-up Starting Bid: $600

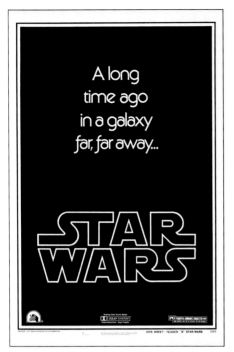

83179 **Star Wars (20th Century Fox, 1977).** One Sheet (27" X 41") Advance Style B. Rolled, Mint.
Estimate: $400-up Starting Bid: $200

83181 **Revenge of the Jedi (20th Century Fox, 1982).** One Sheet (27" X 41") Flat Folded Advance. Very Fine/Near Mint.
Estimate: $600-up Starting Bid: $300

83183 **War of the Colossal Beast (American International, 1958).** Insert (14" X 36"). Rolled, Very Fine/Near Mint.
Estimate: $500-up Starting Bid: $250

83180 **The Empire Strikes Back (20th Century Fox, 1980).** One Sheet Style A (27" X 41"). Near Mint/Mint.
Estimate: $300-up Starting Bid: $150

83182 **Return of the Jedi (20th Century Fox/Polfilm, 1984).** Polish One Sheet (26" X 38.5") Style B. Very Fine+ on Linen.
Estimate: $400-up Starting Bid: $200

83184 **Them! (Warner Brothers, 1954).** Window Card (14" X 22"). Folded, Fine-.
Estimate: $400-up Starting Bid: $300

83185 The Deadly Mantis (Universal International, 1957). Insert (14" X 36"). Rolled, Very Fine.
Estimate: $500-up Starting Bid: $250

83188 Day the World Ended (American Releasing Corp., 1956). One Sheet (27" X 41"). Fine/Very Fine.
Estimate: $500-up Starting Bid: $250

83187 The Monster that Challenged the World (Atlantis Films, 1958). Italian 2 - Foglio (39" X 55"). Very Fine+ on Linen.
Estimate: $500-up Starting Bid: $250

83186 The She-Creature (American International, 1956). Lobby Card Set of 8 (11" X 14"). Very Fine-.
Estimate: $600-up Starting Bid: $300

83189 Queen of Outer Space (Allied Artists, 1958). Half Sheet (22" X 28"). Very Fine on Linen.
Estimate: $500-up Starting Bid: $250

83190 Terror from the Year 5000 (American International, 1958). Half Sheet (22" X 28"). Rolled, Very Fine+.
Estimate: $600-up Starting Bid: $300

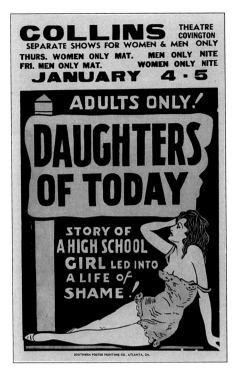

83191   Daughters of Today (Unknown, Early 1930s). Window Card (14" X 22"). Fine+.
Estimate: $500-up Starting Bid: $250

83192   Teaserama (Beautiful Productions Inc., 1955). One Sheet (27" X 41"). Very Fine+ on Linen.
Estimate: $600-up Starting Bid: $300

83193   Nude on the Moon (J.E.R. Pictures, 1961). One Sheet (27" X 41"). Very Fine-.
Estimate: $1,500-up Starting Bid: $750

83194   Pickup (Columbia, 1951). Insert (14" X 36"). Folded, Very Fine-.
Estimate: $500-up Starting Bid: $250

83195   Blonde Sinner (Allied Artists, 1956). One Sheet (27" X 41"). Very Fine- on Linen.
Estimate: $400-up Starting Bid: $200

83196   Blonde Sinner (Allied Artists, 1956). Insert (14" X 36"). Folded, Fine/Very Fine.
Estimate: $700-up Starting Bid: $350

83197   Running Wild (Universal International, 1955). Half Sheet (22" X 28") Style B. Rolled, Very Fine/Near Mint.
Estimate: $400-up Starting Bid: $200

83198 Blonde Bait (Associated Film, 1956). Half Sheet (22"X 28"). Very Fine- on Paper.
Estimate: $400-up Starting Bid: $200

83199   Dragstrip Girl (American International, 1957). One Sheet (27"X 41"). Mint.
Estimate: $500-up Starting Bid: $250

83200   Reform School Girl (American International, 1957). One Sheet (27"X 41"). Fine/Very Fine.
Estimate: $400-up
Starting Bid: $200

83201   Faster, Pussycat! Kill! Kill! (Eve Productions, 1965). One Sheet (27" X 41") Style A. Voluptuous Tura Satana leads a gang of go-go dancers on a murderous crime spree in this Russ Meyer exploitation classic. Tura plays Varla, who hits the road with her girlfriend Rosie (Haji), and the reluctant Billie (Lori Williams) and mayhem ensues. This is the classic "style A" one sheet with an impressive image of Satana's assets. Condition issues on this unrestored sheet include minor edge wear on the left, a few light smudges in the border, and crossfold separation. Very Fine.
Estimate: $1,500-up Starting Bid: $750

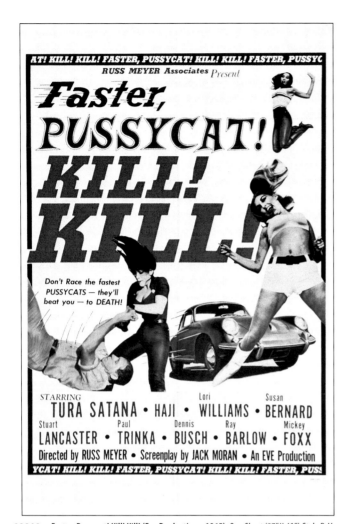

83202   Faster, Pussycat! Kill! Kill! (Eve Productions, 1965). One Sheet (27" X 41") Style B. Very Fine+.
Estimate: $1,500-up Starting Bid: $750

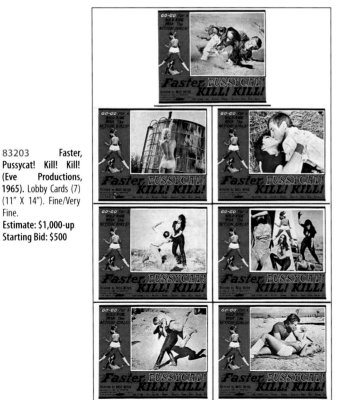

83203   Faster, Pussycat! Kill! Kill! (Eve Productions, 1965). Lobby Cards (7) (11" X 14"). Fine/Very Fine.
Estimate: $1,000-up Starting Bid: $500

83204   Flirtation (J.D. Trop, 1934). One Sheet (27" X 41"). *From the Theaters of Old Detroit Collection.* Fine/Very Fine.
Estimate: $700-up
Starting Bid: $350

83205   Girl With An Itch (Howco, 1958). One Sheet (27" X 41"). Kathy Marlowe stars as a scheming blonde hitchhiker who thinks she's found her new sugar daddy in ranch owner Ben Cooper (Robert Armstrong), while she is really attracted to his son Orrie (Robert Clarke). One of the classic bad girl films of the 1950s, this film was directed by Ronald V. Ashcroft who also directed *The Astounding She-Monster* (1957). This sensational poster is perhaps the rarest title from this genre and has minor fold wear, pinpoint crossfold separations, and a crease in the lower right border which happened after it was paper-backed. This poster never shows up! Very Fine on Paper.
Estimate: $1,500-up Starting Bid: $750

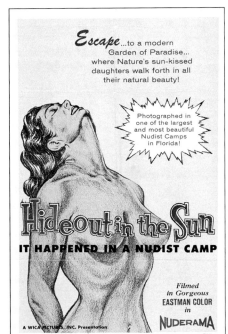

83206 Hideout in the Sun (Wica Pictures, 1960). One Sheet (27" X 41"). Folded, Fine.
Estimate: $250-up
No Minimum Bid

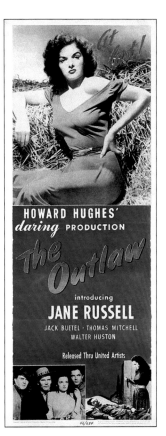

83209 The Outlaw (United Artists, 1946). Insert (14" X 36"). Fine/Very Fine on Paper.
Estimate: $500-up Starting Bid: $250

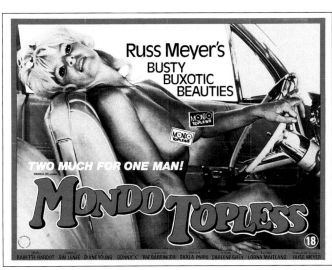

83207 Mondo Topless (Eve Productions, 1966). British Quad (30" X 40"). Very Fine.
Estimate: $400-up Starting Bid: $200

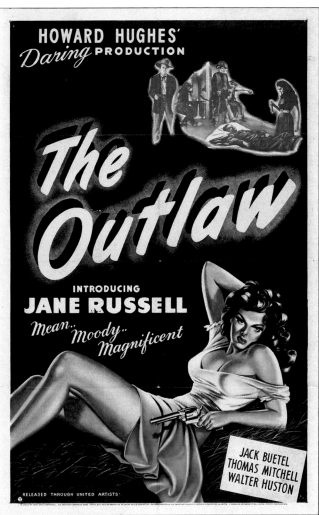

83208 The Outlaw (United Artists, 1946). One Sheet (27" X 41"). Long noted for its intensely controversial history, posters from *The Outlaw*, with some of the sexiest images ever connected with a mainstream Hollywood film, have always been avidly collected. This colorful one sheet, from the general release in 1946, doesn't disappoint, with its art based on famed pinup artist Zoe Mozert's original. The film was made in 1941, but due to censorship issues with Jane Russell's bosoms having too much screen time, there was only a very small release in 1943 before the film was pulled again. There are minor pinholes in the corners with a few in the background. The credits have minor smudges and there is pain on the reverse of the poster not affecting the front of the poster. Above Russell's name there is a small scratch and one above the title. Fine/Very Fine.
Estimate: $1,700-up Starting Bid: $850

83210   Jesse James (20th Century Fox, 1939). One Sheet (27" X 41") Style B. It took the talent and finesse of a great cast and a creative and savvy director to make us forget the historical inaccuracies and just enjoy this as a terrific film. And it didn't hurt to have one of the best illustrators of the 1930's, Frederic C. Madan, handling the colorful poster artwork. Note how skillfully Madan weaves no fewer than six key elements together to make a great piece of art for this ever elusive Style B one sheet. Especially effective is the color coordinated faces of the characters on the left. The sinister "Bob Ford" (John Carradine) is in garish green, while Jesse's gentle mother (Jane Darwell) is in soft pink. The color is very bright for a 1939 poster with the main issues the top and left white borders. There are small missing chips in the top and right corners, and small tears along the top border. There are small cross fold separations, and a slight smudging in the bottom border. The surface has slight crinkling in several places. Very Good+..

Estimate: $12,000-up Starting Bid: $9,500

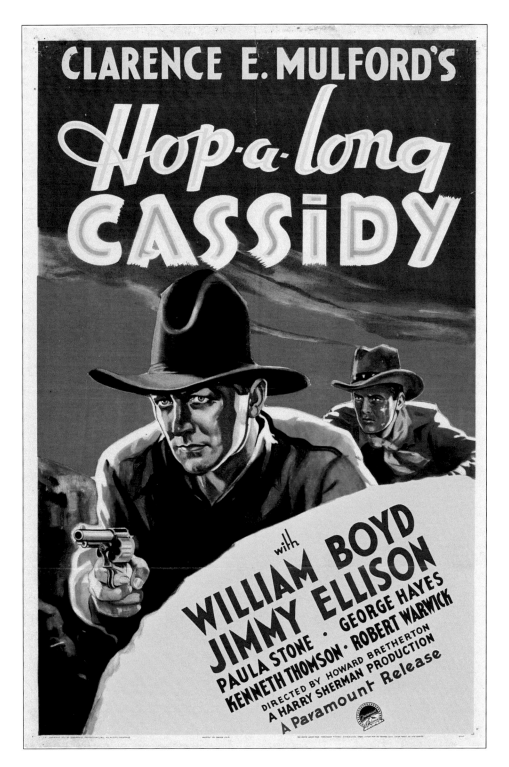

83211 **Hop-a-long Cassidy (Paramount, 1935).** One Sheet (27" X 41"). Clarence E. Mulford's cowboy character Hopalong Cassidy first appeared in a series of novels at the turn of the century. Hopalong made his screen debut in 1935 in this film, with silent star William Boyd in the lead role. Bill Cassidy earns his nickname after being shot in the leg trying to aid his young friend Johnny Nelson (Jimmy Ellison) at the Bar 20, in the midst of a war between cattle ranchers. With the aid of oldtimer Uncle Ben (George "Gabby" Hayes) Hopalong is able to discover who the real rustlers are and to clear Nelson's sweetheart's (Mary Meeker) father's name. This picture began the most successful series of the era, its immediate and enormous popularity launched over sixty subsequent Hopalong pictures through 1948, each featuring trusty sidekick Gabby. William Boyd, very astutely purchased the rights to the character and the films, approaching NBC in 1949 to develop what would be the first network Western television series, making Hopalong Cassidy a household name that would endure for generations. Original paper from this seminal Western is nearly impossible to come by, with probably less than a handful of posters existing today, as we know of only one other copy. This colorful sheet shows pinholes, mainly in the corners, edge wear and small stains at the top, small tears in the borders, bends in the lower right corner, and a minor chip in the lower left corner. To offer such a clean, unrestored one sheet from this important title is a real delight, and we know this gem deserves a place of honor in a top collection. Fine.

Estimate: $10,000-up Starting Bid: $8,000

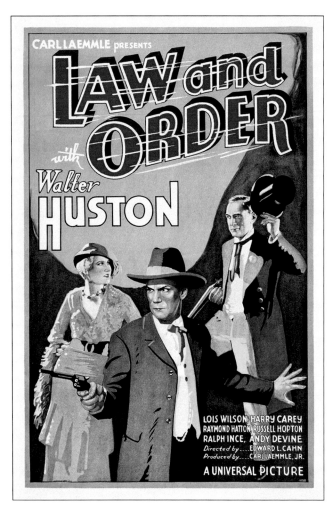

83212 Law and Order (Universal, 1932). One Sheet (27" X 41"). The names have been changed, but any Western fan will recognize this as the story of Wyatt Earp, Doc Holiday, and the gunfight at the O.K. Corral. Walter Huston, Russell Hopton, Raymond Hatton, and Harry Carey are the gunfighters. This gorgeous stone litho one sheet has fantastic, colorful artwork and a very fresh appearance. There were small tears in the left border, and a small bit missing from the top right corner, all of which has been smoothed over with professional restoration. This is a very rare A- Western poster. Fine+ on Linen.
Estimate: $2,000-up Starting Bid: $1,000

83213 Destry Rides Again (Universal, 1932). One Sheet (27" X 41"). Cowboy hero Tom Mix, as Tom Destry, is framed and thrown into jail. He lives to ride again and with help from Sally Dangerfield (Claudia Dell), goes after his partner Tom Brand (Earle Foxe) who was behind the murderous plot from the beginning. One of the most popular Cowboy stars of the era, Mix had a brief retirement from films, but made his comeback in a big way with this picture, his first talkie, which makes this a very special item for Western collectors. This stunning poster has been professionally restored to address pinholes, a chip in the bottom border, and a nick in the left border. The top few inches of white border and just into the yellow field was trimmed, but after excellent conservation the poster appears mint. The posters from Mix's nine Westerns for Universal are some of the hardest from his career to find. In 2005 we sold a three sheet from this film for over $10,000! Very Good/Fine on Linen.
Estimate: $5,000-up Starting Bid: $2,500

83214 The Heart Buster (Fox, 1924). One Sheet (27" X 41"). Fine+ on Linen.
Estimate: $2,000-up Starting Bid: $1,000

83215   Destry Rides Again (Universal, 1939). One Sheet (27" X 41"). With a stellar cast and a first rate script, Universal brought James Stewart and Marlene Dietrich together and created one of the classics of the greatest year in the Golden Age of Hollywood! This lovely one sheet with vibrant colors has some wear to the borders and a couple of small chips in the middle horizontal fold on the left border. Professional conservation has restored the poster to its original glory. *From the Theaters of Old Detroit Collection.* Very Good/Fine on Linen.
Estimate: $4,000-up Starting Bid: $2,000

83216   Silent Men (Columbia, 1933). One Sheet (27" X 41"). Fine/Very Fine on Linen.
Estimate: $2,000-up Starting Bid: $1,000

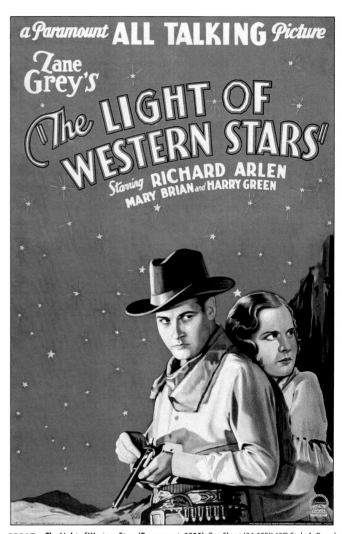

83217   The Light of Western Stars (Paramount, 1930). One Sheet (26.25" X 40") Style A. Based on a Zane Grey novel, Richard Arlen stars as Dick Bailey, a ranch hand who is out for revenge when his friend is murdered by the corrupt businessman Stack (Fred Kohler). Perky star Mary Brian plays Ruth Hammond, the new owner of Bailey's ranch, who needs his help when Stack attempts to steal her property. In all, Arlen and Brian would star in eleven pictures together, and were a popular pairing for Paramount. This unique and gorgeous stone litho is a full-bleed one sheet, as originally printed and has not been trimmed. Paramount did these full-bleeds for only a couple of seasons before discontinuing them. It has been professionally restored to address a few small tack holes in the background. The lithographic colors are stunning and this gem will be a rare find for a lucky collector. Very Fine- on Linen.
Estimate: $2,000-up Starting Bid: $1,000

83218 **The Life of Buffalo Bill (Pawnee Bill Film Co., 1912).** One Sheet (27" X 41"). William F. Cody (a.k.a. Buffalo Bill) was one of the most colorful figures of the Old West. Before Cody went into show business he had a number of occupations including: trapper, Colorado "Fifty-Niner," Pony Express rider, wagon master, stagecoach driver, Civil War soldier, and even hotel manager. He was awarded the Congressional Medal of Honor in 1872 for his role as a scout for the United States Army (1868-1872). Cody's Wild West Shows were an enormous success in the late 1880s and remained a popular subject in the early 1900s when this very early silent three-reeler was made. Prior to restoration, there were small chips in the right border, tears in the borders, two of which go into the art, and a top left corner chip. There is a small bit of surface paper loss on the left side which occurred after restoration. This is a gorgeous stone litho one sheet displaying a dashing figure of Cody in his prime. Fine/Very Fine on Linen.
Estimate: $2,700-up Starting Bid: $1,350

83220 **The Trail of '98 (MGM, 1928).** Pre-War Australian Daybill (15" X 40"). Fine/Very Fine on Linen.
Estimate: $600-up Starting Bid: $300

83219 **Tumbleweeds (United Artists, 1925).** Window Card (14" X 22"). Fine+.
Estimate: $800-up Starting Bid: $750

83221 **Silent Men (Columbia, 1933).** Lobby Card Set of 8 (11" X 14"). Fine+.
Estimate: $600-up Starting Bid: $300

83224   Man of the Forest (Paramount, 1933). Lobby Card Set of 8 (11" X 14"). Very Fine.
Estimate: $600-up Starting Bid: $300

83222   Justice of the Range (Columbia, 1935). Lobby Card Set of 8 (11" X 14"). Very Fine.
Estimate: $600-up Starting Bid: $300

83225   Ride, Ranger, Ride (Republic, 1936). One Sheet (27" X 41"). Very Fine- on Linen.
Estimate: $600-up Starting Bid: $300

83226   Strawberry Roan (Universal, 1933). One Sheet (27" X 41"). Very Good/Fine on Linen.
Estimate: $600-up Starting Bid: $300

83223   Wild Horse Mesa (Paramount, 1932). Lobby Card Set of 8 (11" X 14"). Very Fine+.
Estimate: $500-up Starting Bid: $250

83227 Yodelin' Kid from Pine Ridge (Republic, 1937). One Sheet (27" X 41"). Fine/Very Fine on Linen.
Estimate: $600-up
Starting Bid: $300

83229 Shine On Harvest Moon (Republic, 1938). One Sheet (27" X 41"). Fine on Linen.
Estimate: $700-up
Starting Bid: $350

83228 In Old Caliente (Republic, 1939). One Sheet (27" X 41"). Very Fine- on Linen.
Estimate: $2,000-up
Starting Bid: $1,000

83230 San Fernando Valley (Republic, 1944). One Sheet (27" X 41"). Fine on Linen.
Estimate: $500-up
Starting Bid: $250

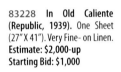

For full lot descriptions, enlargeable images and online bidding, visit HA.com/7025

83231 The Santa Fe Trail (Paramount, 1930). Half Sheet (22" X 28"). Rolled, Fine-.
Estimate: $600-up Starting Bid: $300

83232 **The Spoilers** (Paramount, 1930). Half Sheet (22" X 28"). The second of four film versions of Rex Beach's Western tale of the Alaskan gold rush, this version stars Gary Cooper as Roy Glenister, a prospector whose gold mine is in jeopardy of being stolen by crooked politician Alec McNamara (William Boyd). The poster had tack holes in the image, a few light wrinkles, and a small tear at the bottom edge. These minor issues have been repaired with expert restoration and this colorful half sheet, with its original varnish, and a terrific early image of Gary Cooper, is a stunner. Rolled, Fine/Very Fine.
Estimate: $800-up Starting Bid: $400

83233 **One Man Law** (Columbia, 1932). Insert (14" X 36") Style D Stock. Very Good on Paper.
Estimate: $600-up Starting Bid: $300

83234 **My Darling Clementine** (20th Century Fox, 1946). One Sheet (27" X 41"). Henry Fonda stars as the reluctant marshal, Wyatt Earp, in John Ford's classic version of the gunfight at the OK Corral. Victor Mature, in one of his best performances, is memorable as Doc Holliday, and Cathy Downs stars as Earp's sweetheart, Clementine. Holliday teams with Earp for the legendary showdown with the Clanton family, led by Old Man Clanton (Walter Brennan). This ranks as one of the top Hollywood Westerns. This stunner had only pinholes in the corners, fold wear, and a small tear in the top border, but all has been professionally restored. The artwork, featuring the seductive Linda Darnell, was done by Sergio Gargiulo. Very Fine on Linen.
Estimate: $2,000-up Starting Bid: $1,800

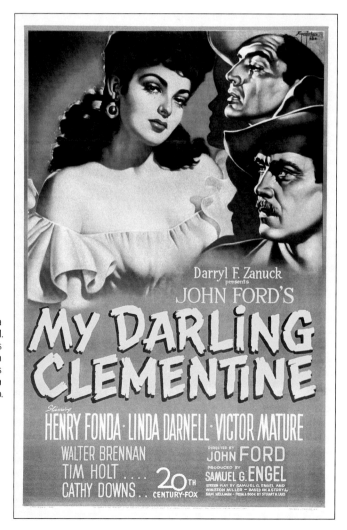

83235 **My Darling Clementine (20th Century Fox, 1946).**
Insert (14" X 36"). Folded, Fine/Very Fine.
Estimate: $400-up Starting Bid: $200

83237 **Shane (Paramount, 1953).** Belgian (13.75" X 21.75").
Folded, Fine+.
Estimate: $500-up Starting Bid: $250

83238 **Winchester '73 (Universal International, 1950).** Belgian (14" X 21.5"). Folded, Fine.
Estimate: $500-up Starting Bid: $250

83236 **Shane (Paramount, 1953).** One Sheet (27" X 41").
Fine+ on Linen.
Estimate: $1,200-up Starting Bid: $600

83239 **Winchester '73 (Universal International, 1950).** Lobby Card Set of 8 (11" X 14"). The first of five collaborations between director Anthony Mann and star James Stewart, this riveting Western is a groundbreaking look at the harsh realities of frontier life. Following the lives of each owner of a prized Winchester rifle, the story unveils the violence and death that is inevitable. Shelley Winters, Dan Duryea, and Stephen McNally co-star in this superb classic. In great condition, each card in the set shows only corner bumps, and a minimal dust shadow at the edges. One card has a light scratch at the top of the image, and one has a small tear in the right border. Rarely seen in a full set, these cards will garner much deserved attention. Fine/Very Fine.
Estimate: $1,200-up
Starting Bid: $600

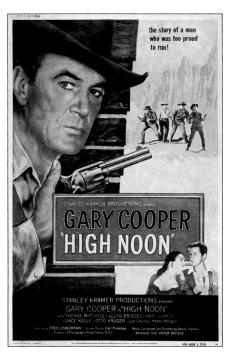

83240 High Noon (United Artists, 1952). Poster (40" X 60")
Style Y. Very Good- on Paper.
Estimate: $1,000-up Starting Bid: $500

83241 The Plainsman (Paramount, 1936). French Affiche
(23.5" X 31.5"). Fine/Very Fine on Linen.
Estimate: $500-up Starting Bid: $250

83242 **The Lone Ranger** (Warner
Brothers, 1956). Three Sheet (41" X 81").
The Masked Rider of the Plains gallops
onto the silver screen in the form of the
great Clayton Moore. This was the first of
two Technicolor features made to cash in
on the popularity of the TV series, which
began in 1949 and was still running when
this feature was released; the series would
continue until 1957. Jay Silverheels is of
course Tonto, the Ranger's sidekick who
helps him bring crooked land baron Re-
ece Kilgore (Lyle Bettger) to justice, while
Bonita Granville stars as the heroine. This
dramatic three sheet, perhaps the best
image of the beloved hero, has had some
restoration to address a chip and a tear in
the top border that extends into the background, a tear in the left border, and small
chips and two tears in the artwork. Fine/
Very Fine on Linen.
Estimate: $1,200 Starting Bid: $600

83243 **The Lone Ranger and the Lost City of Gold** (United
Artists, 1958). 40" X 60". Rolled, Fine-.
Estimate: $400-up Starting Bid: $200

83244   Duel in the Sun (United Artists, 1947). Lobby Card Set of 8 (11" X 14"). Fine+.
Estimate: $600-up Starting Bid: $300

83247   Butch Cassidy and the Sundance Kid (20th Century Fox, 1969). Insert (14" X 36"). Rolled, Near Mint/Mint.
Estimate: $600-up Starting Bid: $300

83245   Shane (Paramount, 1953). Italian 4 - Foglio (55" X 78"). Fine on Linen.
Estimate: $800-up Starting Bid: $400

83246   Butch Cassidy and the Sundance Kid (20th Century Fox, 1969). British Quad (30" X 40"). Very Fine+.
Estimate: $600-up
Starting Bid: $400

83248   Butch Cassidy and the Sundance Kid (20th Century Fox, 1969). One Sheet (27" X 41") Style B. Folded, Very Fine.
Estimate: $500-up Starting Bid: $400

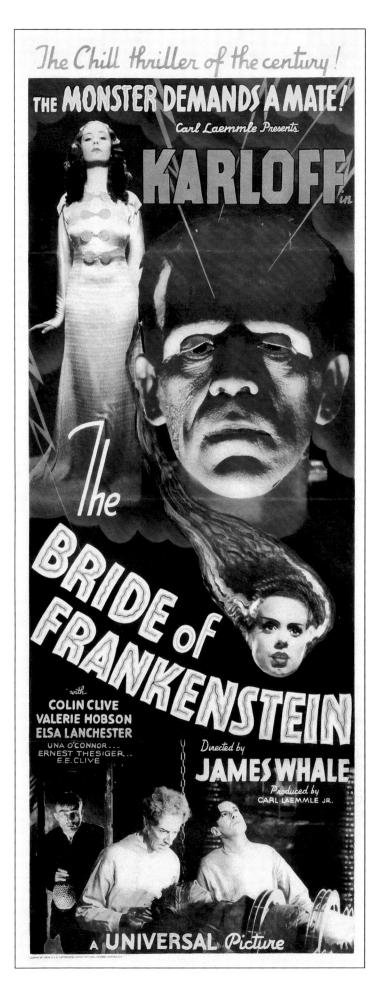

83249   The Bride of Frankenstein (Universal, 1935). Insert (14" X 36").
One cannot overstate the rarity and desirability of original release poster material for this, one of the greatest classic horror films of all time. Only a handful of these insert posters have ever surfaced, and this poster features some of the best art designed for this release. Boris Karloff as the Frankenstein Monster has never looked more menacing, and all the other main characters, from Elsa Lanchester as "the Bride", to Colin Clive, Valerie Hobson, Ernest Thesiger and Dwight Frye, are all well represented on this strikingly eerie poster. There was expert touchup work on the folds. There was very thin masa paper applied on the reverse of the entire poster. There were small chips in three of the borders, with some small tears, a top right corner chip, and a one small tack hole each in the left and the right border, all of which have been expertly restored. One of the most iconic items in all of movie poster collecting, one rarely gets a chance to bid on this outstanding rarity. Fine+.
Estimate: $95,000-up Starting Bid: $85,000

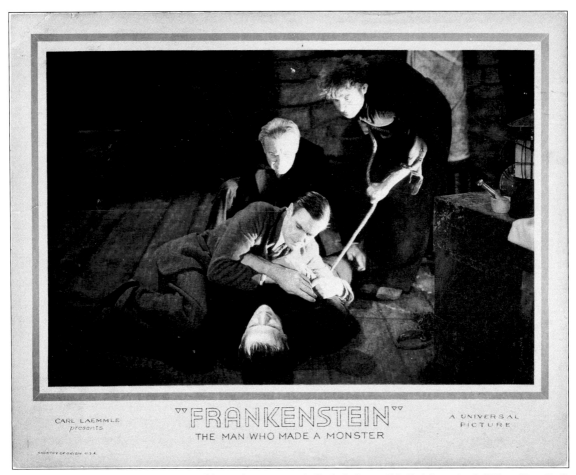

83250   **Frankenstein (Universal, 1931).** Lobby Card (11" X 14"). In one of the most dramatic scenes in the film, Dr. Frankenstein (Colin Clive), his associate, Dr. Waldman (Edward Van Sloan), and Fritz, the hunchback assistant (Dwight Frye) pin down the monster (Boris Karloff) after they realize he is incapable of logic or reason. The Gothic laboratory and the ominous lighting make this card a standout. Original cards with the Monster are on just about everyone's wish list. There are pinholes in the top center, light top border edge wear, and a faint dust shadow along the border edges. On the lower left and top left corners there are small bends. The back has some tempura paint and archival tape on the reverse edges. Fine+.
Estimate: $5,500-up **Starting Bid: $2,750**

83251   **The Black Cat (Universal, 1934).** Pressbook (Multiple Pages). Incest, murder, torture, devil worship and perverse psychological obsessions are layered throughout this film as Boris Karloff and Bela Lugosi (in their first co-starring feature) play a game of chess to determine the fate of a young couple. Edgar G. Ulmer directs, and the script has little or nothing to do with Edgar Allan Poe's classic tale. This terrific pressbook is chock-full of cool ad material for the title. The book has fold wear and separations, tape and a price sticker remnant on the front cover, and corner creases. Also included is a publicity supplement, folded inside the pressbook. Fine+.
Estimate: $2,000-up **Starting Bid: $1,500**

83252   **Dracula (Universal, 1931).** Jumbo Lobby Card (14" X 17"). Producing the best of the horror genre, first with *The Hunchback of Notre Dame* and *The Phantom of the Opera*, Universal studios quickly set its sights on Bram Stoker's *Dracula*. With Tod Browning directing, a relatively unknown Hungarian actor, Bela Lugosi, was cast in the lead role, having already successfully played the vampire on Broadway. The result was one of the most iconic films in cinematic history and one of the top titles for poster collectors to own. This rare and very impressive jumbo lobby card features Count Dracula dominating his henchman Renfield (Dwight Frye) with the lovely Mina Harker (Helen Chandler) in a helpless trance. It is in extremely nice condition with only a few light creases, and minimal wear at the corners. Opportunities to obtain paper from this horror classic rarely come along and this beauty will be a star item in any serious collection. Very Fine.
Estimate: $20,000-up Starting Bid: $10,000

83253 **Dracula (Universal, 1931).** British Front of House Photos (8) (8" X 10"). This is an amazing find of 8 original issue photos from the British release of this time honored film. Three of the photos prominently feature Bela Lugosi as Dracula, including one with perhaps one of the most important images in sci-fi/horror history, that of Dracula being repelled by the cross being held in front of him by the vampire hunter, Van Helsing (Edward van Sloan). There are pinholes in the corners, one has a small stain in the top border, one has a small chip in the lower right corner, and several have minor surface scuffs and mild creases. It is important to note that these are not faded as we see most photos from this are. Only the brides photo shows a bit of toning. The black and white is crisp and they are all on double weight paper. Fine+.
Estimate: $4,000-up Starting Bid: $2,000

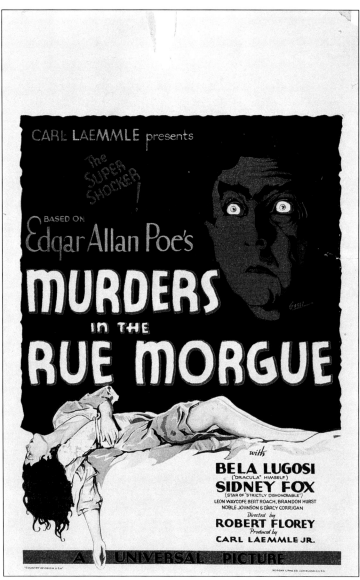

83254 **Murders in the Rue Morgue (Universal, 1932).** Window Card (14" X 22"). Robert Florey, having lost the chance to direct *Frankenstein* (1931) when James Whale was selected for the job, was offered this equally horrifying project, an adaptation of Edgar Allan Poe's classic tale. Bela Lugosi, a year after his success in *Dracula,* is terrific as Dr. Mirakle, a carnival showman/ mad scientist who experiments with mixing the blood of his pet gorilla with that of a series of prostitutes he murders. When he realizes he needs a virgin for the tests to work, he sets his sights on Camille L'Espanaye (Sidney Fox). Poor Camille's mother is murdered by the gorilla, the girl is imprisoned in Mirakle's lab, and only her boyfriend Pierre Dupin (Leon Ames a.k.a. Waycoff) can solve the case. With the dark and expressionistic cinematography of Karl Freund, this eerie thriller is a masterpiece of the genre and widely admired by critics today. Paper from this top title is scarce, especially in its original unrestored condition such as this wonderful item, which is guaranteed to be an authentic original release window card. It shows a chip at the top, a smaller one in the top right corner, and light edge wear at the bottom. There are two tears at the right border and one in the left, backed by archival tape. The dramatic artwork is by Karoly Grosz. For serious fans of the horror genre, images of Lugosi from his early classics are always the ultimate prize. Very Good/Fine.
Estimate: $10,000-up Starting Bid: $5,000

83255 Mark of the Vampire (MGM, 1935). Lobby Card (11" X 14"). Director Tod Browning has said that he remade his 1927 thriller, *London After Midnight*, with Lon Chaney, duplicating shot-for-shot for this still hotly debated horror classic. Unfortunately the 1927 version has no known extant prints. Posters for this title have been just as nonexistent for this film, particularly this Bela Lugosi portrait card, which many consider the gem of the set. Lugosi is giving it his vampire best in this scene playing straight horror. He wasn't told until just a few day's before the film wrapped of the twist ending that still sets off many a lively debate at film festival retrospective showings. That's Henry Wadsworth and lovely Elizabeth Allen in the card with Lugosi. This card had the left and right borders trimmed prior to being beautifully and expertly restored by laying the card atop another card and carefully airbrushing in the seams. This overlay leaves a mild vertical crease along the left border. The original image was completely intact. There has been some great touch up for a small tear in the bottom border, and a faint smudge in the title. The card is authentic, displays beautifully and one of the rarest

cards from the set. We have never offered another copy of this card.. *From the collection of Kirk Hammett*. Good+ on Cardstock.
Estimate: $9,000-up Starting Bid: $8,500

83256 White Zombie (United Artists, 1932). Lobby Card (11" X 14"). Fine/Very Fine on Paper.
Estimate: $6,000-up Starting Bid: $3,000

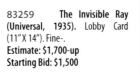
83259   The Invisible Ray (Universal, 1935). Lobby Card (11" X 14"). Fine-.
Estimate: $1,700-up
Starting Bid: $1,500

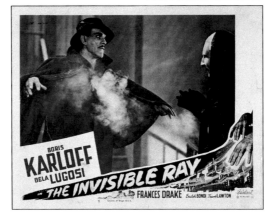

83260   The Invisible Ray (Realart, R-1948). Lobby Card (11" X 14"). Fine+.
Estimate: $200-up No Minimum Bid

83257   The Invisible Ray (Universal, 1935). Pre-War Australian Daybill (15" X 40"). Fine on Linen.
Estimate: $3,000-up Starting Bid: $2,250

83258   The Invisible Ray (Universal, 1935). Lobby Card (11" X 14"). Fine/Very Fine.
Estimate: $600-up Starting Bid: $500

83261   Son of Frankenstein (Universal, 1939). Turkish One Sheet (28" X 39.5"). Very Fine+ on Linen.
Estimate: $1,400-up Starting Bid: $700

83262 **House of Frankenstein (Universal, 1944).** One Sheet (27" X 41"). It's been almost five years since we've had an original one sheet on this great title. Glenn Strange, not Karloff, is the Frankenstein monster this time around, but Karloff turns in a terrific performance as the evil Doctor Niemann. John Carradine is on hand as Dracula, and Lon Chaney Jr. returns as The Wolfman. The other evil man on the poster is J. Carroll Naish, the hunchback assistant to Karloff. This is one of the best villain groups ever put together! There has been some restoration and the poster placed on linen. There were pinholes in the borders and center of the artwork, small chips in the borders and corners, small tears in the right border, and a few tears into the artwork at the bottom. There are some minor crossfold separations and fold wear. Very Good/Fine on Linen.
Estimate: $8,000-up Starting Bid: $6,000

83263 **House of Frankenstein (Universal, 1944).** Half Sheet (22" X 28"). The most entertaining and gleefully macabre of Universal's "monster team up" films, *House of Frankenstein* cast Karloff as the mad scientist, Glenn Strange as the Monster, Lon Chaney Jr. as the Wolf Man, J. Carrol Naish as the Hunchback, and John Carradine as Dracula, "all together!" Minor condition issues included some minor chipping in the left and bottom borders, pinholes in the corners and the image, all of which has been addressed with professional restoration. Fine/Very Fine on Paper.
Estimate: $7,000-up Starting Bid: $6,500

83264　House of Frankenstein (Universal, 1944). Title Lobby Card (11" X 14"). Very Good-.
Estimate: $1,700-up Starting Bid: $1,500

83265　House of Frankenstein (Universal, 1944). Lobby Card (11" X 14"). Fine+.
Estimate: $1,000-up Starting Bid: $500

83266　The Ghost of Frankenstein (Universal, 1942). Title Lobby Card (11" X 14"). Fine-.
Estimate: $3,200-up Starting Bid: $3,000

83267   **The Ghost of Frankenstein (Universal, 1942).** Lobby Card (11" X 14"). Fine+.
Estimate: $1,200-up Starting Bid: $600

83268   Frankenstein Meets the Wolf Man (Universal, 1943). Title Lobby Card (11" X 14"). Fine.
Estimate: $2,500-up Starting Bid: $1,250

83269   Frankenstein Meets the Wolf Man (Universal, 1943). Lobby Card (11" X 14"). Very Fine-.
Estimate: $1,500-up Starting Bid: $750

83270   Frankenstein Meets the Wolf Man (Universal, 1943). Lobby Card (11" X 14"). Fine/Very Fine.
Estimate: $1,000-up Starting Bid: $500

83271 Frankenstein Meets the Wolf Man (Universal, 1950s). First Post-War Release Belgian (15.5" X 20"). Folded, Fine/Very Fine.
Estimate: $600-up
Starting Bid: $450

83273 The Wolf Man (Universal, 1941). Lobby Card (11" X 14"). Fine on Paper.
Estimate: $500-up Starting Bid: $250

83272 The Wolf Man (Universal, 1941). Lobby Card (11" X 14"). Fine on Paper.
Estimate: $4,500-up Starting Bid: $2,250

83274 The Mummy's Hand (Universal, 1940). Lobby Card (11" X 14"). Very Good.
Estimate: $2,400-up Starting Bid: $2,250

83275 The Mummy's Ghost (Universal, 1944). Half Sheet (22" X 28"). John Carradine, as an Egyptian high priest, travels to America to reclaim the soul of Princess Anaka and her guardian, the Living Mummy. Lon Chaney, Jr. reprises his role as the stalking terror of the sands and adds depth to the character for the first time. This terrific poster has pinholes in the border and artwork, fold wear with crossfold separations, a tear in the bottom border, chip in the top border at the fold, and a lower right corner crease; the poster has had some touch-up paint applied. Fine on Paper.
Estimate: $4,000-up Starting Bid: $3,000

83276   The Mummy's Curse (Universal, 1944). Lobby Card (11" X 14"). Fine-.
Estimate: $600-up Starting Bid: $500

83277   The Mummy's Curse (Universal, 1944). Lobby Card (11" X 14"). Fine-.
Estimate: $700-up Starting Bid: $650

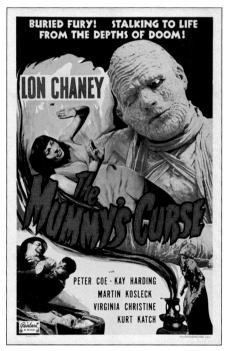

83278   The Mummy's Curse (Realart, R-1951). One Sheet (27" X 41"). Very Fine on Linen.
Estimate: $1,000-up Starting Bid: $500

83279   The Mummy (Universal International, 1959). Six Sheet (81" X 81"). Near Mint-.
Estimate: $700-up Starting Bid: $350

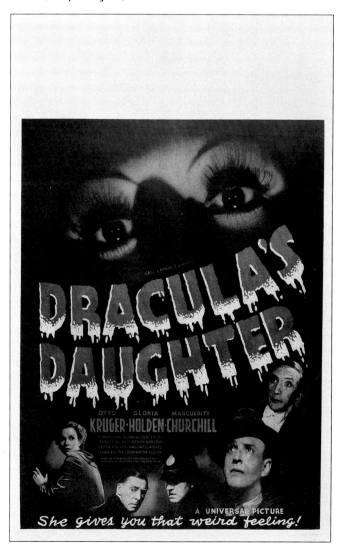

83280   Dracula's Daughter (Universal, 1936). Window Card (14" X 22"). Fine+ on Cardstock.
Estimate: $1,400-up Starting Bid: $1,150

83281 Dracula's Daughter (Universal, 1936). Lobby Card (11" X 14"). Fine+.
Estimate: $1,000-up
Starting Bid: $500

83284 Bela Lugosi Stage Production of "The Tell-Tale Heart" (Late 1940s). Window Card (14" X 22"). Fine/Very Fine on Cardstock.
Estimate: $600-up Starting Bid: $300

83282 The Human Monster (Monogram, 1939). Insert (14" X 36"). Fine- on Linen.
Estimate: $1,000-up Starting Bid: $500

83283 Spooks Run Wild (Monogram, 1941). One Sheet (27" X 41"). *From The Theatres of Old Detroit Collection.* Fine/Very Fine on Linen.
Estimate: $1,000-up Starting Bid: $500

83285 Bride of the Monster (Filmmakers Releasing, 1956). One Sheet (27" X 41"). Fine-.
Estimate: $1,000-up Starting Bid: $500

83288   The Uninvited (Paramount, 1944). One Sheet (27" X 41"). Very Good on Linen.
Estimate: $800-up Starting Bid: $700

83286   Before I Hang (Columbia, 1940). One Sheet (27" X 41"). *From the Theaters of Old Detroit Collection.* Fine on Linen.
Estimate: $1,200-up Starting Bid: $600

83289   The Uninvited (Paramount, 1944). Half Sheet (22" X 28") Style A. Very Good/Fine on Paper.
Estimate: $700-up Starting Bid: $600

83290   Dante's Inferno (Jawitz Pictures Corp., 1921). Title Lobby Card (11" X 14"). Fine-.
Estimate: $400-up Starting Bid: $200

83287   The Bride of Frankenstein (Realart, R-1953). One Sheet (27" X 41"). Fine/Very Fine on Linen.
Estimate: $800-up Starting Bid: $400

83293   El Vampiro (Alemeda Films, 1957). Mexican One Sheet (29" X 43.5"). Fine/Very Fine on Linen.
Estimate: $1,200-up
Starting Bid: $600

83291   The Hate Ship (First National, 1929). Swedish One Sheet (27.5" X 39.5"). Rolled, Fine/Very Fine.
Estimate: $500-up Starting Bid: $250

83292   The Nude Vampire (Les Distrubuteurs Associes, 1970). French Grande (45" X 62"). Very Fine+.
Estimate: $600-up Starting Bid: $300

83294   Horror of Dracula (Universal International, 1958). British Double Crown (19" X 28"). Released in England as *Dracula*, many consider this to be the ultimate adaptation of the Bram Stocker horror novel. Christopher Lee portrays Count Dracula in what would become a career defining role. This country-of-origin poster is the only one we have ever seen and is assuredly rare. Condition includes corner pinholes, slight water stains in the bottom right corner. Slight fold wear and very minor top left corner chip and minor soiling. The poster has slight tanning color overall and has been supported with a very thin masa paper backing which is hard to detect. Folded, Fine/Very Fine.
Estimate: $1,800-up Starting Bid: $1,500

83295 The Invisible Man (Realart, R-1951). One Sheet (27" X 41"). *From the collection of Wade Williams.* Fine+. Estimate: $2,500-up Starting Bid: $1,250

83296 Creature From the Black Lagoon (Universal International, 1954). Insert (14" X 36"). Folded, Fine+. Estimate: $4,000-up Starting Bid: $2,000

83297 Creature From the Black Lagoon (Universal International, 1954). Half Sheet (22" X 28") Style B. Very Fine+ on Paper. Estimate: $4,000-up Starting Bid: $3,500

83298   Creature From the Black Lagoon (Universal International, 1954). Window Card (14" X 22"). Very Fine-.
Estimate: $1,400-up Starting Bid: $1,250

83299   Creature From the Black Lagoon (Universal International, 1954). Title Lobby Card (11" X 14"). Very Fine-.
Estimate: $1,200-up Starting Bid: $600

For full lot descriptions, enlargeable images and online bidding, visit HA.com/7025

83300   Creature From the Black Lagoon (Universal International, 1954). Lobby Card (11" X 14"). Very Fine-.
Estimate: $800-up Starting Bid: $400

83301   Creature From the Black Lagoon (Universal International, 1954). Lobby Card (11" X 14"). Very Fine.
Estimate: $600-up Starting Bid: $300

83302   Creature From the Black Lagoon (Universal International, 1954). Lobby Cards (2) (11" X 14"). Very Fine-.
Estimate: $600-up Starting Bid: $300

83303   Creature From the Black Lagoon (Universal International, 1954). Lobby Cards (3) (11" X 14"). Very Fine.
Estimate: $500-up Starting Bid: $250

83304   Revenge of the Creature (Universal International, 1955). Three Sheet (41" X 81"). *From the collection of Wade Williams.* Fine+ on Linen.
Estimate: $3,000-up Starting Bid: $1,500

83306   Revenge of the Creature (Universal International, 1955). Lobby Card (11" X 14"). Fine+.
Estimate: $400-up Starting Bid: $200

83305   Revenge of the Creature (Universal International, 1955). Half Sheet (22" X 28") Style B. Rolled, Very Fine-.
Estimate: $2,200-up Starting Bid: $1,800

83307 Revenge of the Creature/ The Creature Walks Among Us Lot (Universal International, 1955-1956). Window Cards (2) (14" X 22"). Fine. Estimate: $1,000-up Starting Bid: $500

83309 The Creature Walks Among Us (Universal International, 1956). Half Sheet (22" X 28") Style B. Folded, Fine/Very Fine. Estimate: $600-up Starting Bid: $300

83310 The Creature Walks Among Us (Universal International, 1956). Lobby Card Set of 8 (11" X 14"). Fine/Very Fine. Estimate: $1,000-up Starting Bid: $500

83308 The Creature Walks Among Us (Universal International, 1956). One Sheet (27" X 41"). Very Fine- on Linen. Estimate: $1,000-up Starting Bid: $600

83311   All Quiet on the Western Front (Universal, 1930). Half Sheet (22" X 28") Style B. Winning Academy Awards for Best Picture and Director, this seminal war epic stars Lew Ayres as Paul Baumer, one of a group of friends who heads to the front during WWI. A masterpiece of cinematography, director Lewis Milestone films the action sequences with unbelievable reality, which is even more heart-breaking as we get to know the characters in quieter scenes. Influencing war pictures for generations to come, this gripping early film has earned a special place in cinematic history. This rare poster had two tack holes in the top border and one in the title area, two tears in the top right of the image area, and creasing in the right side. Professional restoration has addressed these issues and it now displays very well. Presented here for the first time, this striking style B half sheet will be a highlight to any serious collector. Fine+ on Paper.
Estimate: $4,500-up Starting Bid: $2,250

83312   All Quiet on the Western Front (Universal, 1930). Swedish One Sheet (27.5" X 39.5"). Rolled, Fine/Very Fine.
Estimate: $500-up Starting Bid: $250

83313   The Great Ziegfeld (MGM, 1936). Insert (14" X 36"). The winner of the Best Picture Academy Award, Luise Rainer also won the first of her two Oscars for this fictionalized three-hour epic about the great showman Florenz Ziegfeld. William Powell has the title role, a smooth-talking impresario who convinces a European stage actress (Rainer) to appear in his new "Follies" show. The film looked as if it would be beyond the scope of Universal Studios finances at the time, so they sold the rights to MGM for $300,000. The film would ultimately cost MGM $2 million to produce, a huge sum for that day! It would earn over $40 million! This colorful insert has light foxing, and soiling in the borders, a small tear in the right border, and some creasing in the top right corner. We have never sold this glorious insert before and this rolled copy is fantastic. Rolled, Very Fine.
Estimate: $2,000-up Starting Bid: $1,000

83314 Casablanca (Warner Brothers, 1940s). First Post-War French Affiche (31.5" X 46.5"). American expatriate Rick Blaine (Humphrey Bogart) runs the top night spot in Casablanca during the early years of WWII, but gets more than he bargained for when a European resistance fighter comes to town, with Rick's old flame (Ingrid Bergman) in tow. Ranked as the #3 film of all time in the American Film Institute's 2007 poll, this is certainly a classic, loved by film fans everywhere. Sublime Pierre Pigeot artwork graces this French poster, including a lovely profile of Ms. Bergman. Condition includes pinholes in the image area, fold wear with crossfold separations, a tear through Bogart's name in the title area, and a tear above Paul Henreid, all of which has been smoothed over with professional restoration. Fine+ on Linen.
Estimate: $10,000-up Starting Bid: $9,500

83315 Casablanca (Warner Brothers, 1942). Window Card (14" X 22"). Although the script was unfinished when shooting began, and the process of making the film was unusually chaotic, the result was a true American film classic. Rick Blaine (Humphrey Bogart) is the proprietor of Ricks' American Cafe, located in the mysterious city of Casablanca, trying to maintain an air of neutrality during the Second World War. When old flame Ilsa Lund (Ingrid Bergman) walks through his door seeking to flee the country with her husband, resistance leader Victor Laszlo (Paul Henreid), Blaine's world is turned upside down. The film won three Academy Awards, including Best Picture and Best Director (Michael Curtiz). It should come as no surprise, then, that paper on this title is extremely rare and desirable. This lovely window card had a few small tears in the borders, a crease in the imprint area, and corner bends in the top right and bottom left, but these are all minor flaws that do nothing to detract from the overwhelming beauty and desirability of this great piece. There has been airbrush work in the upper and lower imprint areas. Minimal restoration on a very desirable piece! Fine/Very Fine.
Estimate: $8,000-up Starting Bid: $7,500

83316 Casablanca (Warner Brothers, 1942). Lobby Card (11" X 14"). Fine.
Estimate: $2,400-up Starting Bid: $2,200

83317 Casablanca (Warner Brothers, 1942). Lobby Card (11" X 14"). Fine-.
Estimate: $2,000-up Starting Bid: $1,600

83318 Casablanca (Warner Brothers, 1942). Lobby Card (11" X 14"). Fine.
Estimate: $1,000-up Starting Bid: $800

83319 Casablanca (Warner Brothers, Late 1940s). First Post-War German A1 (24" X 34"). Very Fine on Linen.
Estimate: $400-up Starting Bid: $200

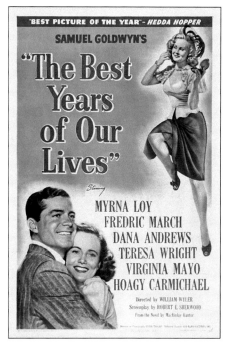

83320 The Best Years of Our Lives (RKO, 1946). One Sheet (27" X 41") Style B. Fine/Very Fine on Linen.
Estimate: $700-up Starting Bid: $350

83321 All the King's Men (Columbia, 1949). Six Sheet (81" X 81"). Broderick Crawford brilliantly portrays the ever-popular but corrupt politician Willie Stark in this dramatic film, which started as a novel by Robert Penn Warren, and is loosely based on the life of Louisiana governor Huey P. Long. Crawford and co-star Mercedes McCambridge both won Academy Awards and the film won Best Picture. This impressive poster has only minor fold wear and two pieces of paper tape on the reverse. Very Fine+.
Estimate: $500-up Starting Bid: $250

83322   All the King's Men (Columbia, 1949). CGC Graded Lobby Card Set of 8 (11" X 14"). Near Mint+.
Estimate: $400-up Starting Bid: $200

83323   All About Eve (20th Century Fox, 1950). One Sheet (27" X 41"). Very Fine- on Linen.
Estimate: $1,500-up Starting Bid: $750

83324   All About Eve (20th Century Fox, 1950). Insert (14" X 36"). Rolled, Fine/Very Fine.
Estimate: $1,200-up Starting Bid: $600

83325   All About Eve (20th Century Fox, 1950). Lobby Card (11" X 14"). Fine/Very Fine.
Estimate: $500-up Starting Bid: $450

83326   **An American in Paris** (MGM, 1951). Three Sheet (41" X 81"). Very Fine on Linen.
Estimate: $1,200-up Starting Bid: $600

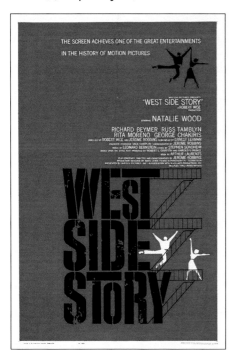

83327   **West Side Story** (United Artists, 1961). One Sheet (27" X 41"). Near Mint-.
Estimate: $500-up Starting Bid: $250

83328   **Lawrence of Arabia** (Columbia, 1962). One Sheet (27" X 41") Roadshow Style A. Earning seven Academy Awards, David Lean's monumental epic is based on T. E. Lawrence's autobiography, *Seven Pillars of Wisdom*, and stars Peter O'Toole, in a role of a lifetime, as the conflicted adventurer. The outstanding supporting cast includes Alec Guinness, Anthony Quinn, Omar Sharif, Jack Hawkins, and Claude Rains. With an unforgettable score by Maurice Jarre, eye popping cinematography by Freddie Young, and themes of identity, war, patriotism, and loyalty, this picture is one of the all-time greats. Posters from this classic always demand attention and this rare Style A Roadshow one sheet is no exception. It features artwork by Howard Terpning and is in spectacular condition, showing only a minute dust shadow at the top of the vertical fold. Near Mint/Mint.
Estimate: $8,000-up Starting Bid: $4,000

83330   Lawrence of Arabia (Columbia, 1962). Lobby Card Set of 8 (11" X 14"). Near Mint-.
Estimate: $900-up Starting Bid: $450

83329   **Lawrence of Arabia (Columbia, 1962).** Insert (14" X 36") Roadshow
Style. Very Fine+ on Paper.
Estimate: $1,500-up Starting Bid: $750

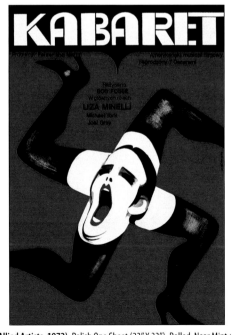

83331   **Cabaret (Allied Artists, 1972).** Polish One Sheet (23" X 33"). Rolled, Near Mint+.
Estimate: $1,600-up Starting Bid: $800

83332 It Happened One Night (Columbia, 1934). Window Card (14" X 22"). Claudette Colbert and Clark Gable make movie magic with this flawless screwball comedy from beloved director Frank Capra. Spoiled socialite Colbert has a hard time running away from her father (Walter Connolly) since she has no conception of money or of how common people live. Ace reporter Clark Gable is only too happy to show her the realities of life in exchange for a front page story. Each scene is classic- from the hitchhiking contest, the art of dunking doughnuts, the singing of "The Man on the Flying Trapeze," to the walls of Jericho. Both stars won Academy Awards for their performances, which perfectly blend romance, comedy, and witty dialogue. Offered by Heritage for the first time is this gorgeous window card, which has been professionally restored to address a few pinholes in the image, a small tear in the right side of the blue background, with some touch-up in the white areas. These issues are no longer apparent, and this very special poster displays magnificently. Fine+ on Cardstock.
Estimate: $5,000-up Starting Bid: $3,500

83333 Gone with the Wind (MGM, 1939). Lobby Displays (4) (18" X 19"). Noted artist Armando Seguso created most of the major artwork for the posters and promotional displays for Selznick's triumphant film. One of his most sought after creations was a series of four "oilette" portraits, featuring Clark Gable, Vivien Leigh, Leslie Howard and Olivia de Havilland. This lot contains all four, in the desired "recessed frame" edition, with original tassel and linen type tape hangers on the reverse. Near the end of his career, Seguso would remark that he was prouder of his paintings for *Gone With the Wind* (done in a hectic three weeks with the legendary taskmaster Selznick breathing down his neck) than any of his other film work in over 30 years in the business. The artwork is clean and intact with only a horizontal scratch in de Havilland's dress and small nicks in her hair. There are minor chips and wear in the frames themselves, except for Leigh's. The Gable has minor staining in three edges. The Leigh portrait has the artist's signature clearly displayed, and on the back of the Gable handwritten in pencil is a stern underlined "MUST BE RETURNED" (We're betting they weren't!) We sold a pristine set of these rare posters in 2004 for $27,600! Fine-.
Estimate: $2,500-up Starting Bid: $1,250

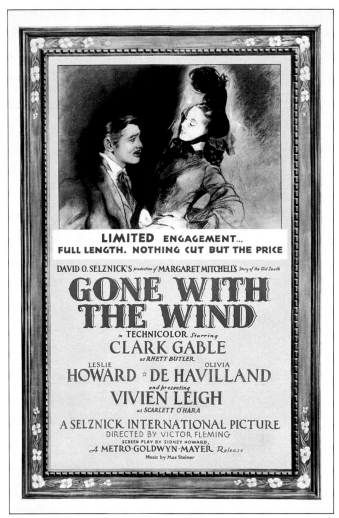

83334 **Gone with the Wind (MGM, 1939).** One Sheet (27" X 41") Style CF. Clark Gable and Vivien Leigh star in one of the most important pictures ever made. The film went on to win Oscars for Best Picture, Actress, Director, Screenplay and Supporting Actress among others. Shortly after the film's initial release the film went into a wider release and to allay the public's fears that the film would be abridged, MGM announced that the only thing that had been cut were the ticket prices. Some of the first one sheets printed were shipped out with paper snipes attached to them announcing the "Full Length, Nothing Cut" information while others were printed with the sniped information printed on the poster. This example has the printed information, identifying it as a poster printed during the second month of the film's release. This is the very rare style CF and is one of the more desirable of the four styles done. The poster had some border chips and a missing lower right corner. There was a large tear from the center of the top border extending into the right border, and two smaller tears at the top. After professional restoration, these issues are no longer apparent. The original release posters for this film do not come to auction often so get one while you can. Fine- on Linen.
Estimate: $6,000-up Starting Bid: $3,000

83335 **Gone with the Wind (MGM, 1939).** Roadshow Lobby Card (11" X 14"). Fine/Very Fine.
Estimate: $600-up Starting Bid: $300

83336   Gone with the Wind (MGM, 1939). Roadshow Lobby Cards (4) (11" X 14"). Fine+.
Estimate: $600-up Starting Bid: $300

83337   Gone with the Wind (MGM, 1939). Pressbook (17" X 19") (Multiple Pages). What more can be said about the film or the explosion of praise that followed the release of this ground-breaking film! David Selznick's magnificent retelling of the Margaret Mitchell novel is the stuff of legends. Offered here for the first time by Heritage is the magnificent deluxe press book for the initial showing of this film. All of the promotional pieces are shown including all of the posters produced and shown here in full color! The three style 24 sheets and six sheets, the five style one sheets and three sheets. Also shown are the standees, the 40" X 60" cutout figures, the 30" X 72" uprights, the merchandising such as the candy, the scarves, perfume, the stationary, the jewelry and tons more. It is all here. There are small stains on the front cover and a few pages on the inside, the covers have separated and have been repaired with archival tape. There is a lower right corner bend on the cover and there are creases on the left side near the spine in the publicity and premiere sections. Fine+.
Estimate: $1,200-up Starting Bid: $600

83338   **Men In White (MGM, 1934).** One Sheet (27" X 41") Style C. Very Fine+ on Linen.
Estimate: $2,500-up Starting Bid: $1,250

83339   **Strange Cargo (MGM, 1940).** One Sheet (27" X 41") Style C. *Strange Cargo* remains easily one of Clarke Gable's most complex and thought provoking films. Gable stars as a convict who leads a group of escapees from a French penal colony on a perilous trek towards freedom. Along for the ride are girlfriend Joan Crawford and holy man Ian Hunter. This would be Crawford's eighth and final teaming with Gable. After being linen-backed there is still some evidence of light fold wear. There were small chips on the bottom left corner and left border. This is a very scarce poster with artwork by Armando Seguso. Very Fine on Linen.
Estimate: $2,000-up Starting Bid: $1,000

End of Session One

VINTAGE MOVIE POSTERS

SESSION TWO

Floor, Telephone, HERITAGE Live!™, Internet, Fax, and Mail Auction #7025
Friday, July 16, 2010 • 5:00 PM CT • Lots 83340-83718

A 19.5% Buyer's Premium Will Be Added To All Lots.
To view full descriptions, enlargeable images and bid online, visit HA.com/7025

83341   The 39 Steps (International Film Renters, Late 1930s). British Quad (28" X 39"). Fine on Linen.
Estimate: $1,000-up Starting Bid: $500

83340   Blackmail (British International Pictures, 1929). Australian Daybill (15" X 40"). Considered by most to be the first British talkie and directed by the man who would become one of the country's most famous exports, Alfred Hitchcock, the film has taken on legendary status. But with poster collectors, the scarcity of material from this film's first release is even more legendary! We offered a U.S. lobby card last July which sold for $14,340. This beautiful Australian daybill is one of the only very few large posters for this film that we are aware of. Done in beautiful stone lithography and printed by W.E. Smith in Sydney with artwork by Charles H. Barrie, this poster is assuredly a rare find for the Hitchcock completist. There were three chips in the borders and wear to both fold lines but is otherwise completely intact and has been magnificently conserved on linen. Fine+ on Linen.
Estimate: $7,000-up Starting Bid: $3,500

83342   Rebecca (United Artists, 1940). Insert (14" X 36"). Folded, Very Fine-.
Estimate: $1,500-up Starting Bid: $750

83343   Foreign Correspondent (Sangraf, late 1940s). First Post-War Italian 2 - Foglio (39" X 55"). Very Fine- on Linen.
Estimate: $600-up Starting Bid: $300

83345   Saboteur (Universal, 1958). German A1 (23" X 33"). Folded, Very Fine/Near Mint.
Estimate: $500-up
Starting Bid: $450

83346   To Catch a Thief (Paramount, 1955). Belgian (14.25" X 21.5"). Folded, Very Fine-.
Estimate: $700-up
Starting Bid: $350

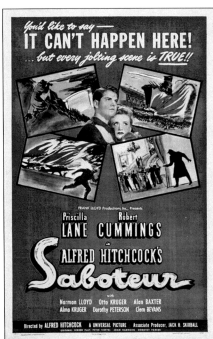

83344   Saboteur (Universal, 1942). One Sheet (27" X 41") Style D. Very Fine on Linen.
Estimate: $700-up Starting Bid: $600

83347   To Catch a Thief (Paramount, 1955). Half Sheet (22" X 28") Style B. Folded, Very Fine-.
Estimate: $1,000-up Starting Bid: $500

83348 To Catch a Thief (Paramount, 1955). Half Sheet (22" X 28") Style A. Rolled, Fine/Very Fine.
Estimate: $1,000-up Starting Bid: $500

83349 North by Northwest (MGM, 1959). Color Photos (8) (8" X 10"). *From the collection of Wade Williams.* Very Fine-.
Estimate: $500-up Starting Bid: $250

83350 Vertigo (Paramount, 1958). One Sheet (27" X 41"). Much has been made of the deceptively intricate styling of the work of poster artist Saul Bass for one of Hitchcock's best. The genius begins with the selection of the "nervous font" Bass uses in the top credits, simply calling the film "Alfred Hitchcock's Masterpiece". But the cleverest part of the poster is the uneven plane the central characters find themselves swept into as they spiral into a vortex that spreads across 3/5ths of the poster. The man in black is harming/helping, depending on your mood. The woman is in a police-styled drawn outline, with a pool of blood between them. So engaging is the design one noted director said that, for him, the film began when he first saw the poster. There are pinholes in the top corners and top center border and background. The centerfolds have pinpoint separations and there is a small tear in the upper vertical fold. The top left corner has a small crease, and there is soft extra vertical creasing. Very Fine.
Estimate: $4,000-up Starting Bid: $2,000

83351 **Notorious (RKO, 1946).** One Sheet (27" X 41"). This taut love story set amongst Nazi spies and counter spies in South America is one of Alfred Hitchcock's best films and one of the director's own personal favorites. Cary Grant stars as T.R. Devlin, an American agent who does everything he can to keep his distance from enlisted spy and playgirl Alicia Huberman (Ingrid Bergman), even as she gets closer to danger with husband Sebastian (Claude Rains) and his conspirators. Prior to restoration, this poster had a few pinholes in the image and borders as well as minor crossfold separations, but now displays extremely well and will be a standout in any collection. Very Fine+ on Linen.
Estimate: $4,000-up Starting Bid: $2,000

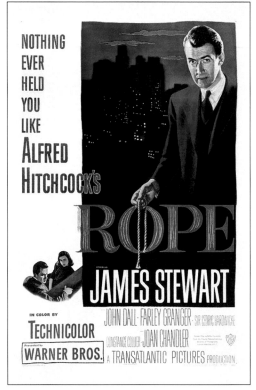

83352 **Rope (Warner Brothers, 1948).** One Sheet (27" X 41"). Fine on Linen.
Estimate: $1,200-up Starting Bid: $600

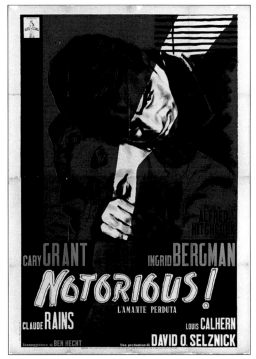

83353 **Notorious (Cei Incom, R-1960).** Italian 4 - Foglio (55" X 78"). Fine+.
Estimate: $600-up Starting Bid: $300

83354   Rear Window (Paramount, 1954). Insert (14" X 36"). Fine-on Paper.
Estimate: $1,200-up Starting Bid: $600

83356   Dial M For Murder (Warner Brothers, 1954). One Sheet (27" X 41"). Fine on Linen.
Estimate: $2,000-up Starting Bid: $1,000

83357   The Wrong Man (Warner Brothers, 1957). Lobby Card Set of 8 (11" X 14"). Very Fine-.
Estimate: $600-up Starting Bid: $300

83355   Rear Window (Paramount, 1954). Lobby Card Set of 8 (11" X 14"). *From the collection of Wade Williams.* Fine/Very Fine.
Estimate: $1,200-up Starting Bid: $600

83358   North by Northwest (MGM, 1959). Lobby Cards (2) (11" X 14"). Fine+.
Estimate: $600-up Starting Bid: $300

83359 **North by Northwest (MGM, 1959).** One Sheet (27" X 41"). Very Fine- on Linen.
Estimate: $1,000-up **Starting Bid: $500**

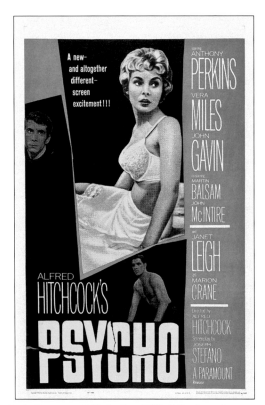

83360 **Psycho (Paramount, 1960).** One Sheet (27" X 41"). Very Fine on Linen.
Estimate: $1,200-up **Starting Bid: $600**

83361 **Psycho (Paramount, 1960).** CGC Graded Lobby Card (11" X 14"). Near Mint.
Estimate: $1,600-up **Starting Bid: $800**

83362 **Psycho (Paramount, 1960).** CGC Graded Lobby Cards (3) (11" X 14"). Near Mint+.
Estimate: $800-up **Starting Bid: $400**

83363 **Psycho (Paramount, 1960).** CGC Graded Lobby Cards (4) (11" X 14"). Near Mint+.
Estimate: $800-up **Starting Bid: $400**

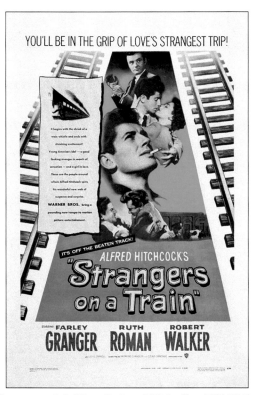

83364   Strangers on a Train (Warner Brothers, 1951). One Sheet (27" X 41"). Very Fine+ on Linen.
Estimate: $1,000-up Starting Bid: $500

83366   Notorious (Columbia, R-1954). French Affiche (23.5" X 31.5"). Very Fine+.
Estimate: $400-up Starting Bid: $200

83365   The Paradine Case (Selznick, 1948). Lobby Card Set of 8 (11" X 14"). Very Fine.
Estimate: $600-up Starting Bid: $300

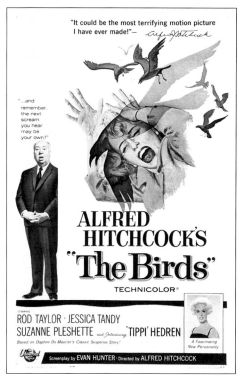

83367   The Birds (Universal, 1963). One Sheet (27" X 41"). Very Fine on Linen.
Estimate: $800-up Starting Bid: $400

83368   **The Birds (Universal, 1963).** Half Sheet (22" X 28"). Rolled, Very Fine+.
Estimate: $400-up Starting Bid: $200

83370   **North by Northwest (MGM, R-1976).** Italian 2 - Foglio (39" X 55"). Very Fine+.
Estimate: $500-up Starting Bid: $250

83369   **North by Northwest (MGM, 1959).** Insert (14" X 36"). Rolled, Very Fine-.
Estimate: $600-up Starting Bid: $300

83371   **Psycho (Universal, R-1965).** Italian Photobustas (6) (17.5" X 25"). . Folded, Fine.
Estimate: $300-up Starting Bid: $150

83372   The Range Feud (Columbia, 1931). Lobby Card Set of 8 (11" X 14"). Fine/ Very Fine.
Estimate: $1,500-up Starting Bid: $750

83373   The New Frontier (Republic, 1935). One Sheet (27" X 41"). When Monogram Studios merged with Lone Star Productions and several other producers to form Republic Studios in 1935, John Wayne was one of the stars used to launch the new franchise. This Western was Wayne's second with Republic, a studio with which he would remain until the early 1950s. Republic produced some of the most attractive lobby cards and posters in the 1930s, and this beautiful example shows what makes them so collectible. There was a small chip in the left side of the top border, a small tear in the lower left, and one in the upper right border. All has been expertly restored. It is one of the best Wayne images available on any poster, with a portrait of a smiling Wayne taking up a full two-thirds of the image area, in stunning stone litho color. Very Fine- on Linen.
Estimate: $8,000-up Starting Bid: $4,000

83374   The Big Trail (Fox, 1930). Title Lobby Card (11" X 14"). Before filming even began, behind-the-scenes crew member and on-the-spot extra, Marion Michael Morrison, was spotted by director Raoul Walsh. He took the inexperienced actor under his wing, changed his name and John Wayne was born. Wayne stars as Breck Coleman, who joins a wagon train heading West in order to spy on suspected murderer Red Flack (Tyrone Power Sr.). He falls in love with Ruth Cameron (Marguerite Churchill) along the way. One of the first films to be shot in both widescreen and standard formats, this top Western is truly an important historical masterpiece and posters from this title are top prizes for collectors. This stunning title card, with artwork by Marion Jochimsen, is a rare gem, showing only slightly rounded corners, and a light scuff above Walsh's name. Very Fine+.
Estimate: $2,000-up Starting Bid: $1,000

83375   The Big Trail (Fox, 1930). Lobby Card (11" X 14"). Many top collectors have spent years looking for the wonderful art work lobby cards by noted portraitist Marion Jochimsen for John Wayne's first starring role in 1930. This romantic painting by Jochimsen captures the young Wayne and his costar Marguerite Churchill faithfully and has always been one of the most sought after cards in the set. Fortunately the studio chose a small imprint title credit to preserve the art and with the almost full bleed format the cards look as much like the original fine paintings as possible. This terrific piece has only slightly rounded corners with small bends, a tiny chip in the lower left corner, and some very minor edge tears in the left and right borders. We're sure this may be one of the few times we see this card. Fine+.
Estimate: $1,500-up Starting Bid: $750

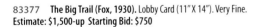

83376   The Big Trail (Fox, 1930). Lobby Card (11" X 14"). Fine/Very Fine.
Estimate: $1,200-up Starting Bid: $600

83377   The Big Trail (Fox, 1930). Lobby Card (11" X 14"). Very Fine.
Estimate: $1,500-up Starting Bid: $750

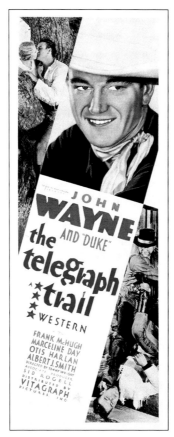

83378   The Big Trail (Fox, 1930). Lobby Cards (2) (11"X 14"). Fine/Very Fine.
Estimate: $800-up Starting Bid: $400

83381   The Telegraph Trail (Warner Brothers, 1933). Insert (14"X 36"). Fine on Paper.
Estimate: $800-up Starting Bid: $400

83382   Angel and the Badman (Republic, 1947). Insert (14"X 36"). Rolled, Fine/Very Fine.
Estimate: $1,200-up Starting Bid: $600

83379   The Big Trail (Fox, 1930). Lobby Card (11"X 14"). Very Fine-.
Estimate: $500-up Starting Bid: $250

83383   Red River (United Artists, 1948). Lobby Card Set of 8 (11"X 14"). Very Fine+.
Estimate: $1,200-up
Starting Bid: $600

83380   The Big Stampede (Vitagraph, 1932). Title Lobby Card (11"X 14"). Fine+.
Estimate: $800-up Starting Bid: $400

83384 **Rio Grande (Republic, 1950).** Standee (32.5" X 59"). John Ford directed this romantic action film set just after the Civil War, when the U.S. Army turned its attention to the Apaches in the Southwest, who had been roaming at will while the Army was busy elsewhere. John Wayne and Maureen O'Hara star, with Claude Jarman Jr., Chill Wills, Victor McLaglen, and Harry Carey, Jr. turning in nice supporting performances, in Ford's last film in his "Cavalry Trilogy." This is a very rare standee, used in theater lobbies to advertise an upcoming film. These pieces are rare due to the fact that they were oversized and would be more difficult to store. Thus most of them went to the trash heap. This poster is silk-screened artwork in the bottom two-thirds and a large black and white portrait of the two stars glued at the top third. The bottom two corners are impacted and there is some soiling and color paint transfer shown in horizontal lines as the poster is printed on corrugated cardboard. The poster displays beautifully and still has the string easel hangers on the verso. This is one we have never seen before and offers a fabulous image of Wayne and O'Hara together! Fine-.
Estimate: $800-up Starting Bid: $400

83385 **The Searchers (Warner Brothers, 1956).** Lobby Card (11" X 14"). Fine+.
Estimate: $400-up Starting Bid: $350

83386 **The Searchers (Warner Brothers, 1956).** Window Card (14" X 22"). Folded, Fine.
Estimate: $500-up Starting Bid: $250

83387 **The Man Who Shot Liberty Valance (Paramount, 1962).** Italian 4 - Foglio (55" X 78"). Folded, Very Fine-.
Estimate: $600-up Starting Bid: $300

83388   The Man Who Shot Liberty Valance (Paramount, 1962). Lobby Card Set of 8 (11"X 14").
Very Fine+.
Estimate: $500-up Starting Bid: $250

83390   The Alamo (United Artists, 1961). Italian 4 - Foglio (55"X 78"). Fine/Very Fine on Linen.
Estimate: $400-up Starting Bid: $200

83389   Rio Bravo (Warner Brothers, 1959). Lobby Card Set of 8 (11"X 14"). Fine/Very Fine.
Estimate: $800-up Starting Bid: $400

83391   Sands of Iwo Jima (Republic, 1950). Insert (14"X 36"). Rolled, Very Fine+.
Estimate: $600-up Starting Bid: $300

83392 **The Hurricane Express (Mascot, 1932).** Lobby Card (11" X 14") Episode 1— "The Wrecker." Fine/Very Fine.
Estimate: $700-up Starting Bid: $350

83393 **The Shadow of the Eagle (Mascot, 1932).** Lobby Card Set of 8 (11" X 14") Chapter 1 — "The Carnival Mystery." A young John Wayne stars as a strong-willed pilot searching for a missing carnival owner known as "the eagle" in this first chapter of the Mascot serial. Some of the cards have pinholes in the corners, three cards have small pinholes in the center background, another card has a scuff in the right background, and the title card has slight surface paper loss. This has to be one of the rarest sets of cards from any of the early John Wayne titles. This Chapter one set, the only in color as the other chapters were done in doutone, we have never seen a single card from, much less a whole set! Fine/Very Fine.
Estimate: $2,000-up Starting Bid: $1,000

83394 **The Three Musketeers (Mascot, 1933).** One Sheet (27" X 41") Chapter 1: "The Fiery Circle." Fine+ on Linen.
Estimate: $1,200-up Starting Bid: $600

83395 **The Batman (Columbia, 1943).** One Sheet (27" X 41") Chapter 14 — "The Executioner Strikes." Very Good on Linen.
Estimate: $1,800-up Starting Bid: $1,500

83396   The New Adventures of Batman and Robin (Columbia, 1949). One Sheet (27" X 41") Chapter 14 — " Batman vs. Wizard." Very Fine-.
Estimate: $1,500-up Starting Bid: $750

83398   Batman (20th Century Fox, 1966). Italian 4 - Foglio (55" X 78"). Very Fine- on Linen.
Estimate: $500-up Starting Bid: $250

83397   Batman (20th Century Fox, 1966). Japanese B2 (20" X 29"). Rolled, Near Mint/Mint.
Estimate: $500-up Starting Bid: $375

83399   The Iron Claw (Pathé, 1916). One Sheet (27" X 41") Episode 6 — "The Spotted Warning." Fine- on Linen.
Estimate: $1,500-up Starting Bid: $750

83400 **Conan the Barbarian (20th Century Fox, 1982).** Advance (22" X 36"). This art was done for the book trade by one of the best illustrators ever to hold a paintbrush, Frank Frazetta, in 1974. With additional Robert E. Howard books being reissued in 1980, the art was again used to promote the the upcoming film based on Howard's stories and the books. Very rare!! There are only soft folds and very light edge wear. Folded, Near Mint.
Estimate: $500-up Starting Bid: $400

83401 **Superman and the Mole Men (Lippert, 1951).** One Sheet (27" X 41"). After two successful serials, the Man of Steel was recruited into his first feature film, with George Reeves replacing Kirk Alyn in the title role. *Mole Men* served as a de facto pilot for the TV series that followed, and in fact was eventually edited down and broadcast as a two-part episode of the series. Clark Kent, Jimmy Olsen, and Lois Lane arrive in a small town to find that denizens of the underworld have been terrorizing the citizens, in response to recent drilling operations that has disturbed their hidden lair. This outstanding poster has a great shot of George Reeves in an iconic pose. Pinholes in the background corners, edge wear with tears in the top left, fold wear with crossfold separations and some splitting along the fold lines, a small hole in the background at the bottom, some tape on the reverse, and a faint stain in the center of the image are the condition issues of note. Fine.
Estimate: $2,000-up Starting Bid: $1,000

83402 **Superman and the Mole Men (Lippert, 1951).** Lobby Card (11" X 14"). Fine+.
Estimate: $500-up Starting Bid: $250

83403 **Superman and the Mole Men (Lippert, 1951).** Lobby Card (11" X 14"). Fine/Very Fine.
Estimate: $500-up Starting Bid: $250

83404   **Superman in Exile (20th Century Fox, 1954).** One Sheet (27" X 41"). Fine/Very Fine.
Estimate: $800-up Starting Bid: $600

83405   **Captain America (Republic, 1944).** Lobby Card (11" X 14") Chapter 1 — "The Purple Death." Fine/Very Fine.
Estimate: $500-up Starting Bid: $250

83406   **The Lost Planet (Columbia, 1953).** Six Sheet (81" X 81"). *From the collection of Wade Williams.* The last of the great space adventure chapter serials, this 15-chapter drama stars Judd Holdren as newspaper reporter Rex Barrow, Vivian Mason as Professor Dorn's (Forrest Taylor) daughter, and Michael Fox as the villainous Dr. Ernst Grood. Offered here is the rarely seen six sheet which is in excellent condition showing only fold wear and a small chip at the title. Very Fine.
Estimate: $800-up Starting Bid: $400

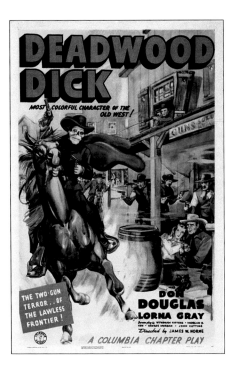

83407   Deadwood Dick (Columbia, 1940). One Sheet (27" X 41"). Very Fine.
Estimate: $600-up Starting Bid: $300

83408   The Good, the Bad and the Ugly (PEA, 1966). Italian 4 - Foglio (55" X 77").
Clint Eastwood gives a seminal performance as The Man With No Name, who isn't particularly "good," in this classic Spaghetti Western from Sergio Leone, but he is smarter and
faster than the "bad" (Lee Van Cleef) and the "ugly" (Eli Wallach) in the third and best of
the "Dollars" trilogy. This incredibly rare, original release, Italian four foglio has a unique
design similar to the 2-Foglio with its reflective silver background and was used only for
the Rome premiere and its limited run in that city. It was designed by F. Fiorenzi. The poster,
which is in two sections, has an area of missing paper at the left edge, edge wear, light
wrinkles, and a corner crease at the top of the bottom section. If you are looking for the
rarest of posters from this iconic title, this one is it! Fine.
Estimate: $7,000-up Starting Bid: $3,500

83409   The Good, the Bad and
the Ugly (PEA, 1966). Italian Foglio
Set of 3 (26" X 36"). Clint Eastwood,
Lee Van Cleef, and Eli Wallach star
in this highly praised film by Sergio
Leone, which has become one of
the most beloved Westerns of all
time. The trio forms an uneasy al-
liance in order to unearth a buried
fortune in gold. The original music
score is unforgettable and was created by Ennio Morricone. Offered
here is the set of country-of-origin
foglios from the original release
which is an extremely rare find.
They show wrinkles, edge wear
with small tears, and small chips at
the right edge. Highlighting each
star on his own poster, this unique
set will garner much deserved attention. Fine.
Estimate: $3,000-up
Starting Bid: $1,500

83410   The Good, the Bad and the Ugly (PEA, 1966). Italian Program Hard-Cover Book (8.5" X 12") (18 Pages). Very Fine-.
Estimate: $800-up Starting Bid: $400

83412   A Fistful of Dollars (United Artists, 1967). One Sheet (27" X 41") Teaser Style A. Very Fine-.
Estimate: $2,000-up Starting Bid: $1,500

83413   A Fistful of Dollars (PEA, 1965). French Grande (47" X 63"). Very Fine-.
Estimate: $600-up Starting Bid: $300

83411   For a Few Dollars More (PEA, 1965). Italian Program (13" X 13") and Italian Theater Mobile (8.5" X 12"). Very Fine/Near Mint.
Estimate: $800-up Starting Bid: $400

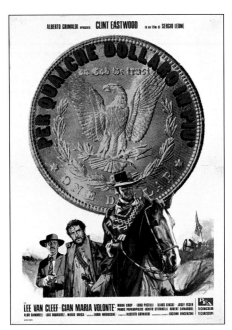

83414 For a Few Dollars More (PEA, R-1970's). Italian 4 - Foglio (55" X 78"). Very Fine-.
Estimate: $600-up Starting Bid: $300

83416 A Fistful of Dollars (United Artists, 1967). Insert (14" X 36"). Folded, Fine+.
Estimate: $600-up Starting Bid: $300

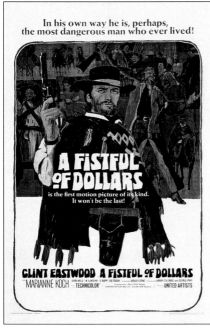

83417 A Fistful of Dollars (United Artists, 1967). One Sheet (27" X 41"). Very Fine/Near Mint on Linen.
Estimate: $500-up Starting Bid: $400

83415 A Fistful of Dollars (United Artists, 1967). CGC Graded Lobby Card Set of 8 (11" X 14"). Very Fine/Near Mint.
Estimate: $600-up Starting Bid: $300

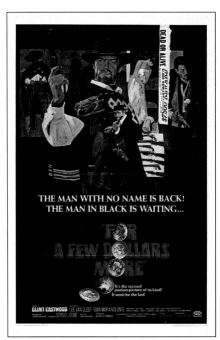

83418 For a Few Dollars More (United Artists, 1967). One Sheet (27" X 41"). Near Mint-.
Estimate: $400-up Starting Bid: $200

83419   The Outlaw Josey Wales (Warner Brothers, 1976). Three Sheet (41" X 81"). Very Fine+ on Linen.
Estimate: $800-up Starting Bid: $400

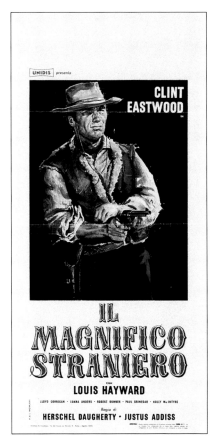

83420   The Magnificent Stranger (Unidas, 1966). Italian Locandina (13" X 27"). Fine+.
Estimate: $400-up Starting Bid: $200

83421   Waterloo Bridge (Universal, 1931). Lobby Card Set of 8 (11" X 14"). Mae Clarke, Kent Douglass and relative unknown Bette Davis star in the film adaptation of Robert E. Sherwood's award-winning play. Clarke turns in a stellar performance as Myra Deauville, a down-on-her-luck beauty who in desperation turns to prostitution before meeting the man of her dreams (Douglass). Universal had just signed Davis in 1931 and quickly put her to work in three films with *Waterloo Bridge* being the first produced and last of the three to be released. All cards have pinholes in the corners and a slight crease in the lower right corner. A few cards have pinholes in the bottom border. The title card has a faint dust shadow, and a scuff in the right side. One card has a minor chip in the top left corner while the one Bette Davis card is in excellent shape other than a very tiny chip in the top right corner. It is exceedingly rare to find a total set intact for this early historical film. Very Fine-.
Estimate: $2,500-up Starting Bid: $1,750

For full lot descriptions,
enlargeable images and
online bidding, visit
HA.com/7025

83422 **The Golden Arrow (Warner Brothers - First National, 1936).** One Sheet (27" X 41"). Bette Davis was in her heyday when she starred in this comedy with frequent co-star George Brent, with whom she made a dozen pictures. Davis recently had two critical successes which garnered one Academy Award nomination and one win— *Of Human Bondage* (1933) and *Dangerous* (1934). In this lighter film, Davis is Daisy Appleby, an heiress who weds a fellow socialite (Brent). All seems well until Daisy, who is really a penniless waitress posing for a publicity stunt for a perfume company, realizes she was equally duped by her husband, who is a penniless news reporter. Paper for this early title rarely appears, and this one sheet is a stunning portrait of the legendary star. It shows faint staining in the borders, a tiny corner chip at the top left, pinholes in the corners, a few minor tears at the top and bottom edges, and small pieces of tape on the reverse. This unrestored beauty has vibrant colors and rarely shows up, being on of Davis' better one sheets. Fine+.

Estimate: $7,500-up Starting Bid: $3,750

83423   Of Human Bondage (RKO, 1934). Pre-War Australian Daybill (14.5" X 40"). Fine/Very Fine on Linen.
Estimate: $1,200-up Starting Bid: $800

83425   Jezebel (Warner Brothers, 1939). Italian 2 - Foglio (39" X 55"). Film posters done by the Italian masters of design, Ballester, Capitani, Brini, and Luigi Martinati, during the war torn era of the late 1930's are a difficult group to obtain. They were never in abundance, due to the instant collectability of the fine art work itself, and the high attrition rate of a country at war. This wonderful find has us marveling at the brilliant artistry of Martinati's magnificent rendition of the final scene of an Oscar winning performance by Bette Davis. With her eyes turned to the heavens as she faces sure death from yellow fever, she cradles a dying Henry Fonda in her arms, in fulfillment of the promise she has just made to Fonda's wife..."Help me make myself clean again, as you are clean". Chances to obtain a true art triumph such as this are few and far between. Prior to professional restoration the poster had fold wear and crossfold separations, and a tear in the top that extends into the field. Very Fine- on Linen.
Estimate: $6,000-up Starting Bid: $3,000

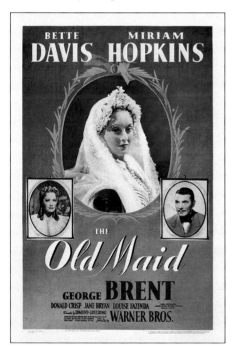

83424   The Old Maid (Warner Brothers, 1939). One Sheet (27" X 41"). Fine+ on Linen.
Estimate: $700-up Starting Bid: $400

83426   Juarez (Warner Brothers, late 1940s). First Post-War Italian Poster (27.75" X 39.5"). Fine/Very Fine on Linen.
Estimate: $1,400-up Starting Bid: $700

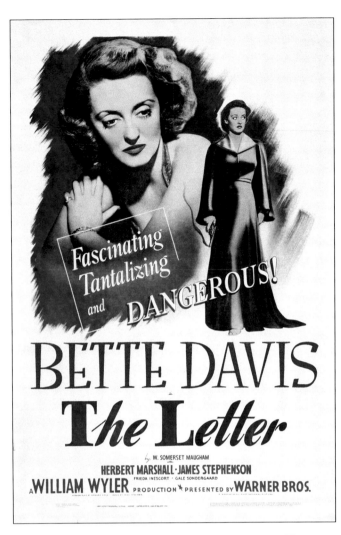

83427   The Letter (Warner Brothers, 1940). One Sheet (27" X 41"). Bette Davis has never been so dangerous or so self-destructive as in this William Wyler *film noir*, which is based on Somerset Maugham's novel. Set on a Malayan plantation, Leslie Crosbie murders her boyfriend Geoffrey Hammond (David Newell), and then gives a moving performance to her husband (Herbert Marshall) and their lawyer friend Howard Joyce (James Stephenson) explaining why it was self-defense. Despite her wealth, loving and forgiving husband, and a sympathetic jury, Leslie cannot escape her punishment, declaring "With all my heart, I still love the man I killed." This desirable one sheet had fold wear, tears in the top left corner and the top border with a few extending into the artwork, a tear at the bottom border, an area of paper loss in the top right corner, and chips in the bottom corners. Most of these issues have been addressed with restoration, and the artwork is in extremely nice condition, with a striking image of Davis at her finest. Fine+ on Linen.
Estimate: $2,000-up Starting Bid: $1,000

83428   Now, Voyager (Warner Brothers, 1942). Lobby Card Set of 8 (11" X 14"). Very Fine-.
Estimate: $1,500-up Starting Bid: $750

83429   Kid Galahad (Warner Brothers, 1937). One Sheet (27" X 41"). In this Michael Curtiz-directed melodrama, Edward G. Robinson plays a manager looking for a new pugilist after losing his best fighter to crooked promoter Humphrey Bogart. Robinson discovers a bellhop (Wayne Morgan) who is adept at the sweet science, and dubs him Kid Galahad. Bette Davis plays Robinson's sister. This striking and rare duo-tone one sheet features terrific artwork of Robinson and Davis. There were pinholes in the background, tears in the center of the image, and fold wear, all of which has been smoothed over with professional restoration. Fine+ on Linen.
Estimate: $2,500-up Starting Bid: $2,000

83430   Tiger Shark (First National, 1932). One Sheet (27" X 41"). Master filmmaker Howard Hawks directs the great Edward G. Robinson in one of his earliest roles in this nautical melodrama. As Mike Mascarenhas, Robinson is a heroic fisherman who saves his best friend's (Richard Arlen) life when he is attacked by a shark, resulting in the loss of Mike's hand. Mike eventually marries young orphan Quita Silva (Zita Johnson, best known for her role in the 1932 classic, *The Mummy*) and all is well until she falls in love with his rescued friend, and Mike is out for revenge. This love triangle plot of this film was so successful that Warner Brothers reused it several times in different variations. Prior to professional restoration, this gorgeous poster had a corner crease, pinholes in the corners and bottom border, an extra horizontal crease and an extra vertical crease, and a small tear at the left edge. Minor edge wear at the top and light staining are still evident, and the linen has been trimmed to the edge of the poster. This unique stone litho one sheet is one of the rarest Robinson titles to find, and we are proud to offer one in such nice condition, a truly unique prize for fans of the top star! Fine/Very Fine on Linen.
Estimate: $6,000-up Starting Bid: $3,000

83431 Confessions of a Nazi Spy (Warner Brothers, 1939). One Sheet (27" X 41"). Very Good/Fine on Linen.
Estimate: $700-up
Starting Bid: $350

83432 Smart Money (Warner Brothers, 1931). Lobby Card (11" X 14"). Very Fine-.
Estimate: $800-up Starting Bid: $700

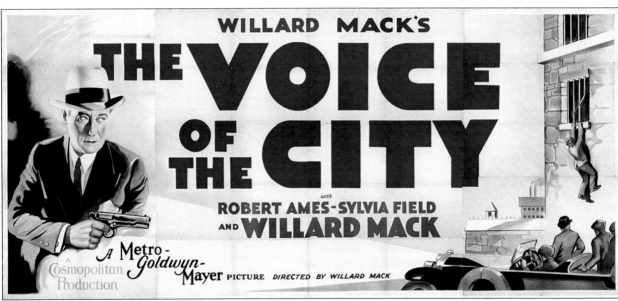

83433 The Voice of the City (MGM, 1929). 24 Sheet (104" X 232"). Mainly known for his writing prowess, Willard Mack not only wrote the screenplay, but he also directs and stars in this early gangster film, which is a part-talkie. Mack plays detective Biff Myers who discovers that a juvenile convict named Bobby (Robert Ames) is actually innocent, and he uses any means necessary to bring the real killer to justice. Sylvia Field stars as Bobby's girl Beebe. Mack had a string of writing successes on Broadway, where he met a young actress who had a small role in his play *The Noose*. With encouragement and coaching from the playwright, Ruby Stevens moved to Hollywood to try her luck in pictures and changed her name... to Barbara Stanwyck. This magnificent poster, in its original twelve sections, is in exceptional condition showing only light fold wear with small chips, edge wear with tears at the folds, and a lower right corner crease. The gorgeous stone litho artwork retains its vivid color and features a gun-totting Mack, ready to take on the world. Very Fine-.
Estimate: $1,000-up Starting Bid: $500

83434 20,000 Years in Sing Sing (First National, 1932). Title Lobby Card and Lobby Cards (3) (11" X 14"). Formerly incorrigible prisoner Tommy Connors (Spencer Tracy) has a change in attitude after a stretch in solitary, and soon wins the trust of the warden, who allows him a brief period of freedom to see his girlfriend (Bette Davis), who has been injured in an auto accident. Offered here are the title card and three scene cards from one of the rarest titles in the early crime genre. Original paper from the titles is exceedingly scarce! All the cards have pinholes in the corners, and a faint top right corner crease. Very Fine+.
Estimate: $700-up Starting Bid: $350

83435   I Am a Fugitive From a Chain Gang (Warner Brothers, 1932). Lobby Card (11" X 14"). Fine+.
Estimate: $1,000-up Starting Bid: $500

83436   Scarface (United Artists, R-1954). French Grande (47" X 63"). Fine+.
Estimate: $400-up
Starting Bid: $350

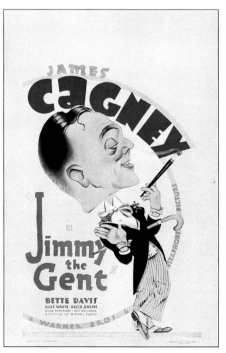

83437   Jimmy the Gent (Warner Brothers, 1934). Window Card (14" X 22"). Fine/ Very Fine on Cardstock.
Estimate: $1,000-up
Starting Bid: $1,000

83438   The Roaring Twenties (Warner Brothers, 1939). Half Sheet (22" X 28"). Very Good/Fine on Paper.
Estimate: $3,000-up Starting Bid: $1,500

83439   Angels with Dirty Faces (Warner Brothers, 1938). Lobby Card (11" X 14"). Very Good/ Fine.
Estimate: $2,000-up Starting Bid: $1,000

83440   Each Dawn I Die (Warner Brothers, 1939). French Grande (47" X 63"). Very Fine-.
Estimate: $1,200-up Starting Bid: $1,000

83442 James Cagney Personality Poster (Warner Brothers, 1934). Poster (22" X 28"). Fine+.
Estimate: $500-up Starting Bid: $250

83441 City for Conquest (Warner Brothers, 1940). Insert (14" X 36"). Fine on Paper.
Estimate: $2,100-up Starting Bid: $1,050

83443 White Heat (Warner Brothers, 1949). Insert (14" X 36"). Fine/Very Fine on Paper.
Estimate: $800-up Starting Bid: $400

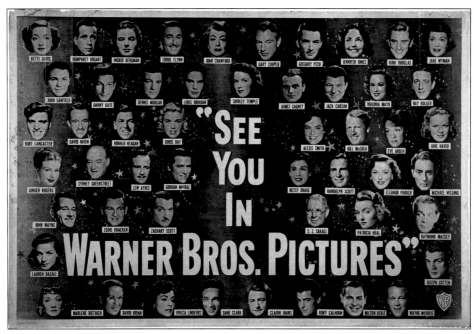

83444 Warner Brothers Stars of 1949 Promotional Poster (Warner Brothers, 1949). Horizontal Format Poster (60" X 40"). This is a very rare and unusual poster which we have never seen before. This original 1949 promotional poster produced by Warner Brothers, pictures their stars from that year including Humphrey Bogart, who was finishing his contract out with the studio, Bette Davis, whose contract with the studio would end this very year and John Wayne, who wouldn't appear in a Warner's film until 1951! A young Kirk Douglas is shown as is the future president Ronald Reagan, a big star with the studio in these years. Enjoy this wonderful look back at a time when a studio's worth was in its roster of stars. The poster has wear to the corners and borders as well as a bit of staining and soiling. This poster is generally in very good condition. Get this rarity while you can! Rolled, Fine-.
Estimate: $700-up Starting Bid: $500

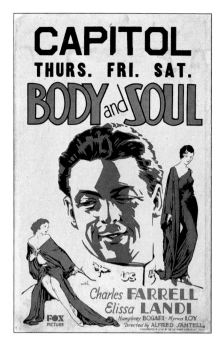

83447 Body and Soul (Fox, 1931). Window Card (14" X 22"). Fine-.
Estimate: $500-up Starting Bid: $250

83445 A Devil With Women (Fox, 1930). Window Card (14" X 22"). In on of his earliest screen appearance, Humphrey Bogart plays wastral heir Tom Standish who joins up with playboy soldier Jerry Maxton (Victor McLaglen) in South America to rescue kidnapped beauty Rosita (Mona Maris). Once they do, they fight each other for her love. This bright Art Deco window card shows only pinholes in the corners, a horizontal crease at the bottom, light stains in the right and bottom borders, and one corner bump. Rarely do posters from this film come to market so get this one while you can! Very Fine-.
Estimate: $500-up Starting Bid: $250

83448 Crime School (Warner Brothers, 1938). Three Sheet (41" X 81"). This film co-stars the "Dead End Kids", who actually received top billing in all of the film's advertising. That is due to the big success of their film Dead End the previous year. Though Humphrey Bogart played his character as a by-the-book good guy, he of course made it work spectacularly. This poster has a few edge tears, and light fold separations. There was a paper loss at the join with the bottom panel and there is a tear that runs diagonally in the lower left corner. All of these issues have been addressed with professional restoration and are no longer apparent. This is the only three sheet for this film known to exist and is a beautiful rendering of Warner Brothers' rising star. Fine+ on Linen.
Estimate: $6,000-up
Starting Bid: $3,000

83446 Up the River (Fox, 1930). Window Card (14" X 22"). Very Fine-.
Estimate: $1,500-up Starting Bid: $750

83449 Isle of Fury (Warner Brothers, 1936). Window Card (14" X 22"). Very Good/Fine.
Estimate: $300-up
Starting Bid: $150

83452 The Big Shot (Warner Brothers, 1942). Half Sheet (22" X 28") Style B. Very Fine on Paper.
Estimate: $400-up Starting Bid: $200

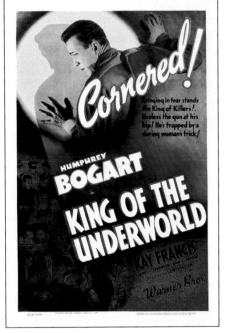

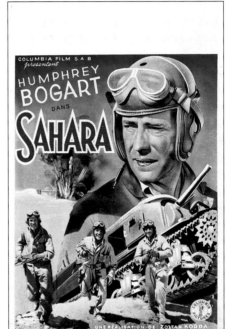

83450 King of the Underworld (Warner Brothers, 1939). One Sheet (27" X 41"). Very Fine- on Linen.
Estimate: $1,000-up
Starting Bid: $500

83453 Sahara (Columbia, late 1940's). First Post-War Belgian (10.5" X 216.5"). Very Fine-.
Estimate: $400-up
Starting Bid: $200

83454 High Sierra (Warner Brothers, R-1947). Belgian (10.5" X 13.75"). Fine/Very Fine on Linen.
Estimate: $500-up
Starting Bid: $250

83451 It All Came True (Warner Brothers, 1940). Lobby Card (11" X 14"). Very Fine-.
Estimate: $400-up Starting Bid: $200

83456   The Big Sleep (Warner Brothers, 1946). Banner (24" X 82"). Fine-.
Estimate: $1,000-up Starting Bid: $1,000

83455   Dark Passage (Warner Brothers, 1947). Window Card (14" X 22"). Very Good+ on Cardstock.
Estimate: $800-up Starting Bid: $400

83458   Dead Reckoning (Columbia, 1947). One Sheet (27" X 41") Style A. Fine+ on Linen.
Estimate: $1,000-up Starting Bid: $500

83457   The Big Sleep (Warner Brothers, 1946). Insert (14" X 36"). Famed screenwriters William Faulkner, Jules Furthmann, and Leigh Brackett adapted Raymond Chandler's novel, but even though they consulted with the author, the story is still somewhat confusing at times. In addition, the studio was somewhat unsure of Lauren Bacall's performance, and several of her scenes were re-shot to emphasize her chemistry with Humphrey Bogart. Ultimately, the film's release was delayed for more than a year and a half to accommodate these tweaks. They need not have feared: infused with the star power of B&B, *The Big Sleep* went on to become on of the classic *film noirs* of all time. This terrific insert has great images of Bogie and Bacall, and is in terrific shape. Condition issues include corner and surface creases, light edge wear, small chip in left border held in place with cellophane tape, and minor smudging in the bottom left border. Rolled, Very Fine-.
Estimate: $3,500-up Starting Bid: $1,750

83459   Key Largo (Warner Brothers, 1948). One Sheet (27" X 41"). Fine-.
Estimate: $1,200-up Starting Bid: $600

83460 Key Largo (Warner Brothers, 1948). Lobby Card Set of 8 (11" X 14"). Fine.
Estimate: $1,600-up
Starting Bid: $800

83461 Key Largo (Warner Brothers, 1948). Half Sheet (22" X 28") Style A. Folded, Fine.
Estimate: $500-up Starting Bid: $250

83462 The Treasure of the Sierra Madre (Warner Brothers, 1948). Half Sheet (22" X 28") Style A. Fine- on Paper.
Estimate: $1,200-up Starting Bid: $800

83463 The Treasure of the Sierra Madre (Warner Brothers, R-1952). French Grande (47" X 63"). Fine-.
Estimate: $500-up
Starting Bid: $300

83464 In a Lonely Place (Columbia, 1950). One Sheet (27" X 41"). Fine on Linen.
Estimate: $700-up
Starting Bid: $350

83465 The African Queen (United Artists, 1952). One Sheet (27" X 41"). Fine- on Linen.
Estimate: $1,000-up
Starting Bid: $500

83466   The African Queen (United Artists, 1952). Insert (14" X 36"). Fine+ on Paper.
Estimate: $900-up Starting Bid: $450

83468   The Grapes of Wrath (20th Century Fox, 1940). Window Card (14" X 22"). Fine+ on Cardstock.
Estimate: $700-up Starting Bid: $500

83469   The Grapes of Wrath (20th Century Fox, 1940). Title Lobby Card (11" X 14"). Fine/Very Fine.
Estimate: $1,800-up Starting Bid: $1,200

83467   The African Queen (United Artists, 1952). Lobby Cards (6) (11" X 14"). Fine.
Estimate: $800-up Starting Bid: $400

83470   The Grapes of Wrath (20th Century Fox, 1940). Lobby Cards (2) (11" X 14"). Fine.
Estimate: $600-up Starting Bid: $500

83471   The Grapes of Wrath (20th Century Fox, 1940). Lobby Card (11" X 14"). Fine.
Estimate: $400-up Starting Bid: $200

83472   Citizen Kane (RKO, 1941). Lobby Card (11" X 14"). Fine/Very Fine.
Estimate: $700-up Starting Bid: $350

83473   Citizen Kane (RKO, 1941). Lobby Card (11" X 14"). Very Fine.
Estimate: $700-up Starting Bid: $350

83474   Citizen Kane (RKO, 1941). Lobby Card (11" X 14"). Very Fine.
Estimate: $700-up Starting Bid: $350

83475   The Rescue (United Artists, 1929). One Sheet (27" X 41"). Based on Joseph Conrad's adventurous novel set on the South Seas, this early talking drama is helmed by noted director Herbert Brenon and stars screen idol Ronald Colman and German born actress Lili Damita in her American debut. Colman had been working in Hollywood for a decade when this film was released, often in heroic swashbuckling roles. A rising star in silent films, with his smooth English speaking voice Colman easily made the transition to talking pictures. This absolutely stunning stone litho one sheet is from his first sound picture, in which he plays adventurer Tom Lingard, who aids a prince and his sister who have been chased from their village. In gorgeous, unrestored color, this striking sheet shows edge wear in three borders, a small tear and a minor pinhole at the center fold, a chip in the right border, and a chip in the lower right corner. There is an extra crease at the top and a few stains in the right border. Early posters of this quality and beauty rarely come available, and the last restored copy we had of this poster sold in our auction in March of 2008 for $35,850. Fine+.
Estimate: $5,000-up Starting Bid: $2,500

83476 Beau Geste (Paramount, 1939). One Sheet (27" X 41") Style A. A true film classic, this picture stars Gary Cooper as Michael "Beau" Geste, who, in order to protect a beloved aunt, confesses to a crime he did not commit, and joins the French Foreign Legion in disgrace. There, he is reunited with his brothers, John (Ray Milland) and Digby (Robert Preston), and eventually redeems his honor at the hour of his death. This fantastic one sheet has a great artwork of Cooper, Milland and Preston. There are pinholes in the top background area, fold wear with crossfold separations, a chip in the top right corner, creases in all the corners, and edge wear. Fine/Very Fine.
Estimate: $4,500-up
Starting Bid: $2,250

83477 The Fountainhead (Warner Brothers, 1949). Insert (14" X 36"). Good/Very Good on Paper.
Estimate: $1,200-up Starting Bid: $600

83478 The Adventures of Robin Hood (Warner Brothers, 1938). Half Sheet (22" X 28") Style B. Michael Curtiz and William Keighley co-direct this upbeat swashbuckler set in the famed Sherwood forest and filmed in brilliant Technicolor. In perhaps his most iconic role, Errol Flynn stars as the dashing bandit Robin Hood, doing good for the Saxon poor and rallying his men to stop the evil Prince John (Claude Rains) and Guy of Gisbourne (Basil Rathbone) from taking over the country. Olivia de Havilland is sublime as Maid Marian and she and Flynn would make eight top films together. Alan Hale co-stars as the trustworthy Little John in this high adventure, which won three Academy Awards. With its high production value, thrilling action, romance and superb acting, this has become a timeless classic. This gorgeous half sheet, with its original linen finish, has been professionally restored to address fold wear, small tears in the borders, and a small chip in the top right corner. A stunning showpiece, this poster features some of the best artwork for this beloved title. Fine/Very Fine on Paper
Estimate: $7,000-up
Starting Bid: $3,500

83479   **The Adventures of Robin Hood (Warner Brothers, 1938).** One Sheet (27" X 41"). From the classic title painted on a shield, to the colorful image of the dashing Errol Flynn loosing an arrow while "Maid Marian" (Olivia de Havilland) is tucked safely behind him, this poster stands out as one of the defining moments in Hollywood's storied history. Flynn was born to play Robin Hood and this always elusive poster has been ardently sought for decades by even the most casual of collectors. The poster has been linenbacked and there has been some color touchup in the image area. There were surface abrasions and small chips in the borders. This would be a showpiece in any collection. Fine+ on Linen.
Estimate: $8,000-up Starting Bid: $4,000

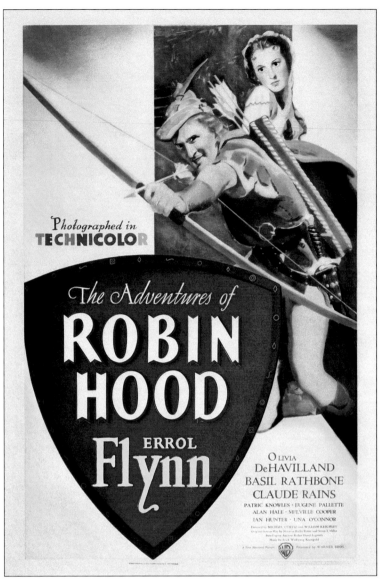

83480   **The Private Lives of Elizabeth and Essex (Warner Brothers, 1939).** Three Sheet (41" X 81"). Very Fine on Linen.
Estimate: $3,000-up Starting Bid: $1,500

83481   The Sea Hawk (Warner Brothers, 1940). Insert (14" X 36"). Fine/Very Fine on Paper.
Estimate: $1,800-up Starting Bid: $900

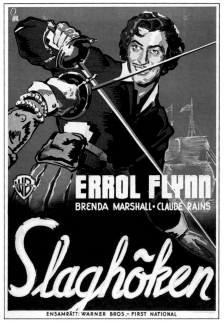

83482   The Sea Hawk (Warner Brothers, 1940). Swedish One Sheet (27.5" X 39.5") Art Style. Rolled, Fine+.
Estimate: $500-up Starting Bid: $250

83483   The Sea Hawk (Warner Brothers, late 1940s). First Post-War Belgian (14" X 22"). Folded, Very Fine-.
Estimate: $500-up Starting Bid: $250

For full lot descriptions, enlargeable images and online bidding, visit HA.com/7025

83484   Dodge City (Warner Brothers, 1938). Half Sheet (22" X 28"). Top stars Errol Flynn and Olivia de Havilland bring this classic Western tale to life, with expert direction from Michael Curtiz. Set in the frontier of Kansas in the early years of civilization brought by the railroads, it is up to newly arrived sheriff Wade Hatton (Flynn) and his pal Rusty (Alan Hale) to bring order to the anarchy and gunfights of the lawless cattlemen of Dodge City. This epic American Technicolor film was a big hit for Warner Brothers, and cemented Flynn's reputation as a top screen idol. This gorgeous half sheet has its original linen finish and has been professionally restored to address pinholes in the borders and art, an area of missing paper and a small chip at the bottom, edge wear, and light creases. For Western fans, it doesn't get much better than this beauty. Fine- on Paper.
Estimate: $3,000-up Starting Bid: $1,500

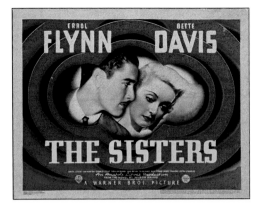

83485
Dodge City (Warner Brothers, 1938). Lobby Card (11" X 14"). Fine+.
Estimate: $600-up
Starting Bid: $300

83486 **The Charge of the Light Brigade (Warner Brothers, 1936).** One Sheet (27" X 41"). Very Fine on Linen.
Estimate: $1,500-up
Starting Bid: $750

83489 **Virginia City (Warner Brothers, 1940).** One Sheet (27" X 41"). Fine/Very Fine on Linen.
Estimate: $1,200-up
Starting Bid: $600

83487 **The Adventures of Robin Hood (Warner Brothers, 1938).** Pressbook (35 Pages, 17" X 22"). Errol Flynn, Olivia DeHavilland, Claude Rains and Basil Rathbone star in one of the greatest action films ever made! A thrilling musical score by Erich Wolfgang Korngold and the three strip Technicolor filming process round out this masterful work by director Michael Curtiz. This exceedingly rare pressbook has excellent interior pages with no blemishes, defects, or cuts. The cover shows some spine wear, with a 2.5" area of separation at the bottom, some dust shadowing on the front and back, a tear on the right side, bends in the bottom corners, and some edge wear on the right side. Also included is a separate ad supplement (no cuts) and an original herald, both in excellent condition. This is a very scarce and attractive piece, making this a tempting lot that any Flynn fan will covet. Fine/Very Fine.
Estimate: $1,000-up Starting Bid: $1,000

83490 Virginia City (Warner Brothers, 1940). Insert (14" X 36"). Rolled, Fine-.
Estimate: $800-up Starting Bid: $400

83491 Virginia City (Warner Brothers, Late 1940s). Post-War French Grande (47" X 63"). Fine/Very Fine on Linen.
Estimate: $500-up Starting Bid: $250

83492 The Prisoner of Zenda (United Artists, 1937). Lobby Card Set of 8 (11" X 14"). Very Fine.
Estimate: $600-up Starting Bid: $300

83493 The Black Pirate (United Artists, 1926). Lobby Cards (3) (11" X 14"). Very Fine+.
Estimate: $600-up Starting Bid: $300

83494 The Knickerbocker Buckaroo (Artcraft, 1919). One Sheet (27" X 41"). Fine on Linen.
Estimate: $800-up Starting Bid: $400

83495   The Gaucho (United Artists, 1927). Lobby Card Set of 8 (11" X 14"). Very Good+.
Estimate: $1,000-up Starting Bid: $500

83496   The Gaucho (United Artists, 1927). Window Card (14" X 22"). Very Fine-.
Estimate: $800-up Starting Bid: $400

83497   Dirigible (Columbia, 1931). Lobby Card (11" X 14"). Near Mint+.
Estimate: $300-up Starting Bid: $150

83498   Cock of the Air (United Artists, 1932). One Sheet (27" X 41"). *From the Theaters of Old Detroit Collection.* Chester Morris and Billie Dove star in this romantic comedy about a vain French actress who is "set up" with a charming aviation officer in Italy. Dove's character sets out to ensnare and deny the debonair officer and what ensues between the frustrated fellow and the alluring femme is the crux of the film. This lovely stone litho one sheet has art attributed to "Hap" Hadley and is one of only two known copies! This was a Howard Hughes release and as with many of the young millionaire's films he printed his own posters as is evidenced by the printer, M.R. Litho of New York and distributed, at least initially, by himself. Evidence survives that the Hays office compiled a list of suggestions for Hughes to bring the film into conformity with the censorship code. But Hughes had already shipped a positive print of the film, no doubt with this poster, to every state in the union before even securing an MPPDA approval from the Hays office. Hays learned from the preview that Hughes had ignored all of his suggestions concerning conforming to the code! The poster had some fold wear, crossfold separations with some chipping and small chips in three borders, all of which has been addressed with professional restoration. *From the Theaters of Old Detroit Collection.* Fine on Linen.
Estimate: $2,000-up Starting Bid: $1,000

83499 **Air Hawks (Columbia, 1935).** One Sheet (27" X 41"). Famed aviator Wiley Post stars in this aviation action film as himself. Post had just completed a sensational around-the-world flight. The plot involves a rivalry between two airlines over an infra-red "death ray." Tragically, two months after this film was released, Post and close friend Will Rogers died in a plane crash off the coast of Alaska. Prior to restoration, there were pinholes in the borders, a chip in the lower left corner, and small chips in the left border. Very Fine- on Linen.
Estimate: $1,000-up Starting Bid: $500

83500 **Young Eagles (Paramount, 1930).** One Sheet (27" X 41") Style A. Very Fine on Linen.
Estimate: $1,000-up Starting Bid: $500

83501 **Wall Street (Columbia, 1929).** One Sheet (27" X 41"). Ralph Ince was a very talented and prolific actor, writer, and director in Hollywood from its earliest days, and was brother to two other well-known directors, John and Thomas H. This early and topical look at the tycoons and swindlers of Wall Street was released just two months after the great Crash of 1929, with Ince starring as the ruthless steel mogul Roller McCray, who drives his rival to commit suicide. Things become more complicated when his victim's widow Ann (Aileen Pringle) teams up with John Willard (Sam De Grasse) to get revenge and ruin McCray. Prior to professional restoration, this rare sheet had a few tears in the left border with two that extended into the yellow background, a tear in the bottom border going into the black, and one at the top border. There were also a few small tack holes in the background. These issues are no longer apparent, and this exquisite stone litho poster is a unique beauty to behold. Fine+ on Linen.
Estimate: $2,500-up Starting Bid: $1,250

83502   Dynamite (MGM, 1929). One Sheet (27" X 41") Sound Style. In his first all-talking picture, Cecil B. DeMille directs this very modern melodrama about a spoiled rich girl, Cynthia Crothers (Kay Johnson in her film debut) who loves Roger (Conrad Nagel) who is married to Marcia (Julia Faye) who is willing to give Roger up, for a price... Cynthia then realizes she has to marry quickly in order to inherit her fortune and settles on soon-to-be-executed convicted killer Buddy (Charles Bickford). DeMille knew how to pack a lot of drama into one film, and this one has it all, which also makes for a stunner of a poster. The film was released both as a silent, to accommodate theaters that did not have the latest sound technology, and as a "talkie," and this copy is from the sound release. A gorgeous stone litho, the poster has been professionally restored to address a small tack hole in the lower right, two minor ones in the yellow field, a small tack hole in Johnson's neck, and pinholes in the corners. None of these issues are now apparent and this beauty displays extremely well. Very Fine- on Linen.
Estimate: $1,000-up Starting Bid: $500

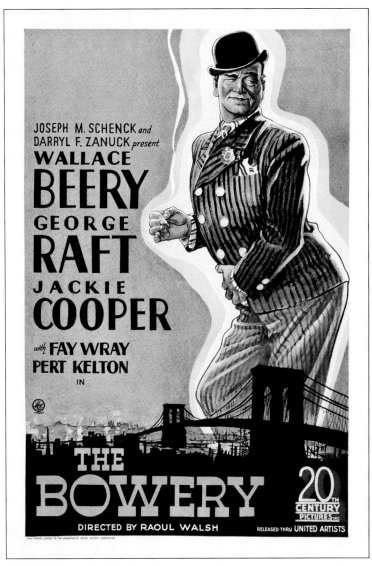

83503   The Bowery (United Artists, 1933). One Sheet (27" X 41"). Wallace Beery and George Raft star as two buddies living at the turn of the century who compete for everything in their Bowery neighborhood, including the love of Lucy Calhoun (Fay Wray). Beery is saloon owner Chuck Connors, who is raising orphan Swipes McGurk (Jackie Cooper) and dares pal Brodie (Raft) to jump off the Brooklyn Bridge to prove his love to Lucy. In a small bit part, Lucille Ball can be seen making her film debut. Paper from this title is rare indeed, and we are proud to offer this sensational stone litho artwork of Beery for the first time. It has been expertly restored to address tears at the crossfolds, minor crossfold separations with a few tiny chips, and small chips in the borders and two corners. Fine/Very Fine on Linen.
Estimate: $2,000-up Starting Bid: $1,000

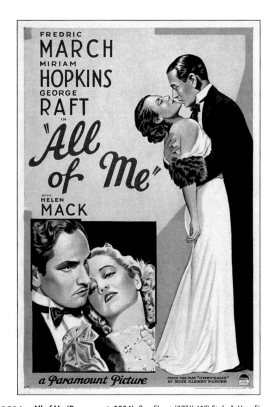

83504   All of Me (Paramount, 1934). One Sheet (27" X 41") Style A. Very Fine- on Linen.
Estimate: $2,500-up Starting Bid: $1,250

83505   Anthony Adverse (Warner Brothers, 1936). Lobby Card Set of 8 (11" X 14"). Very Fine+.
Estimate: $600-up Starting Bid: $300

83506   The Barretts of Wimpole Street (MGM, 1934). Lobby Card Set of 8 (11" X 14"). Very Fine.
Estimate: $500-up Starting Bid: $250

83507   Merrily We Go to Hell (Paramount, 1932). One Sheet (27" X 41"). Sylvia Sidney stars as Joan Prentice, a spoiled heiress who runs away and marries reporter Jerry Corbett (Fredric March) a ne'er-do-well who is also an abusive drunk. Fed up with his flirting with *femme fatale* Claire Hempstead (Adrianne Allen), and his drinking, Joan leaves her new husband, only to find she is pregnant. The tragic title and melodramatic plot of this top film is leavened with humor and the combination works. Cary Grant can be seen in a small role as Charlie Baxter, one of his earliest screen appearances. This terrific poster has pinholes in the corners, edge wear, crossfold separations with minor paper loss, two small chips at the top, and wrinkles in the borders. With its striking stone litho artwork of these top stars, this Pre-Code beauty is sure to be a hit with collectors. Fine+.
Estimate: $2,000-up Starting Bid: $1,000

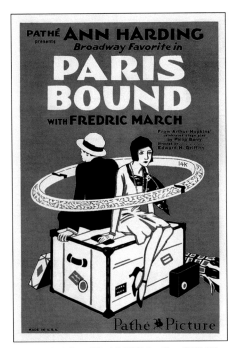

83508 Paris Bound (Pathé, 1929). One Sheet (27" X 41"). Fine+ on Linen.
Estimate: $1,200-up Starting Bid: $600

83509 Smilin' Through (MGM, R-1935). One Sheet (27" X 41") Style C. Fine-.
Estimate: $800-up Starting Bid: $400

83510 Man Trouble (Fox, 1930). One Sheet (27" X 41"). Fine- on Linen.
Estimate: $1,000-up Starting Bid: $500

83511 Gigolettes of Paris (Majestic, 1933). One Sheet (27" X 41"). Madge Bellamy stars as party girl Suzanne Ricord who gets in over her head when she accepts an marriage proposal of convenience from the wealthy count Balraine (Theodore von Eltz) who has no intention of going through with his promise. A dejected Suzanne takes up a singing career at a cabaret, where she falls for gigolo Antoine Ferand (Gilbert Roland), which complicates her life even further. This terrific pre-Code stone litho one sheet was designed by renowned artist Hap Hadley, who created many of the memorable posters for Charlie Chaplin and Buster Keaton films, as well as cartoons for New York newspapers. It shows fold wear with separations, edge wear with small chips, tack holes in the borders, and two pieces of paper tape in the borders. Do not let this rare beauty pass you by. Fine.
Estimate: $1,200-up Starting Bid: $600

83512 Melody Cruise (RKO, 1933). One Sheet (27" X 41"). In his twenty year career, Mark Sandrich earned a reputation as one of the top musical directors in Hollywood, with Fred Astaire/ Ginger Rogers classics such as *Top Hat, Follow the Fleet, Shall We Dance*, along with Bing Crosby's Christmas perennial *Holiday Inn*, amongst his many credits. Sandrich started his career directing comedy shorts, winning an Academy Award for the short *So This is Harris!* (1933), which launched him in the genre of musicals. Offered here is a true gem, a breathtaking one sheet from his first full-length musical feature film. It stars bandleader Phil Harris as a millionaire bachelor, whose presence aboard a cruise ship gains him too much attention from fortune-hungry females. This very colorful and detailed stone litho one sheet has been professionally restored to address the main issue of the missing top 1/4 portion of the poster, including anything above the top horizontal fold which extends through the middle of the word "Cruise." There are also small tears in the bottom border, and some fold wear. The restoration of all of theses issues is exquisite, and no flaws are noticeable until looked at it under strong light. A striking work of art, it will be a long time coming before paper from this very special pre-Code title is available again. Good+ on Linen.
Estimate: $4,000-up Starting Bid: $2,000

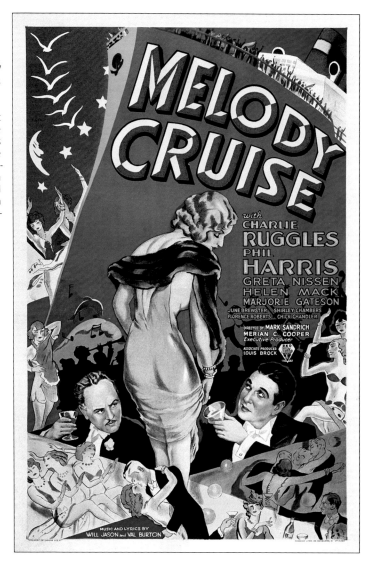

83513 Transatlantic Merry-Go-Round (United Artists, 1934). Lobby Card Set of 8 (11" X 14"). Fine/Very Fine.
Estimate: $500-up Starting Bid: $250

83514 Love in the Rough (MGM, 1930). Half Sheet (22" X 28"). Rolled, Fine+.
Estimate: $500-up Starting Bid: $250

83515 Strangers May Kiss (MGM, 1931). Half Sheet (22" X 28"). Rolled, Very Good+.
Estimate: $600-up Starting Bid: $300

83516   Central Park (Warner Brothers - First National, 1932). One Sheet (27" X 41"). Fine/Very Fine.
Estimate: $1,400-up Starting Bid: $700

83517   Central Park (Warner Brothers - First National, 1932). CGC Graded Lobby Card Set of 8 (11" X 14"). Near Mint/Mint.
Estimate: $1,200-up Starting Bid: $600

83518   Crazy That Way (Fox, 1930). One Sheet (27" X 41"). Fine/Very Fine on Linen.
Estimate: $1,200-up Starting Bid: $600

83519   Vigil in the Night (RKO, 1940). Title Lobby Card (11" X 14"). Fine/Very Fine.
Estimate: $400-up Starting Bid: $300

83520   The Princess Comes Across (Paramount, 1936). Insert (14" X 36"). Rolled, Fine/Very Fine.
Estimate: $1,800-up Starting Bid: $1,200

83522   Give Me Your Heart (Warner Brothers, 1936). One Sheet (27" X 41"). Fine+.
Estimate: $400-up
Starting Bid: $200

83523   Norma Shearer Personality Poster (MGM, 1930s). Poster (22" X 28"). Very Good+.
Estimate: $600-up
Starting Bid: $300

83521   To Be or Not to Be (Metropole, 1947). First Post-War French Grande (47" X 63"). Very Good/Fine on Linen.
Estimate: $600-up Starting Bid: $300

83524   Camille (MGM, 1937). Window Card (14" X 22"). Fine/Very Fine.
Estimate: $600-up Starting Bid: $300

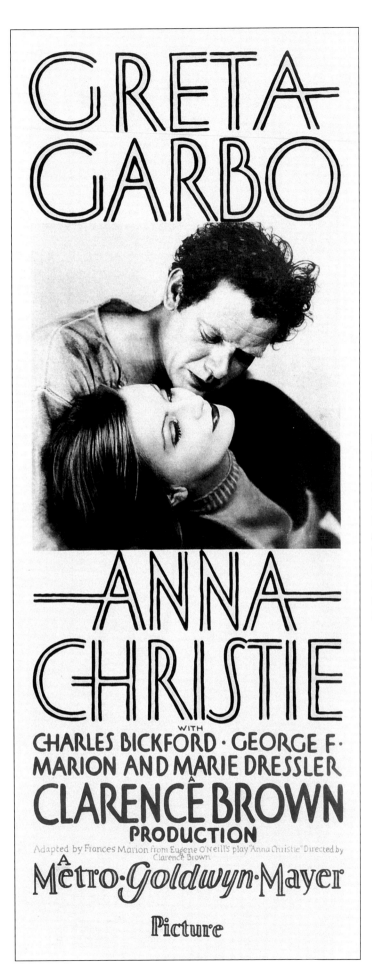

83525   Anna Christie (MGM, 1930). Insert (14"X 36"). Greta Garbo gives one of her greatest performances as the Swedish Anna Christie, a woman with an unsavory past returning to her father's home only to fall in love with Irish sailor Matt Burke (Charles Bickford). Will her father (George F. Marion) and new beau forgive her her sins? Based on an Eugene O'Neill play, this was another huge success for Garbo. Her first talking picture, it was advertised with the famous line "Garbo Talks" and is an important film in the history of cinema. This incredible insert had only two enlarged pinholes in Garbo's name, two pinholes at the bottom corners, and a small chip in the right border. All of these issues have been corrected with professional restoration, leaving this beauty in excellent condition, and we are proud to offer this rare and very special insert for the first time. Very Fine- on Paper.
Estimate: $5,000-up Starting Bid: $2,500

83526   Anna Christie (MGM, 1930). Title Lobby Card (11" X 14"). MGM mounted a massive ad campaign to promote this, the very first sound film to star silent film siren Greta Garbo, with the legendary ad line, "Garbo talks!" Based on the play by Eugene O'Neill (and filmed once before in 1923), Anna Christie tells of a young woman trying to hide her past (prostitution) from her newly-found father (George F. Marion), as well as the charming Irish sailor (Charles Bickford) she has fallen for. This sublime title lobby card is exceedingly rare, and highly coveted by Garbo collectors and posters are rarely found. Corner pinholes and one in her hat have been corrected with professional restoration. This card is not paper backed and appears near mint! Fine/Very Fine.
Estimate: $4,000-up Starting Bid: $2,000

83527   Anna Christie (MGM, 1930). Lobby Card (11" X 14"). Fine/Very Fine.
Estimate: $1,500-up Starting Bid: $750

83528   Anna Christie (MGM, 1930). Lobby Card (11" X 14"). Fine/Very Fine.
Estimate: $1,500-up Starting Bid: $750

83529   The Temptress (MGM, 1926). Insert (14" X 36"). Good on Paper.
Estimate: $1,000-up Starting Bid: $1,000

83531   Iron Man (Universal, 1931). Lobby Card (11" X 14"). Fine-.
Estimate: $600-up Starting Bid: $300

83530   Ninotchka (MGM, 1939). Title Lobby Card and Lobby Cards (6) (11" X 14"). Fine+.
Estimate: $1,200-up Starting Bid: $900

83532   Reckless (MGM, 1935). Locally Produced Jumbo Window Card (22" X 28"). Very Good+.
Estimate: $800-up Starting Bid: $400

83533 Belle of the Nineties (Paramount, 1934). Jumbo Lobby Card (14" X 17"). Very Fine+.
Estimate: $500-up Starting Bid: $250

83536 Not Quite Decent (Fox, 1929). Swedish One Sheet (27.5" X 39.5"). Rolled, Very Good/Fine.
Estimate: $300-up
Starting Bid: $150

83534 Amor am Steuer (UFA, 1921). Swedish One Sheet (23" X 35"). Rolled, Very Fine.
Estimate: $400-up
Starting Bid: $200

83537 Java Head (First Division Pictures, 1934). Title Lobby Card (11" X 14"). Very Fine+.
Estimate: $500-up
Starting Bid: $300

83535 Words and Music (1929) (Fox, 1929). Swedish One Sheet (27.5" X 39.5"). Rolled, Fine.
Estimate: $500-up
Starting Bid: $400

83538 Private Number (20th Century Fox, 1936). Three Sheet (41" X 81"). Very Fine on Linen.
Estimate: $800-up
Starting Bid: $400

83539 **Man's Castle (Columbia, 1933).** One Sheet (27" X 41"). Fine- on Linen.
Estimate: $1,000-up **Starting Bid: $500**

83541 **We Went to College (MGM, 1936).** One Sheet (27" X 41"). Very Fine.
Estimate: $500-up **Starting Bid: $250**

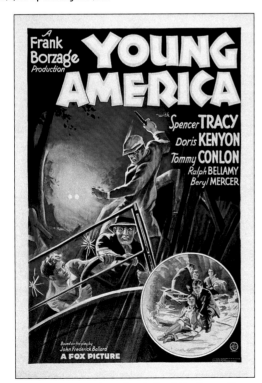

83540 **Young America (Fox, 1932).** One Sheet (27" X 41"). Very Fine+ on Linen.
Estimate: $800-up **Starting Bid: $400**

83542 **State Fair (Fox, 1933).** One Sheet (27" X 41") Style B. Very Fine- on Linen.
Estimate: $450-up **Starting Bid: $225**

83543   The Silver Streak (RKO, 1934). One Sheet (27" X 41"). Fine+ on Linen.
Estimate: $1,000-up Starting Bid: $500

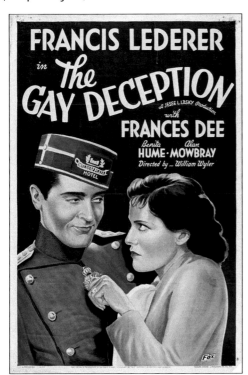

83544   The Gay Deception (Fox, 1935). One Sheet (27" X 41"). Fine-.
Estimate: $800-up Starting Bid: $400

83545   The Big Pond (Paramount, 1930). Half Sheet (22" X 28") Style A. Rolled, Very Good.
Estimate: $1,200-up Starting Bid: $600

83546   She Married Her Boss (Columbia, 1935). One Sheet (27" X 41") Style B. Fine/Very Fine on Linen.
Estimate: $1,500-up Starting Bid: $750

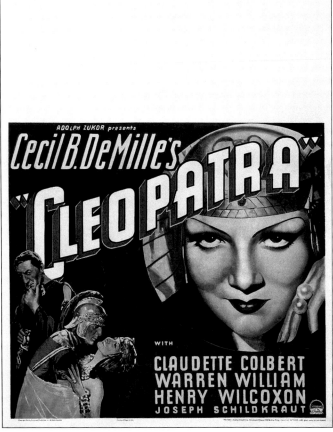

83547   Cleopatra (Paramount, 1934). Jumbo Window Card (22" X 28"). The Hays Code was initiated in 1930 but had little enforcement. By 1934 there was stiffer policing and for films released after July first, a "Certificate of Approval" was required. But Cecil B. DeMille would release *Cleopatra* on October 5th of 1934, replete with a naked woman in the opening titles, and scantily clad sexually suggestive nymphs running amuck in nearly every scene. This wonderful jumbo window card successfully hints at what the film delivered. Claudette Colbert was never lovelier...or naughtier...than as the seductive Queen. The beautiful artist's rendering of her sloe-eyed temptress in her magnificent Travis Banton designed headdress is still one of the most recognizable images in Hollywood film history. This seldom found oversize window card has had expert restoration to replace the top imprint area. There was a long vertical tear, a small tear in the lower left edge, and small tack holes in the borders. There were two tears in Colbert's face, and one in the credits. The result of the first class restoration is a truly desirable example of the Golden Age of Hollywood posters that would improve any collection. Very Good- on Cardstock.
Estimate: $2,000-up Starting Bid: $1,000

83548   Delicious (Fox, 1931). Half Sheet (22" X 28"). Rolled, Very Good+.
Estimate: $600-up Starting Bid: $300

83549   Smartest Girl in Town (RKO, 1936). One Sheet (27" X 41"). Very Fine- on Linen.
Estimate: $1,000-up Starting Bid: $500

83550   Hot Saturday (Paramount, 1932). One Sheet (26" X 40"). Fine/Very Fine on Linen.
Estimate: $600-up Starting Bid: $300

83552   Half A Sinner (Universal, 1934). Lobby Card Set of 8 (11" X 14"). Fine/Very Fine.
Estimate: $600-up Starting Bid: $300

83551   Splendor (United Artists, 1935). Lobby Card Set of 8 (11" X 14"). Very Fine.
Estimate: $400-up Starting Bid: $200

For full lot descriptions, enlargeable images and online bidding, visit HA.com/7025

83553 **Hula (Paramount, 1927).** One Sheet (27" X 41") Style A. On the heels of her success with *Wings*, the effervescent and buoyant Clara Bow was at the height of her fame starring as Hula Calhoun, a free spirit who falls for the very proper and very married English gentleman, Anthony Haldance (Clive Brook). Victor Fleming directs this light romantic tale which showcases Bow's dancing abilities in the exotic locale of Hawaii. This was the second film Fleming and Bow had made together, after the very popular *Mantrap*. The opening sequence features Hula skinny-dipping when she comes to the rescue of Anthony. Full of life and sex appeal, Bow was one of those rare talents, whose personality and charm could transcend even the lightest of plots and she easily captured the hearts of audiences world-wide throughout the 1920s. This spectacular stone litho image of the *It* girl is one of the best we have ever come across, a rare item from her popular hit. It has been professionally restored to address chips which are mainly limited to the border area, with one in the title and one in the image. There was a tear in the left side of the blue background, and fold wear. These issues are no longer apparent, and the gorgeous colors of this beauty make this one sheet really stand out. This will be a prized addition to any early cinema collection. Fine on Linen.
Estimate: $10,000-up Starting Bid: $5,000

83554   The Wild Party (Paramount, 1929). Lobby Card (11" X 14"). Clara Bow, as the quintessential party girl of the '20s, falls for college professor Fredric March. Since he's rather stuffy and low-key, March is unimpressed with Bow, but she eventually finds a way to gain his respect. You could hardly ask for a better image of the legendary "It" girl than this leggy lobby card. The card has pinholes in the corners and one each in the left and right borders. Very Fine-.
Estimate: $600-up Starting Bid: $500

83555   Dangerous Curves (Paramount, 1929). Title Lobby Card (11" X 14"). Fine.
Estimate: $400-up Starting Bid: $350

83557   Rough House Rosie (Paramount, 1927). Jumbo Lobby Card (14" X 17"). Very Fine.
Estimate: $500-up Starting Bid: $250

83556   Call Her Savage (Fox, 1932). Half Sheet (22" X 28"). Fine+ on Paper.
Estimate: $500-up Starting Bid: $250

83558 Rembrandt (United Artists, 1936). One Sheet (27" X 41"). Charles Laughton gives a memorable performance as the legendary artist in this well-executed biopic; Laughton had previously teamed with director Alexander Korda for the similar historic epic *The Private Life of Henry VIII*. This gorgeous stone litho one sheet has terrific artwork and retains excellent color. Condition issues on this unrestored sheet include edge wear with tears in the right and bottom borders, pinholes in the corners, light fold wear, and a scratch in Laughton's banner credit. Fine/Very Fine.
Estimate: $2,500-up Starting Bid: $1,250

83559 That Hamilton Woman (Minerva Film, 1946). First Post-War Italian 2 - Foglio (39" X 55"). Very Fine on Linen.
Estimate: $600-up
Starting Bid: $500

83560 Wuthering Heights (United Artists, 1939). One Sheet (27" X 41"). Very Fine+ on Linen.
Estimate: $700-up Starting Bid: $350

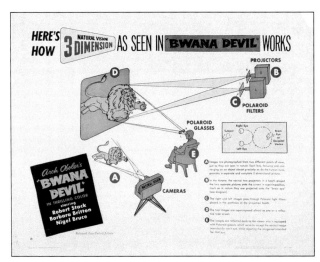

83561 Bwana Devil (United Artists, 1953). Half Sheet (22" X 28") 3-D Style B. Rolled, Fine.
Estimate: $600-up Starting Bid: $300

83562   Cat on a Hot Tin Roof (MGM, 1958). Insert
(14" X 36"). Folded, Fine/Very Fine.
Estimate: $600-up Starting Bid: $300

83563   Cat on a Hot Tin Roof (MGM, 1958). Japanese B2
(20" X 29"). Folded, Fine/Very Fine.
Estimate: $400-up Starting Bid: $350

83564   To Kill a Mockingbird (Universal, 1963). Insert
(14" X 36"). Folded, Very Fine-.
Estimate: $500-up Starting Bid: $250

83565   To Kill a Mockingbird (Universal, 1963). Lobby Card
Set of 8 (11" X 14"). Fine/Very Fine.
Estimate: $600-up Starting Bid: $300

83566   Cool Hand Luke (Warner Brothers, 1967). French
Grande (47" X 63"). Fine/Very Fine on Linen.
Estimate: $600-up Starting Bid: $300

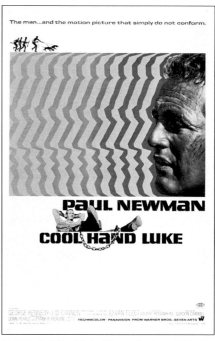

83567   Cool Hand Luke (Warner Brothers, 1967). One
Sheet (27" X 41"). Fine/Very Fine on Linen.
Estimate: $600-up Starting Bid: $300

83568   Ocean's 11 (Warner Brothers, 1960). Poster (40" X 60") Style Z. Eleven friends unite to knock off five of the biggest casinos in Las Vegas in this classic "Rat Pack" film. Frank Sinatra leads the cast as Danny Ocean, ably supported by his friends Dean Martin, Sammy Davis Jr., Peter Lawford, Joey Bishop, Angie Dickinson, and Cesar Romero. It's been said that the point to making this movie was so that Sinatra and his cronies could party in Vegas, and that sense of camaraderie is on full display in this memorable movie, as much of the dialogue between the major characters was ad-libbed. This remarkable poster has pinholes in the top corners, light surface wear, a tear in the top border, a crease in the bottom left corner, and two small tears in the bottom left, but presents very nicely. Paper from this film is always in high demand, especially this image of the boys strolling down the strip. Don't miss out on your chance to add this rare stunner to your collection! Fine/Very Fine.
Estimate: $3,000-up Starting Bid: $1,500

83569   Ocean's 11 (Warner Brothers, 1960). CGC Graded Lobby Card Set of 8 (11" X 14"). Near Mint/Mint.
Estimate: $1,000-up Starting Bid: $500

83570   The Man With the Golden Arm (United Artists, 1955). Banner (24" X 82"). Rolled, Fine.
Estimate: $800-up Starting Bid: $400

83571   The Man With the Golden Arm (United Artists, 1955). Half Sheet (22" X 28") Style B. Very Fine+ on Linen.
Estimate: $400-up Starting Bid: $200

83572   Easy Rider (Columbia, R-1972). One Sheet (27" X 41"). Very Fine+.
Estimate: $450-up Starting Bid: $225

83573   Ciao! Manhattan (Constantin Film, 1974). Rare Advance German A1 (23" X 33"). Folded, Very Fine-.
Estimate: $1,200-up Starting Bid: $1,000

83574   Bonjour Tristesse (Columbia, 1958). One Sheet (27" X 41"). Very Fine-.
Estimate: $500-up Starting Bid: $250

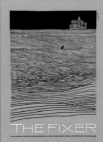

Starring James Stewart/Lee Remick/Ben Gazzara/Arthur O'Connell/Eve Arden/Kathryn Grant and Joseph N. Welch as Judge Weaver/With George C. Scott/Orson Bean/Murray Hamilton/Brooks West. Screenplay by Wendell Mayes/Photography by Sam Leavitt/Production designed by Boris Leven Music by Duke Ellington/Produced and Directed by Otto Preminger/A Columbia release

83576   Anatomy of a Murder (Art Krebs Screen Studio, 1984). Saul Bass Silk-Screen Poster (25.25" X 35.5"). When Saul Bass, the legendary poster/ visuals/ titles designer, submitted his designs for film posters, often the studio would reassemble or alter his original ideas. Here is a rare opportunity to see what Bass originally conceived for the poster for *Anatomy of a Murder*. The studio altered the completely blood red background opting instead for a diluted orange background on top and enlarged actor credits on the bottom in an also diluted red. The closest the Bass conception would come were the oversize posters done in Italy for the Italian release of the film who seemed to have no trouble understanding the importance of "blood red" to the central plot of the film. In frustration, Bass would often go to one of the best print studios in Los Angeles, the Art Krebs Screen Studio, just around the corner from his studio, and privately print his original designs in editions of only 100-400 intended as gifts for friends, Museum of Modern Art, and exhibitions. This silkscreen was done in 1984 in an edition of 300, per a listing from the seller of the remaining few copies who had been engaged by the Bass estate. Minor edge wear in the top and left borders does not depreciate the prominently featured Saul Bass artwork. What a completely unique and grand companion piece this would be, displayed with the American one sheet. Rolled, Near Mint+.
Estimate: $1,500-up Starting Bid: $1,300

83575   Saul Bass Poster Lot (Art Krebs Screen Gallery, 1958-84) (Various printers in Japan/ Italy/ and the US, 1994-99). Sizes range from 22" X 32.5" to 28.75" X 40.5". Fine/Very Fine.
Estimate: $1,000-up Starting Bid: $600

THE MAGNIFICENT SEVEN · DIRECTED BY JOHN STURGES

83577   The Magnificent Seven (Art Krebs Screen Studio, 1960). Saul Bass Silk-Screen Poster (25" X 35.5"). Here is a unique opportunity to be one of the few to own an original silk screen "original concept" poster for *The Magnificent Seven*. It was designed by the legendary Saul Bass and was privately printed by him in 1960, in an addition of 400, per records supplied to the consigned seller of the estate in 2002. The Museum of Modern Art, friends, and exhibitions, were the originally intended recipients of the posters, and those that remained in the estate after the passing of Mr. Bass have long since been distributed. What is very fascinating to poster collectors, is that this image was not used by United Artists. But to those that understand the origins of Bass's brilliant design it is a totally intriguing concept. The design directly relates to the very origins of John Sturges' "remake" of Kurosawa's *Seven Samurai* right down to the tilted ends of the number symbol done in the tilted style of Japanese Kanji script. Surely, there were those at United Artists that thought the concept "too difficult" for the general American public, and that they "just wouldn't get it". Two tiny edge nicks are the only thing keeping this poster from sheer perfection. Rolled, Near Mint/Mint.
Estimate: $1,000-up Starting Bid: $800

83578   Rebel Without a Cause (Warner Brothers, 1955). One Sheet (27" X 41"). Fine+ on Linen.
Estimate: $1,800-up Starting Bid: $900

83579   Rebel Without a Cause (Warner Brothers, 1955). Poster (40" X 60") Style Z. Offered in this lot is the ultra-rare large format poster from the definitive James Dean film. This poster has had a good bit of restoration on the left side of the poster which extends primarily into the white borders and in some areas into the image. There were large areas of tape and a tear at the bottom border and a large section about 6" wide was missing from the left border. The central image area is still in very nice shape and thanks to painstaking professional restoration, poster displays extremely well. Good/Very Good on Paper.
Estimate: $2,500-up Starting Bid: $1,250

83580   Rebel Without a Cause (Warner Brothers, 1955). Half Sheet (22" X 28"). Very Fine- on Paper.
Estimate: $1,000-up Starting Bid: $900

83581   Rebel Without a Cause (Warner Brothers, 1955). Lobby Card Set of 8 (11" X 14"). Fine/Very Fine.
Estimate: $700-up Starting Bid: $350

83582   East of Eden (Warner Brothers, 1955). Color Photo Set of 12 (8" X 10"). *From the collection of Wade Williams.* Very Fine+.
Estimate: $700-up Starting Bid: $350

83583   East of Eden (Warner Brothers, 1955). Lobby Card Set of 8 (11" X 14"). Fine-.
Estimate: $600-up Starting Bid: $300

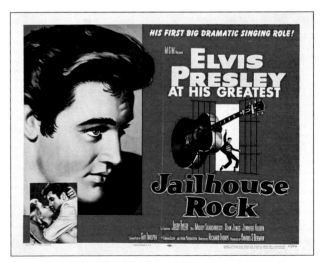

83584   Jailhouse Rock (MGM, 1957). Half Sheet (22" X 28") Style A. Folded, Very Fine.
Estimate: $700-up Starting Bid: $350

83585   King Creole (Paramount, 1958). Six Sheet (81" X 81"). Near Mint+.
Estimate: $800-up Starting Bid: $400

83588   Blue Hawaii (Paramount, 1961). One Sheet (27" X 41"). Fine+.
Estimate: $700-up Starting Bid: $350

83586   Loving You (Paramount, 1957). Three Sheet (41" X 81"). Fine.
Estimate: $600-up Starting Bid: $300

83587   Jailhouse Rock (MGM, 1957). Title Lobby Card (11" X 14"). Fine/Very Fine.
Estimate: $500-up Starting Bid: $250

83589   Viva Las Vegas (MGM, 1964). Six Sheet (81" X 81"). Very Fine+.
Estimate: $1,000-up Starting Bid: $500

83590　G.I. Blues (Paramount, 1960). CGC Graded Lobby Card Set of 8 (11" X 14"). Very Fine+.
Estimate: $400-up　Starting Bid: $200

83591　Sympathy for the Devil (New Line, 1970). Premiere Poster (34.5" X 46.75"). Jean-Luc Godard set off to London in the late 1960s to make a film about the controversial issues of the era—war, power, abortion, religion...In this semi-documentary, he intersperses these topics with footage of the rehearsals and recording of the Rolling Stones' song of the same title. The poster we present here is for the American premiere in April 1970, of the producer Iain Quarrier's cut of the film, an edited version, tacking on a completed version of the title song, completely altering Godard's vision of the film. This led to Godard physically attacking Quarrier at the London premiere in a blind rage! It appears that very few of these graphically charged, over-sized posters were printed. The poster features a marvelous blend of Muybridge photos inset in the top credits and a photo inset of the Stones inside a giant skull wearing recording studio-style headphones. It has light edge wear at the left, two small tears at the top edge, and one at the bottom. This is a scarce major promotional item for the longest lived major rock and roll band in musical history. Rolled, Very Fine-.
Estimate: $3,000-up　Starting Bid: $1,500

83592　Yellow Submarine (United Artists, 1968). British Quad (30" X 40"). The Blue Meanies overthrow Pepperland, draining it of all color and music, bombing it with anti-music missiles, conking people with green apples, and turning the inhabitants to stone by way of the pointed finger of a giant white glove. So Lord Admiral sets off in the yellow submarine to enlist the aide of the Fab Four. The Beatles' third film was a psychedelic cartoon that perfectly embodies the groovy vibe of the '60s. This nifty British quad had edge wear, a hole in the top border, and chips in the right and left borders, all of which has been smoothed over with professional restoration. Fine on Linen.
Estimate: $2,500-up　Starting Bid: $1,250

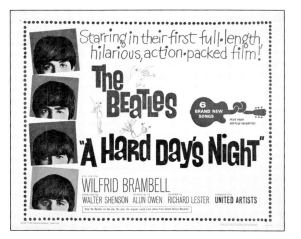

83593 A Hard Day's Night (United Artists, 1964). Half Sheet (22" X 28"). Folded, Fine/Very Fine.
Estimate: $600-up
Starting Bid: $300

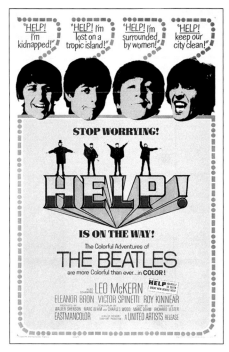

83594 Help! (United Artists, 1965). One Sheet (27" X 41"). Very Fine.
Estimate: $500-up Starting Bid: $250

83596 A Hard Day's Night (United Artists, 1964). Japanese B2 (20" X 28.5"). Very Fine+.
Estimate: $300-up Starting Bid: $150

83595 A Hard Day's Night (United Artists, 1964). Insert (14" X 36"). Folded, Very Fine-.
Estimate: $500-up Starting Bid: $250

83597 Let It Be (United Artists, 1970). One Sheet (27" X 41"). Very Fine/Near Mint.
Estimate: $300-up Starting Bid: $150

83598 Let It Be (United Artists, 1970). CGC Graded Lobby Card Set of 8 (11" X 14"). Near Mint/ Mint.
Estimate: $500-up Starting Bid: $250

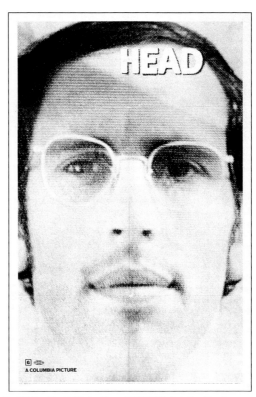

83600 Head (Columbia, 1968). One Sheet (27" X 41") Style A. Fine/Very Fine.
Estimate: $500-up Starting Bid: $250

83599 Yellow Submarine (United Artists, 1968). Three Sheet (41" X 81"). Very Fine on Linen.
Estimate: $1,000-up Starting Bid: $500

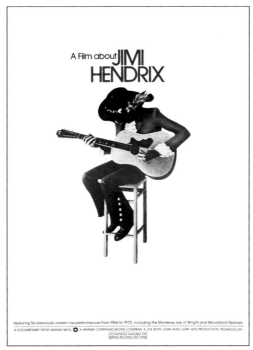

83601 Jimi Hendrix (Warner Brothers, 1973). Soundtrack Poster (21" X 29"). Very Fine+ on Linen.
Estimate: $300-up Starting Bid: $150

83602   L'Avventura (Cino del Duca, 1961). French Grande (47" X 63"). Fine.
Estimate: $600-up Starting Bid: $500

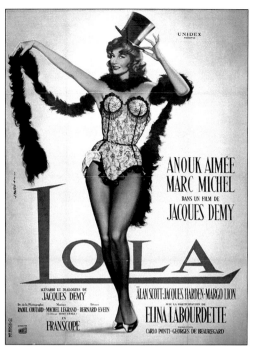

83604   Lola (Unidex, 1961). French Grande (47" X 63"). Very Fine+.
Estimate: $300-up Starting Bid: $150

83605   La Dolce Vita (Astor, 1961). CGC Graded Lobby Card Set of 8 (11" X 14"). Very Fine/Near Mint.
Estimate: $500-up Starting Bid: $250

83603   L'Avventura (Cino del Duca, 1961). Japanese B2 (20" X 29"). Rolled, Very Fine.
Estimate: $800-up Starting Bid: $750

83606   Two Women (Titanus, 1960). Italian 4 - Foglio (55" X 78"). Fine+.
Estimate: $600-up Starting Bid: $300

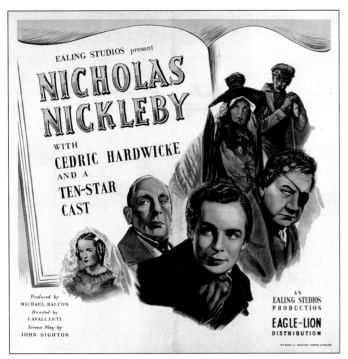

83607　Nicholas Nickleby (Eagle Lion, 1947). British Six Sheet (79" X 79"). Very Fine on Linen.
Estimate: $700-up Starting Bid: $500

83608　A Night to Remember (Rank, 1959). British Three Sheet (40" X 79"). Very Fine.
Estimate: $1,000-up Starting Bid: $500

83609　Tread Softly Stranger (Renown Pictures, 1958). Italian 4 - Foglio (55" X 78"). Very Fine-.
Estimate: $400-up Starting Bid: $200

83610　Blow-Up (MGM, 1967). Italian Photobustas (7) (18" X 27"). Folded, Fine+.
Estimate: $500-up Starting Bid: $250

83611   Romeo and Juliet (Rank, 1954). Italian 2 - Foglio (39" X 55"). Very Fine+.
Estimate: $400-up Starting Bid: $200

83614   Lolita (MGM, 1962). One Sheet (27" X 41"). Very Fine-.
Estimate: $800-up Starting Bid: $400

83612   Lolita (MGM, 1962). British Quad (30" X 40"). Fine/Very Fine.
Estimate: $700-up Starting Bid: $600

83613   Lolita (Dear Film, 1962). Italian Photobusta. Very Fine.
Estimate: $400-up Starting Bid: $200

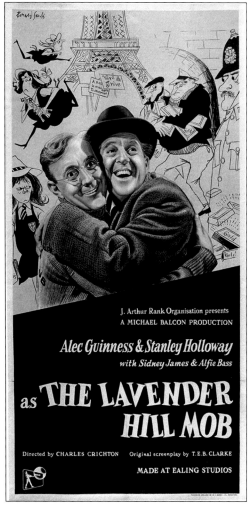

83615   The Lavender Hill Mob (Rank, 1951). British Three Sheet (38" X 76"). Very Fine+ on
Linen.
Estimate: $8,000-up Starting Bid: $4,000

The Seventh Seal (Globe Films International, 1959). Italian 4 - Foglio (55" X 78"). Very Fine.
Estimate: $600-up Starting Bid: $300

83618   The Bride Wore Black (Dear, 1968). Italian 2 - Foglio (39" X 55"). Very Fine+.
Estimate: $600-up
Starting Bid: $300

83617   Le Testament d'Orphee (Cinedis, 1960). French Grande (47" X 63"). Very Fine on Linen.
Estimate: $700-up Starting Bid: $350

83619   The 400 Blows (Cocinor, 1959). French Grande (47" X 63"). The actor on this French grande, drawn with such evocative artwork by prolific artist Boris Grinsson, is the French New Wave *wunderkind* Jean-Pierre Leaud. Loved and hated for the very same aspects of his acting style, he served Truffaut and Godard's improvisational techniques completely . Grinsson wisely chose one of the most memorable closing moments in film history for his poster. The heartbreaking character 'Antoine Doinel' has just escaped from a work camp and runs to the ocean, which he has never seen. Truffaut's camera dollies in and freezes and the actor stares at the sea?..or at us? Leaud's "Doinel" is on several "Top 100 Screen Characters" lists. Professional linenbacking has made negligible minor fold wear and small tears in the left and right borders. This is a poster for anyone that loves great films. Very Fine- on Linen.
Estimate: $1,200-up Starting Bid: $600

83620 **Shoot the Piano Player (Cocinor, 1960).** French Grande (47" X 63"). Very Fine+.
Estimate: $600-up Starting Bid: $300

83621 **Hiroshima, mon amour (Cocinor, 1959).** French Grande (47" X 63"). Very Fine+.
Estimate: $500-up Starting Bid: $250

83622 **Yojimbo (Toho, 1961).** Japanese B2 (20" X 29"). For those that don't think that film is a "collaborative" effort, consider Akira Kurosawa reading the Dashiell Hammett novel, *Red Harvest* (1929), and watching *Glass Key* (1942) in his youth. Later he would recreate some scenes and ideas almost shot-for-shot from those sources in his epic film, *Yojimbo* (Japanese for "bodyguard"). A director from Italy, Sergio Leone, would return the favor, remaking *Yojimbo* as *A Fistful of Dollars* (1964)! Country of origin paper from the 1961 Japanese release has always been in extremely short supply, due mainly to Japanese collectors loathe to part with their finds, coupled with the normal high attrition rate any wildly popular film faces. Here's a great chance to get a high grade original in a size that will fit anywhere. This piece has limited restoration for pinholes in the corners and edges of the fold. There is mild fold wear, an extra horizontal fold, and small chips and tears in the top border. Fine on Masa Paper.
Estimate: $2,500-up Starting Bid: $2,000

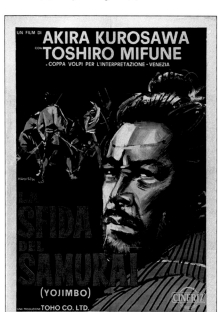

83623 **Yojimbo (Toho, 1961).** Italian 2 - Foglio (39" X 55"). Very Fine-.
Estimate: $600-up
Starting Bid: $300

83625 **Harakiri (Euro International, 1962).** Italian 4 - Foglio (55" X 78") Style B. Considered to be one of the classics of Japanese cinema, Director Masaki Kobayashi's tale of 17th century Japan and the death of the Samurai class has gained international cult status. This magnificent Italian large format poster has wonderful art by Alverado Ciriello and is in excellent condition with just minor fold wear. Very Fine.
Estimate: $600-up Starting Bid: $300

83624 **Throne of Blood (Toho, 1957).** Japanese B2 (20" X 29"). Akira Kurosawa wrote, produced, edited and directed this re-telling of William Shakespeare's *Macbeth*, in which Japanese military commanders become lost in the woods after a major victory. They come across a mysterious woman who predicts one soldier (Toshirô Mifune) will become warlord and the other will rule the military (Takashi Shimura). When events seem to be going in the predicted direction, Wahizu (Mifune) decides to help matters along by killing the current warlord, with the aid of his scheming wife (Isuzu Yamada). Mifune and Shimura often appeared in Kurosawa's epic films, and are powerful in their roles in this masterpiece. This impeccable country-of-origin poster shows only light bends. Rolled, Near Mint/Mint.
Estimate: $600-up Starting Bid: $300

83626 **Kagemusha (20th Century Fox, 1980).** Japanese B0 (41" X 56"). Folded, Fine.
Estimate: $500-up Starting Bid: $300

83627   The Day the Earth Stood Still (20th Century Fox, 1952). Italian 2 - Foglio (39" X 55"). Fine+ on Linen.
Estimate: $1,400-up Starting Bid: $700

83628   The Day the Earth Stood Still (20th Century Fox, 1951). Insert (14" X 36"). Robert Wise's masterful science fiction film is based on the story "Farewell to the Master" by Harry Bates and begins with an alien ship arriving on Earth with Klaatu (Michael Rennie) and Gort (Lock Martin) who wish to warn humans of the dangers of continuing with their war-like behaviors. The only ones to take their message seriously are Helen (Patricia Neal) and Professor Jacob Barnhardt (Sam Jaffe). A thoughtful look into where humans are headed, posters for this title are very special and highly prized, and this beautiful insert is no exception. It has been professionally restored to address fold wear, two tears in the folds, a small tear in the top right field, a few pinholes in the image and corners, and a small area of missing paper in the lower left border. It now displays beautifully in all of its sci-fi glory. Fine+ on Paper.
Estimate: $3,000-up
Starting Bid: $1,500

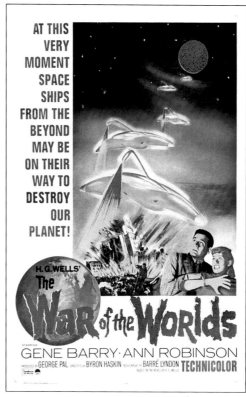

83629   The War of the Worlds (Paramount, R-1965). One Sheet (27" X 41"). Fine/Very Fine on Linen.
Estimate: $3,000-up Starting Bid: $1,500

83630   The War of the Worlds (Paramount, 1953). Lobby Card Set of 8 (11" X 14"). Very Fine-.
Estimate: $2,000-up Starting Bid: $1,000

83631　When Worlds Collide (Paramount, 1951). Half Sheet (22" X 28") Style A. Folded, Fine/
Very Fine.
Estimate: $1,000-up　Starting Bid: $500

83632　The Man
from Planet X (United
Artists, 1951). Lobby
Card Set of 8 (11" X 14").
*From the collection of
Wade Williams.* Very
Fine.
Estimate: $4,000-up
Starting Bid: $2,000

83634　Invaders from Mars (20th Century Fox, 1955). One Sheet (27" X 41"). Very Good/Fine
on Linen.
Estimate: $800-up　Starting Bid: $400

83635　Invaders from Mars (20th Century Fox, 1953). Insert (14" X 36"). Fine+.
Estimate: $1,200-up　Starting Bid: $600

83633　The Man from Planet X (United Artists, 1951). Half Sheet (22" X 28") Style A. *From the
collection of Wade Williams.* Good- on Paper.
Estimate: $1,500-up　Starting Bid: $750

83636   Invaders from Mars (20th Century Fox, 1953). Lobby Card Set of 8 (11"X 14"). *From the collection of Wade Williams.* Fine/Very Fine.
Estimate: $1,200-up Starting Bid: $600

83638   It Came from Outer Space (Universal International, 1953). Lobby Card Set of 8 (11"X 14"). Fine.
Estimate: $1,200-up Starting Bid: $600

83640   Tobor the Great (Republic, 1954). Insert (14"X 36"). Folded, Fine+.
Estimate: $600-up Starting Bid: $300

83637   It Came from Outer Space (Universal International, 1953). Insert (14"X 36") 3-D Style. Folded, Fine/Very Fine.
Estimate: $1,000-up Starting Bid: $500

83639   Rocketship X-M (Lippert, 1950). Three Sheet (41" X 81"). Very Fine- on Linen.
Estimate: $800-up Starting Bid: $400

83641   **Tobor the Great (Republic, 1954).** Lobby Card Set of 8 (11" X 14"). *From the collection of Wade Williams.* Fine/Very Fine.
Estimate: $800-up Starting Bid: $400

83642   **Forbidden Planet (MGM, 1956).** Color Photo Set of 12 (8" X 10"). Fine/Very Fine.
Estimate: $800-up Starting Bid: $400

83643   **Forbidden Planet (MGM, 1956).** Lobby Card (11" X 14"). Very Fine-.
Estimate: $700-up Starting Bid: $350

83644   **Invasion of the Body Snatchers (Allied Artists, 1956).** Half Sheet (22" X 28") Style A. Rolled, Fine+.
Estimate: $1,200-up Starting Bid: $700

83645   **Invasion of the Body Snatchers (Allied Artists, 1956).** Lobby Card Set of 8 (11" X 14"). Fine/Very Fine.
Estimate: $1,000-up Starting Bid: $500

83646 This Island Earth (Universal International, 1955). Insert (14" X 36"). Folded, Fine-.
Estimate: $800-up Starting Bid: $400

83647 Earth vs. the Flying Saucers (Columbia, 1956). One Sheet (27" X 41"). Fine/Very Fine on Linen.
Estimate: $1,500-up Starting Bid: $750

83648 Target Earth (Allied Artists, 1954). Lobby Card Set of 8 (11" X 14"). *From the collection of Wade Williams.* Fine+.
Estimate: $800-up Starting Bid: $400

83649 It Conquered the World (American International, 1956). Insert (14" X 36"). Folded, Fine.
Estimate: $600-up Starting Bid: $300

83650 It Conquered the World/The She-Creature Combo (American International, 1956). Six Sheet (81" X 81"). *From the collection of Wade Williams.* Very Fine+.
Estimate: $800-up
Starting Bid: $400

83651   The She-Creature (American International, 1956). Insert (14" X 36"). Rolled, Very Fine/Near Mint.
Estimate: $600-up Starting Bid: $300

83652   The She-Creature (American International, 1956). Half Sheet (22" X 28"). Rolled, Fine/Very Fine.
Estimate: $600-up Starting Bid: $500

83654   The Blob (Paramount, 1958). One Sheet (27" X 41"). Very Fine-.
Estimate: $700-up Starting Bid: $350

83653   Not of this Earth (Allied Artists, 1957). Three Sheet (41" X 81"). Very Fine on Linen.
Estimate: $1,200-up Starting Bid: $600

83655   The Thing From Another World (RKO, 1951). One Sheet (27" X 41"). Very Fine-.
Estimate: $1,000-up Starting Bid: $500

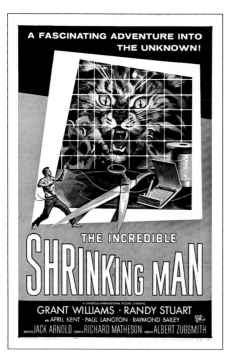

83656 The Incredible Shrinking Man (Universal International, 1957). One Sheet (27" X 41"). Fine.
Estimate: $800-up Starting Bid: $400

83657 The Incredible Shrinking Man (Universal International, 1957). Insert (14" X 36"). Folded, Fine+.
Estimate: $600-up Starting Bid: $300

83658 The Incredible Shrinking Man (Universal International, 1957). Lobby Card Set of 8 (11" X 14"). Fine/Very Fine.
Estimate: $800-up Starting Bid: $400

83659 The Time Machine (MGM, 1960). One Sheet (27" X 41"). Fine- on Linen.
Estimate: $800-up Starting Bid: $400

83660 The Time Machine (MGM, 1960). Color Photo Set of 12 (8" X 10"). Very Fine/Near Mint.
Estimate: $500-up Starting Bid: $250

83661 **Godzilla (Trans World, 1956).** One Sheet (27" X 41"). Very Fine.
Estimate: $2,000-up Starting Bid: $1,000

83663 **The Wasp Woman (Film Group, 1959).** One Sheet (27" X 41"). Very Fine+.
Estimate: $2,500-up Starting Bid: $1,250

83665 **Tarantula (Universal International, 1955).** One Sheet (27" X 41"). Fine+.
Estimate: $1,200-up Starting Bid: $600

83662 **Monster Zero (Toho, 1965).** Japanese STB (20" X 58") Also known as "Invasion of the Astro-Monster." . Folded, Fine.
Estimate: $300-up Starting Bid: $150

83664 **The Wasp Woman (Film Group, 1959).** Insert (14" X 36"). Folded, Fine/Very Fine.
Estimate: $1,500-up Starting Bid: $750

83666 **Tarantula (Universal International, 1955).** Insert (14" X 36"). Fine/Very Fine on Paper.
Estimate: $800-up Starting Bid: $400

83667   Tarantula (Universal International, 1955). Lobby Card Set of 8 (11" X 14"). Very Good/ Fine.
Estimate: $1,600-up Starting Bid: $800

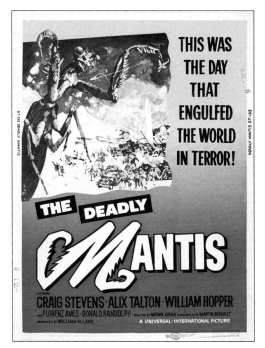

83668   The Deadly Mantis (Universal International, 1957). Poster (30" X 40"). *From the collection of Wade Williams.* Rolled, Fine/Very Fine.
Estimate: $500-up Starting Bid: $250

83669   Them! (Warner Brothers, 1954). One Sheet (27" X 41"). Very Fine+ on Linen.
Estimate: $1,700-up Starting Bid: $850

83670   Them! (Warner Brothers, 1954). Lobby Card Set of 8 (11" X 14"). *From the collection of Wade Williams.* Fine+.
Estimate: $800-up Starting Bid: $400

83671   **Beginning of the End (Republic, 1957).** Autographed Three Sheet (41" X 81"). Very Fine- on Linen.
Estimate: $600-up Starting Bid: $300

83672   **Beginning of the End (Republic, 1957).** Six Sheet (81" X 81"). *From the collection of Wade Williams.* Fine.
Estimate: $1,000-up Starting Bid: $500

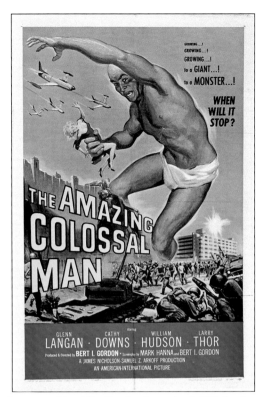

83673   **The Amazing Colossal Man (American International, 1957).** One Sheet (27" X 41"). Fine.
Estimate: $800-up Starting Bid: $400

83674   **The Amazing Colossal Man (American International, 1957).** Lobby Card Set of 8 (11" X 14"). Very Fine.
Estimate: $600-up Starting Bid: $300

83677   The Mole People (Universal International, 1956). One Sheet (27" X 41"). Very Fine+.
Estimate: $800-up Starting Bid: $500

83675   War of the Colossal Beast (American International, 1958). Lobby Card Set of 8 (11" X 14"). *From the collection of Wade Williams.* Very Fine.
Estimate: $600-up Starting Bid: $300

83678   The Mole People (Universal International, 1956). Insert (14" X 36"). Folded, Fine/Very Fine.
Estimate: $600-up Starting Bid: $300

83679   The Beast with 1,000,000 Eyes! (American Releasing Corp., 1955). One Sheet (27" X 41"). Fine/Very Fine.
Estimate: $1,000-up Starting Bid: $500

83676   Attack of the 50 Foot Woman (Allied Artists, 1958). Lobby Card Set of 8 (11" X 14"). Very Fine.
Estimate: $800-up Starting Bid: $400

83680 The Beast with 1,000,000 Eyes! (American Releasing Corp., 1955). Lobby Card Set of 8 (11" X 14"). Very Fine/Near Mint.
Estimate: $600-up Starting Bid: $300

83682 Queen of Outer Space (Allied Artists, 1958). One Sheet (27" X 41"). Very Fine.
Estimate: $1,000-up Starting Bid: $500

83683 Queen of Outer Space (Allied Artists, 1958). Lobby Card Set of 8 (11" X 14"). *From the collection of Wade Williams.* Fine/Very Fine.
Estimate: $600-up Starting Bid: $300

83681 Terror from the Year 5000 (American International, 1958). Insert (14" X 36"). Rolled, Very Fine-.
Estimate: $500-up Starting Bid: $250

83684 Cat-Women of the Moon (Astor Pictures, 1954). Lobby Card Set of 8 (11" X 14"). *From the collection of Wade Williams.* Very Fine-.
Estimate: $700-up Starting Bid: $350

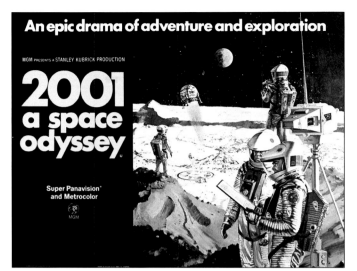

83685   2001: A Space Odyssey (MGM, 1968). British Quad (30" X 40"). Very Fine+.
Estimate: $700-up Starting Bid: $350

83686   2001: A Space Odyssey (MGM, 1968). Three Sheet (41" X 81"). Very Fine+ on Linen.
Estimate: $900-up Starting Bid: $450

83687   Barbarella (Paramount, 1968). Six Sheet (81" X 81"). Fine/Very Fine.
Estimate: $800-up Starting Bid: $400

83688   Robot Monster (Astor Pictures, 1953). Half Sheet (22" X 28") 3-D Style. Fine- on Linen.
Estimate: $1,200-up Starting Bid: $600

For full lot descriptions, enlargeable images and online bidding, visit HA.com/7025

83689 **The Spider/ The Brain Eaters Combo (American International, 1958).** Three Sheet (41" X 81"). Fine/Very Fine.
Estimate: $500-up Starting Bid: $250

83691 **The Giant Leeches (American International, 1959).** Insert (14" X 36"). Rolled, Very Fine-.
Estimate: $500-up Starting Bid: $250

83690 **The Brain Eaters (American International, 1958).** Insert (14" X 36"). Rolled, Very Fine+.
Estimate: $500-up Starting Bid: $250

83692 **The Giant Leeches (American International, 1959).** Lobby Card Set of 8 (11" X 14"). Very Fine/Near Mint.
Estimate: $500-up Starting Bid: $250

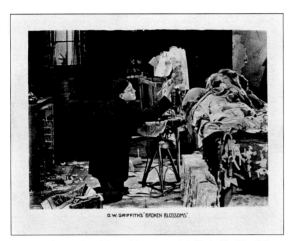

83693   Broken Blossoms (1919) (United Artists, 1919). Lobby Card (11" X 14"). Fine.
Estimate: $800-up Starting Bid: $400

83695   The Son of the Sheik (United Artists, 1926). Lobby Cards (2) (11" X 14"). Fine.
Estimate: $700-up Starting Bid: $350

83694   The Eagle (United Artists, 1925). Lobby Cards (5) (11" X 14"). Good/Very Good.
Estimate: $900-up Starting Bid: $450

83696   Redemption (Triumph, 1917). Window Card (14" X 21"). Actress Evelyn Nesbit is pictured on this very early window card with Russell Thaw, her real life son from her notorious husband Harry Thaw. Much has been written about Nesbit, who was the biggest sensation on the New York stage at the turn of the century, and who was highly sought by artists of the day. Her affair with noted architect Stanford White and his scandalous parties is legendary, and led to her husband Thaw shooting and killing White. After the trials, Nesbit turned to films, many of which have the theme of a woman with a past trying to change her life and do good. This poster has wear associated with much of the paper from this time period, such as edge wear, a small tear in the right border, two tears in the lower left corner, a stain within the left side, and two pinholes. This is a gorgeous stone litho image of one of the most talked about women of the era. Good/Very Good.
Estimate: $600-up Starting Bid: $300

83699   The Girl in the Pullman (Pathé, 1927). Three Sheet (41" X 79"). Fine/Very Fine.
Estimate: $300-up Starting Bid: $150

83697   The Widow's Might (Paramount, 1918). One Sheet (27" X 41"). To understand the importance and rarity of this poster, we need to reflect on the amazing acting ability of Julian Eltinge and how truly gifted a performer he was. There is a reason none less than the editor of *Variety* called him "as great a performer as there is today!". King Edward VII asked for a command performance. His tours in Europe and across the US were consistently sold out and at one point he was the highest paid stage performer in vaudeville and the American stage. His fascinating act succeeded not only in appearance but in manner as well, eschewing the caricature nature of female impersonation but instead presenting his "woman's persona" as a reality. This splendid stone lithograph has Eltinge playing a dual role, but featured in the artwork as the true drawing power he was dressed to the nines in the best 1918 fashion. Few examples of his work survive, especially one this terrific! Fine/Very Fine on Linen.
Estimate: $1,000-up Starting Bid: $700

83698   The Love Mart (First National, 1927). Title Lobby Card and Lobby Cards (5) (11" X 14"). Fine.
Estimate: $400-up Starting Bid: $200

83700   Across the Footlights (Universal, 1915). One Sheet (27" X 41"). Very Good/Fine.
Estimate: $1,000-up Starting Bid: $500

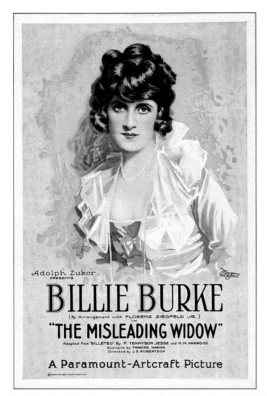

83701 The Misleading Widow (Paramount-Artcraft, 1919). One Sheet (27" X 41"). Very Fine on Linen.
Estimate: $1,000-up Starting Bid: $500

83702 Gloria's Romance (K-E-S-E Service, 1916). One Sheet (27" X 41") "A Modern Pirate". Fine+ on Linen.
Estimate: $600-up Starting Bid: $300

83703 Bluebeard's Eighth Wife (Paramount, 1923). Lobby Card (11" X 14"). Very Fine+.
Estimate: $400-up Starting Bid: $200

83704 The Trespasser (United Artists, 1929). One Sheet (27" X 41"). Throughout the 1920s Gloria Swanson was one of the most glamorous and sought after-actresses in Hollywood, and her popularity with audiences turned her into an icon. She easily made the transition to sound pictures in 1929 with this romantic melodrama, cast here as Marion, a lowly stenographer who endures much heartache when her marriage to her love, Jack Merrick (Robert Ames) is annulled by his intolerant father. Directed by the eminent Edmund Goulding (*A Night at the Opera, Dark Victory, 'Til We Meet Again, Nightmare Alley*, etc.) this film was an early success, garnering an Academy Award nomination for Swanson. One of the reasons early posters are so popular with movie collectors is the gorgeous textures and effects resulting from the process of stone lithography, and this beauty is a prime example. Featuring unbelievable color, art deco design, and fine rendering of the faces, this is one very special and rare poster. It has been professionally restored to address a tear in the lower right at the bottom "R," one in the lower left corner, one in the bottom border, and two in the top border. These issues no longer affect the poster, leaving the artwork in outstanding condition. Fine/Very Fine on Linen.
Estimate: $1,200-up Starting Bid: $600

83705 **The Trespasser (United Artists, 1929).** One Sheet (27" X 41"). Very Good/Fine on Linen.
Estimate: $1,000-up Starting Bid: $500

83706 **What a Widow! (United Artists, 1930).** Half Sheet (22" X 28"). Rolled, Very Good+.
Estimate: $600-up Starting Bid: $300

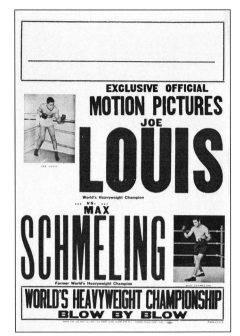

83708 **Joe Louis vs. Max Schmeling Boxing Poster (Empire City, 1937).** One Sheet (28" X 41"). Fine+.
Estimate: $600-up Starting Bid: $300

83707 **Champion (Herald, 1951).** Japanese B0 (35.5" X 60"). Fine+ on Linen.
Estimate: $600-up Starting Bid: $300

83709 **The Endless Summer (Cinema 5, 1966).** Poster (11" X 17"). Rolled, Very Fine+.
Estimate: $600-up Starting Bid: $300

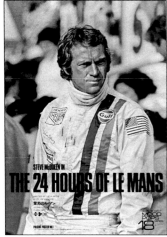

83710   Le Mans (Towa, 1971). Japanese B1 (2) (40" X 29") and Japanese B2 (20" X 29"). Fine/Very Fine.
Estimate: $1,200-up Starting Bid: $1,000

83712   The Sport Parade (RKO, 1932). Lobby Card Set of 8 (11" X 14"). Near Mint-.
Estimate: $600-up Starting Bid: $300

83711   On Any Sunday (Fida Cinematografica, 1972). Italian 2 - Foglio (39" X 55"). Very Fine.
Estimate: $400-up Starting Bid: $200

83713   The Hustler (20th Century Fox, 1961). Japanese STB (20" X 58"). Folded, Very Fine-.
Estimate: $600-up Starting Bid: $300

83714 The Hustler (20th Century Fox, R-1964). One Sheet (27" X 41"). Very Fine.
Estimate: $600-up Starting Bid: $300

83715 The Hustler (20th Century Fox, 1961). Lobby Card Set of 8 (11" X 14"). Fine/Very Fine.
Estimate: $1,000-up Starting Bid: $500

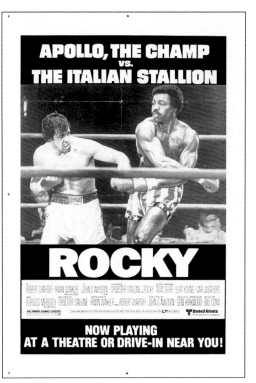

83716 Rocky (United Artists, 1977). One Sheet (27" X 41") Drive-In Style. Very Fine+.
Estimate: $400-up Starting Bid: $200

83717 The White Hell of Pitz Palu (Universal, 1929). (2) Lobby Cards (11" X 14"). Fine+.
Estimate: $500-up Starting Bid: $250

83718 The White Hell of Pitz Palu (Universal, 1929). Lobby Card (11" X 14"). Fine+.
Estimate: $400-up Starting Bid: $200

End of Session Two

VINTAGE MOVIE POSTERS

SESSION THREE

Floor, Telephone, HERITAGE Live!™, Internet, Fax, and Mail Auction #7025
Saturday, July 17, 2010 • 11:00 AM CT • Lots 83719-84026

A 19.5% Buyer's Premium Will Be Added To All Lots.

To view full descriptions, enlargeable images and bid online, visit HA.com/7025

83720 Island of Lost Souls (Paramount, 1933). Lobby Card (11" X 14"). In one of the great early horror classics, Charles Laughton stars as the diabolical Dr. Moreau who experiments on humans and animals on his island, creating mutant creatures that live in the jungle, including the Sayer of the Law (Bela Lugosi). This colorful card features Richard Arlen, Laughton, and Kathleen Burke as Lota the Panther Woman. This great card has been restored to address missing small corner chips, a minor chip in the lower left corner, a few pinholes in the borders and artwork, two tears at the bottom that extend slightly into the artwork, and a larger vertical one in the top right credits area. The card displays extremely well, and is one of the best cards of the horror genre. Very Good/Fine.
Estimate: $6,500-up Starting Bid: $3,250

83719   She (RKO, 1935). Midget Window Card (8" X 14"). Fine/Very Fine on Linen.
Estimate: $400-up Starting Bid: $200

83721   Dr. Jekyll and Mr. Hyde (Paramount, R-1936). Lobby Card (11" X 14"). When this edition of the Robert Louis Stevenson classic was filmed in 1931, the Production Code was not really being enforced. This version is remembered today for a strong sexual content, particularly in the character of the prostitute, "Ivy Pearson", played by Miriam Hopkins.. This card is from the first rerelease in 1936, when the code was in full swing and they demanded that over 8 minutes be removed from the film before they would allow the film to be distributed to theatres. (Fortunately the scenes were replaced for the modern DVD release.) This is one of the few cards, in either set, to depict Fredric March in his Best Oscar winning role as "Mr. Hyde". One of the big differences between these cards and their predecessors five years earlier is that March is seen in a great insert shot on the left side of the card as the mad Hyde. There are pinholes in the corners and artwork, a light stain in the bottom border, and a scratch in the top center of the image. There are small pieces of paper tape on the reverse and some smudging in the left border. Don't miss this chance to get one of the only depictions of one of the top horror figures of all time! Fine.
Estimate: $4,500-up Starting Bid: $4,000

83722   Dr. Jekyll and Mr. Hyde
(Paramount, 1931). Lobby Card (11" X 14").
Fine.
Estimate: $1,200-up Starting Bid: $600

83723   The Vampire Bat (Majestic, 1933). One
Sheet (27" X 41"). Fine on Paper.
Estimate: $2,800-up Starting Bid: $1,000

83724   Mockery (MGM, 1927). Insert (14" X 36"). Good/Very
Good on Paper.
Estimate: $900-up Starting Bid: $450

For full lot descriptions,
enlargeable images and
online bidding, visit
HA.com/7025

83725   The Unholy Three (MGM, 1930). CGC Graded Lobby Card
(11" X 14"). Very Fine/Near Mint.
Estimate: $800-up Starting Bid: $400

83726   The Phantom of the Opera (Universal, 1925). Lobby Card
(11" X 14"). Fine/Very Fine.
Estimate: $2,000-up Starting Bid: $1,000

83727   The Hunchback of Notre Dame (Universal, 1923). Lobby Card
(11" X 14"). Very Good.
Estimate: $2,000-up Starting Bid: $1,000

83730   King Kong (RKO, R-1950s). Belgian (14.5" X 23.5"). Folded, Very Fine+.
Estimate: $600-up Starting Bid: $400

83728   The Hunchback of Notre Dame (RKO, 1939). One Sheet (27" X 41"). *From the Theaters of Old Detroit Collection*. Fine/Very Fine on Linen.
Estimate: $5,000-up Starting Bid: $2,500

83729   King Kong (RKO, R-1946). Title Lobby Card (11" X 14"). Fine-.
Estimate: $3,000-up Starting Bid: $1,500

83731   King Kong (RKO, 1933). Jigsaw Puzzle (150 Pieces) (approx. 11" X 20"). Very Fine/Near Mint.
Estimate: $1,200-up Starting Bid: $1,000

83732 Cat People (RKO, 1942). One Sheet (27" X 41"). Val Lewton produced this moody and magnificent film on a very modest budget, and turned it into one of the most frightening films of the 1940s. Beautiful Simone Simon stars as a woman who turns into a panther when emotionally charged. *Cat People* was the first in a series of films that made Lewton an icon in the genre. The posters for this title are among the most sought after by horror enthusiasts. This wonderful copy had fold wear, pinholes in the corners and right border, and small chips in the top corners, all of which has been addressed with professional restoration. This poster does not come up often so get it while you can! Very Fine- on Linen.
Estimate: $10,000-up Starting Bid: $5,000

83733 The Leopard Man (RKO, 1943). One Sheet (27" X 41"). Near Mint+.
Estimate: $1,500-up Starting Bid: $750

83734 Cat People (RKO, R-1952). One Sheet (27" X 41"). Fine/Very Fine.
Estimate: $1,200-up Starting Bid: $600

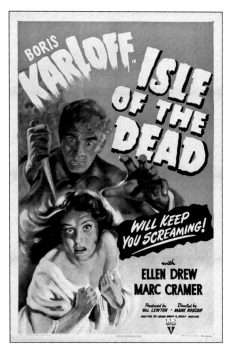

83735 Isle of the Dead (RKO, 1945). One Sheet (27" X 41"). Very Fine+ on Linen.
Estimate: $800-up Starting Bid: $500

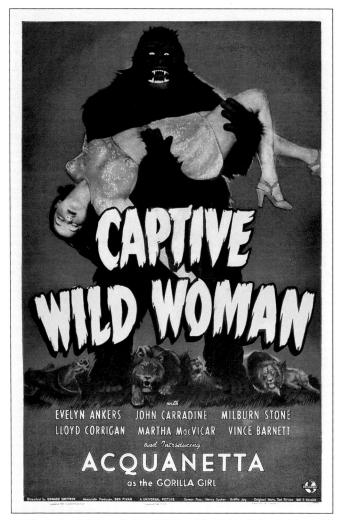

83736 Captive Wild Woman (Universal, 1943). One Sheet (27" X 41"). *From the Theaters of Old Detroit Collection.* Fine/Very Fine on Linen.
Estimate: $2,000-up Starting Bid: $1,000

83737　**Dead of Night (Universal, 1946).** One Sheet (27" X 41"). Fine/Very Fine on Linen.
Estimate: $1,600-up Starting Bid: $800

83739　**Night Tide (American International, 1961).** One Sheet (27" X 41") Style B. Very Fine+ on Linen.
Estimate: $1,000-up Starting Bid: $700

83741　**Curse of the Demon (Columbia, 1957).** Insert (14" X 36"). Folded, Fine+.
Estimate: $800-up Starting Bid: $400

83738　**Dead of Night (Eagle Lion, 1946).** Danish Poster (24" X 33.5"). Fine- on Linen.
Estimate: $600-up Starting Bid: $400

83740　**Curse of the Demon (Columbia, 1957).** One Sheet (27" X 41"). Fine-.
Estimate: $800-up Starting Bid: $400

83742   Curse of the Demon (Columbia, 1957). Lobby Card (11" X 14"). *From the collection of Wade Williams.* Near Mint.
Estimate: $500-up
Starting Bid: $250

83743   Screaming Skull (American International, 1958). One Sheet (27" X 41"). Fine/Very Fine on Linen.
Estimate: $600-up
Starting Bid: $500

83745   I Was a Teenage Frankenstein (American International, 1957). Lobby Card Set of 8 (11" X 14"). Very Good.
Estimate: $600-up Starting Bid: $300

83744   The Wicker Man (Lion International, 1973). British One Sheet (27" X 40"). Very Fine+.
Estimate: $800-up
Starting Bid: $400

83746   I Was a Teenage Werewolf (American International, 1957). CGC Graded Lobby Card Set of 8 (11" X 14"). Near Mint-.
Estimate: $600-up Starting Bid: $300

83747　House on Haunted Hill (Allied Artists, 1959). Half Sheet (22" X 28").
Very Fine- on Linen.
Estimate: $600-up Starting Bid: $500

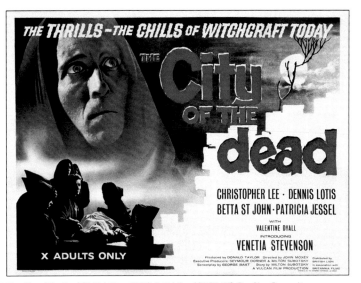

83749　City of the Dead (British Lion, 1960). British Quad (30" X 40"). Fine/Very Fine on Linen.
Estimate: $600-up Starting Bid: $300

83750　Night of the
Living Dead (Continental,
1968). Half Sheet (22" X 28").
Rolled, Fine.
Estimate: $1,000-up
Starting Bid: $500

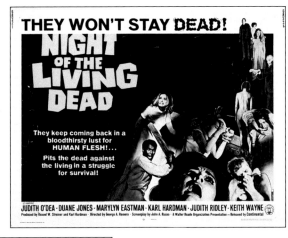

83748　House on Haunted Hill (Allied Artists, 1959). Lobby Card Set of 8
(11" X 14"). Very Fine-.
Estimate: $800-up Starting Bid: $400

83751　The Undead (American
International, 1957). Three Sheet (41" X 81").
Very Fine on Linen.
Estimate: $400-up Starting Bid: $200

83752   Attack of the Mushroom People (Toho, 1963).
Japanese STB (20" X 58"). Folded, Fine/Very Fine.
Estimate: $1,000-up Starting Bid: $500

83753   Kwaidan (Toho, 1965).
Japanese B2 (20" X 28.5") Red Style.
Rolled, Near Mint/Mint.
Estimate: $600-up Starting Bid: $300

83755   The Cat and the Canary (Paramount, 1939). Lobby Cards (5) (11" X 14"). Fine.
Estimate: $1,200-up Starting Bid: $1,200

83754   The Ghost Breakers
(Paramount, 1940). One Sheet
(27" X 41"). Near Mint-.
Estimate: $1,500-up Starting Bid: $750

83756   Abbott and Costello Meet Frankenstein (Universal International, R-1958).
German A1 (23" X 33"). Folded, Very Fine-.
Estimate: $600-up Starting Bid: $450

83757 Abbott and Costello Meet Frankenstein (Realart, R-1956). One Sheet (27" X 41").
Very Fine- on Linen.
Estimate: $2,400-up Starting Bid: $2,000

83758 Abbott and Costello Meet Frankenstein (Universal International, 1948). Lobby Card
(11" X 14"). Fine/Very Fine.
Estimate: $800-up Starting Bid: $400

83759 Abbott and Costello Meet Frankenstein (Universal International, 1948). Lobby Card
(11" X 14"). Near Mint-.
Estimate: $800-up Starting Bid: $400

83760 Abbott and Costello Meet Frankenstein (Universal International, 1948). CGC Graded
Lobby Card (11" X 14"). Fine/Very Fine.
Estimate: $800-up Starting Bid: $400

83761 Abbott and Costello Meet Frankenstein (Universal International, 1948). CGC Graded
Lobby Card (11" X 14"). Very Fine.
Estimate: $900-up Starting Bid: $450

83762 Abbott and Costello Meet Frankenstein (Universal International, 1948). Lobby Card (11" X 14"). Very Good+.
Estimate: $900-up Starting Bid: $450

83763 Buck Privates (Universal, 1941). One Sheet (27" X 41"). Bud Abbott and Lou Costello became the leading comedy team in the U.S. after this film was released. With the addition of the Andrews Sisters and the song "Boogie Woogie Bugle Boy," it cemented their fame and popularity for generations. One of the team's best movies, *Buck Privates* is a true classic, featuring some of the team's best material. Prior to the professional restoration, there were pinholes in the center of the poster, fold wear and crossfold separations with a tear in the right side, a minor chip above and a tear in the title credits, and minor chips in the borders. This colorful and attractive one sheet, with wonderful caricatures of Bud and Lou and Patty, Maxine, and Laverne Andrews, will make a valued addition to any collection, as any poster from this film is very rare. *From the Theaters of Old Detroit Collection.* Fine+ on Linen.
Estimate: $4,000-up Starting Bid: $2,000

83764 Edgar Bergen and Charlie McCarthy Stock Poster (Warner Brothers, R-1938). One Sheet (27" X 41"). After the tremendous surge in popularity of Edgar Bergen's wooden dummy Charlie McCarthy on the Chase and Sanborn radio show (ventriloquism on radio!), Warner Brothers re-released the series of early sound shorts Bergen made for their studio in the early 1930s. This extremely rare poster features an ultra-cute image of Bergen as Charlie's dummy! Prior to restoration, there were pinholes in the borders, a chip in the top left corner, and a minor tear in the lower left corner. Very Fine on Linen.
Estimate: $1,200-up Starting Bid: $600

83765 Doughboys (MGM, 1930). Half Sheet (22" X 28"). Comedic genius Buster Keaton made the transition to talking pictures in 1930 with *Free and Easy*, soon followed with this film, which has Keaton playing Elmer Stuyvesant, a wealthy scion who accidentally signs up for duty during WWI. Based partly on Keaton's own stint in France during the Great War, and filled with iconic scenes of Elmer marching to the beat of his own drum, this is one of Keaton's best films for MGM. Popular leading lady Sally Eilers co-stars as his love interest. This beautifully restored half sheet had three tears at the top that extended into the image area, small tears in the bottom border, and two small tack holes in the image. These issues are no longer evident, and this sensational, rare poster features four images of the comedic legend. Fine+ on Paper.
Estimate: $2,800-up
Starting Bid: $1,400

83766 Free and Easy (MGM, 1930). Half Sheet (22" X 28"). Starring as Elmer Butts, agent to beauty queen and acting hopeful Miss Gopher City, Elvira Plunkett, played by the beautiful real-life MGM star Anita Page, Buster Keaton hilariously mocks the hypocrisy and facade of Tinseltown. In Keaton's first talking picture, he takes his protege and her overbearing Ma (Trixie Friganza) to Hollywood, only to lose his sweetheart to heartthrob Larry Mitchell (Robert Montgomery), ending up as an unwitting Hollywood star himself. This rare half sheet has been professionally restored to address small tack holes in the title and black background. With its portrait of the beloved star and bright colors, this poster will be a highlight to any collection of top films of the era. Rolled, Fine/Very Fine.
Estimate: $2,000-up
Starting Bid: $1,000

83767   College (United Artists, 1929). Austrian (37.5" X 49.75") This is the only image other than the original one sheet we have seen that features Alvan "Hap" Hadley's famous Buster Keaton caricature artwork or a faithful re-creation of the same. This Austrian poster has the great stone faced comedian readying for an attempt at pole vaulting just before he breaks it in half during one of the funniest gags in the film. The poster has been trimmed at the top and bottom, but if you look at the measurements of the folded panels, it appears little of the poster is missing, and certainly none of the art. There is minor edge wear, paper tape on the reverse borders, and a light wrinkling along the left and right border. Don't overlook this important rarity. The colors are excellent and the overall look truly 1920's. Folded, Fine.
Estimate: $4,000-up Starting Bid: $3,500

83769   Buster Keaton by George Hurrell (MGM, 1931). Portrait Photo (10" X 13"). Fine+.
Estimate: $200-up

83768   Hard Luck (Metro, 1921). Title Lobby Card (11" X 13"). Very Good.
Estimate: $800-up Starting Bid: $400

83770   Why Bring That Up? (Paramount, 1929). Insert (14" X 36"). Very Good/Fine on Paper.
Estimate: $600-up Starting Bid: $300

83771   A Night at the Opera (MGM, 1935). Pre-War Belgian (24" X 30.5"). Fine/Very Fine on Linen.
Estimate: $2,500-up   Starting Bid: $2,000

83772   Go West (MGM, 1940). Half Sheet (22" X 28"). Fine+ on Paper.
Estimate: $1,800-up   Starting Bid: $1,500

83773   At The Circus (MGM, 1939). Lobby Card (11" X 14"). Fine-.
Estimate: $1,500-up
Starting Bid: $750

83774   At The Circus (MGM, 1939). Lobby Card (11" X 14"). Fine/Very Fine.
Estimate: $600-up
Starting Bid: $300

83775   A Day At The Races (MGM, 1937). Lobby Card (11" X 14"). Fine/Very Fine.
Estimate: $2,000-up
Starting Bid: $1,000

83776   A Day At The Races (MGM, 1937). Lobby Card (11" X 14"). Fine/Very Fine.
Estimate: $2,000-up
Starting Bid: $1,000

83777   A Night in Casablanca (United Artists, 1946). Insert (14" X 36"). Folded, Fine+.
Estimate: $600-up   Starting Bid: $300

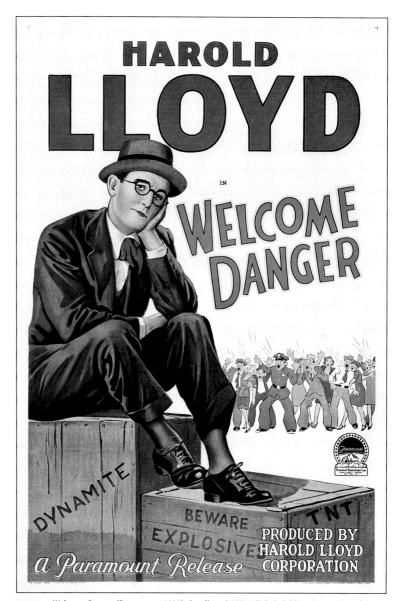

83778   The Freshman (Pathé, 1925). Insert (14" X 36"). This was Harold Lloyd's most successful silent film and it is a main entry in a very thinly populated genre; the funny sports movie. It was wildly popular for years and remained one of Lloyd's only films to be still widely available after the sound era arrived. Lloyd's classic comic hero may *still* be the best depiction of a "nerd" ever filmed! The "Fall Frolic" party-goers all along the sides of the poster have just "outed" Lloyd as being totally unliked. At the bottom of the poster he redeems himself, tackling a real USC football player and hanging on for dear life! Superb restoration has addressed small tears and a chip in the top left corner. If you've only room for one silent insert, you won't do much better than this one. Fine/Very Fine on cardstock.
Estimate: $2,000-up   Starting Bid: $1,500

83779   Welcome Danger (Paramount, 1929). One Sheet (27" X 41") Style B Silent Version. One of the top comedians of the silent era, Harold Lloyd first entered sound pictures with this classic, which was shown in both silent and sound versions, as some theaters in 1929 had not made the transition to the new technology. Lloyd produced his own films at this point in his career, and this was his highest grossing picture to-date, released just weeks before the stock market crash. Lloyd stars as Harold Bledsoe, a botanist who is forced into taking over his father's job as chief of police. Through several death-defying feats, a specialty of Lloyd's, and a romance with in-génue Billie Lee (Barbara Kent), Bledsoe comes through in a big way, taking down a drug ring led by the Dragon (Charles Middleton). Paper for Lloyd titles is always scarce and highly popular, and this stone litho beauty is a real prize. It has been professionally restored to address an area of missing paper on the left side of the image of Lloyd, a chip in the lower left corner, light fold wear, and a tear at the right side. This is truly an unforgettable image of the hapless boy next door. Fine on Linen.
Estimate: $1,500-up   Starting Bid: $750

83780 **Feet First (Paramount, 1930).** Half Sheet (22" X 28"). In Harold Lloyd's second talking picture, the expert stuntman and comedian gets caught up in a series of events that lands him on a window cleaner's scaffolding, several stories above the street. He attempts to get to safety by climbing to the top, where he slips and falls, nearly to the ground. Filled with some his most daring stunts, this comedy is one of Lloyd's most breathtaking. Barbara Kent stars as his love interest, the daughter of his boss, whom he tries desperately to impress with a series of little white lies. Posters with Lloyd are always highly popular, but images of the top comedian in the middle of his daredevil performances, such as this spectacular half sheet, rarely come to auction. The poster has been professionally restored to address three tears at the top, a small tear under Lloyd's name and one in the left side, creasing in the bottom half, and small tack holes in the bottom and left borders. These issues are no longer apparent and this very clean and bright half sheet is a superb image of a genius at work. Fine+ on Paper.
Estimate: $2,500-up Starting Bid: $1,250

83781 **Hot Water (Pathé, 1924).** CGC Graded Lobby Cards (2) (11" X 14"). Near Mint-.
Estimate: $600-up Starting Bid: $300

83782 **Hot Water (Pathé, 1924).** CGC Graded Lobby Cards (2) (11" X 14"). Near Mint.
Estimate: $600-up Starting Bid: $300

83783 **The Bohemian Girl (MGM, 1936).** Italian Foglio (27.75" X 39.25"). Stan Laurel and Oliver Hardy take a hilarious turn in 18th century Austria in this top comedy directed by the great James W. Horne, a veteran of Hal Roach comedies. This film is also notable as Thelma Todd's final screen appearance, as the Gypsy Queen's daughter, performing "Heart of a Gypsy." This very rare pre-war Italian poster has been mounted on linen and shows only a minor chip at the right border, and pinholes in the corners with one in the top border. The linen has been trimmed to the edge of the poster. The gorgeous artwork featuring the hapless pair, is by G. Canestrari. Very Fine on Linen.
Estimate: $5,000-up Starting Bid: $2,500

83784   The Bohemian Girl (MGM, 1936). Title Lobby Card (11" X 14"). Very Fine.
Estimate: $800-up Starting Bid: $400

83785   The Bohemian Girl (MGM, 1936). Lobby Card (11" X 14"). Very Fine+.
Estimate: $600-up Starting Bid: $300

83786   Bonnie Scotland (MGM, 1935). Window Card (14" X 22"). Very Fine.
Estimate: $1,500-up Starting Bid: $750

83787   Way Out West (MGM, 1937). Lobby Card
(11" X 14"). Very Fine-.
Estimate: $800-up Starting Bid: $400

83788   Half-Wits Holiday (Columbia, 1947). One Sheet (27" X 41"). This short marked the last appearance of Jerome Howard as "Curly" in a Three Stooges comedy. He suffered a stroke on the last day of shooting and was never able to return to do a full short again, although he did make cameo appearances. Moe Howard and Larry Fine, along with Curly, are the dim-wits of the title that are being turned into "gentlemen" by Professor Quackenbush (Vernon Dent). The proceedings end with an inevitable pie fight. Prior to the expert linen-backing, this poster only had minor fold wear. Very Fine on Linen.
Estimate: $7,000-up Starting Bid: $3,500

83789   Slap Happy Sleuths (Columbia, 1950). One Sheet
(27" X 41"). Very Fine-.
Estimate: $900-up Starting Bid: $800

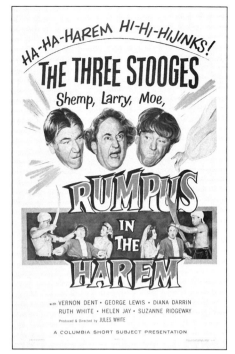

83791   Rumpus in the Harem (Columbia, 1956). One Sheet
(27" X 41"). Very Fine on Linen.
Estimate: $900-up Starting Bid: $700

83793   Miracle on 34th Street (20th Century Fox, 1947).
Insert (14" X 36"). Folded, Fine/Very Fine.
Estimate: $800-up Starting Bid: $400

83790   Tooth Will Out (Columbia, 1951). One Sheet
(27" X 41"). Fine/Very Fine on Linen.
Estimate: $1,200-up Starting Bid: $1,000

83792   Flagpole Jitters (Columbia, 1956). One Sheet
(27" X 41"). Fine.
Estimate: $800-up Starting Bid: $700

83794   Lost Horizon (Columbia, 1937). Pre-War Belgian
(24.5" X 33.5"). Very Fine on Linen.
Estimate: $1,500-up Starting Bid: $1,000

83795   Mr. Deeds Goes to Town (Columbia, 1936). Title Lobby Card (11"X 14"). Fine+.
Estimate: $500-up Starting Bid: $250

83796   Arsenic and Old Lace (Warner Brothers, 1944). Lobby Card (11"X 14"). Fine/Very Fine.
Estimate: $500-up Starting Bid: $250

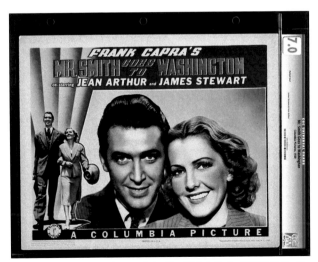

83797   Mr. Smith Goes to Washington (Columbia, 1939). Lobby Card (11"X 14"). Fine/Very Fine.
Estimate: $600-up Starting Bid: $300

83798   It's a Wonderful Life (RKO, 1946). Insert (14" X 36"). Folded, Fine/Very Fine.
Estimate: $8,000-up Starting Bid: $4,000

83799   It's a Wonderful Life (RKO, 1946). Title Lobby Card (11"X 14"). Fine/Very Fine.
Estimate: $800-up Starting Bid: $750

83800   It's a Wonderful Life (RKO, 1946). Lobby Card (11"X 14"). Fine+.
Estimate: $600-up Starting Bid: $300

83801   It's a Wonderful Life (RKO, 1946). Lobby Card (11"X 14"). Fine+.
Estimate: $500-up Starting Bid: $250

83802   It's a Wonderful Life (RKO, 1946). Lobby Card (11"X 14"). Very Fine-.
Estimate: $500-up Starting Bid: $250

83803   Theodora Goes Wild (Columbia, 1936). One Sheet (27"X 41"). Very Fine- on Linen.
Estimate: $2,500-up Starting Bid: $1,250

83804   Penny Serenade (Columbia, 1941). One Sheet (27"X 41") Style B. Fine/Very Fine.
Estimate: $1,000-up Starting Bid: $500

83805   Little Women (RKO, R-1938). One Sheet (27" X 41"). Fine+ on Linen.
Estimate: $1,200-up Starting Bid: $600

83807   The Philadelphia Story (MGM, 1940). Autographed Midget Window Card (8" X 14"). Very Good+.
Estimate: $1,500-up Starting Bid: $750

83806   The Philadelphia Story (MGM, 1940). Half Sheet
(22" X 28"). Based on Philip Barry's Broadway hit, which also starred
Katharine Hepburn, this sensational screwball comedy is helmed
by legendary director George Cukor. Hepburn is sublime as the cold
goddess Tracy Lord who finds love and romance on the eve of her
own wedding. C.K. Dexter Haven, her happy go lucky ex-husband,
is played to perfection by Cary Grant, with James Stewart and Ruth
Hussey co-starring as a pair of cynical party-crashing reporters. This
classic, beautiful poster has been professionally restored to address
corner pinholes, with one enlarged in the lower right corner, a tear
in the lower left corner, minor crossfold wear, a small chip in the top
center border, and creasing in the lower right. This is Hollywood at
its very best. Fine/Very Fine on Paper.
Estimate: $4,500-up Starting Bid: $2,250

83810   Harvey (Universal International, 1950). Title Lobby Card and Lobby Card (11" X 14"). Fine-.
Estimate: $600-up Starting Bid: $500

83808   The Philadelphia Story (MGM, 1940). Lobby Card (11" X 14"). Fine/Very Fine.
Estimate: $600-up Starting Bid: $300

83809   Harvey (Universal International, 1950). Three Sheet (41" X 81"). Fine/ Very Fine on Linen.
Estimate: $1,200-up Starting Bid: $600

83811   The Long, Long Trailer (MGM, 1954). Poster (40" X 60"). Both were stars in their own right before marrying and embarking on a historical journey into early television sitcoms and syndication. By the mid-fifties, Lucille Ball and Desi Arnaz were two of the most famous personalities in the world and Hollywood wanted to cash in on that fame by putting them back on the big screen! This, the most beloved of their screen vehicles, tells the story of a couple who buy a trailer to live in while they see the country. This rare large format poster is in very nice condition with minor edge and handling wear. A couple of tears on the borders have been repaired but none of any significance. Get this one while you can as we have never seen another copy! Rolled, Fine+.
Estimate: $1,000-up Starting Bid: $500

83812 Pillow Talk (Universal International, 1959). Poster (40" X 60"). Rolled, Fine/Very Fine.
Estimate: $800-up Starting Bid: $400

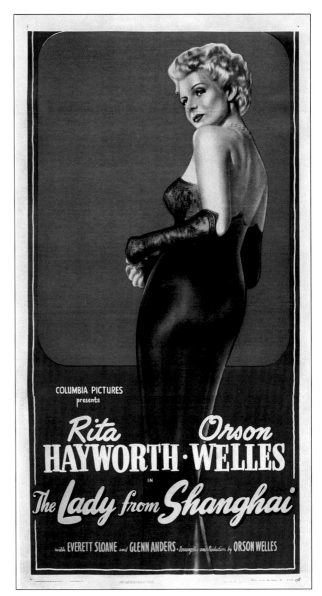

83813 The Lady From Shanghai (Columbia, 1947). Three Sheet (41" X 81"). "Maybe I'll live so long that I'll forget her. Maybe I'll die trying." Few can ever forget the exquisite Rita Hayworth in her sensational role as the devious Elsa Bannister. A beautiful portrait of the femme fatale dominates this exquisite poster promoting one of Orson Welles's *film noir* classics, in which a poor seaman (Welles) falls in with a dangerous crowd of sharks after coming to the aid of a fair maiden (Hayworth) whom he believes is about to be robbed. Everett Sloane and Glenn Anders are terrifically menacing as Bannister and Grisby. A fabulous find for any fan of this legendary icon, this colorful poster had fold wear and crossfold separations, but expert professional restoration has thoroughly addressed these minor issues, returning this poster to a like-new appearance. This will certainly be the high point of any collection! Very Fine on Linen.
Estimate: $6,000-up Starting Bid: $3,000

83814 Gilda (Columbia, R-1959). One Sheet (27" X 41"). Fine/Very Fine on Paper.
Estimate: $1,000-up Starting Bid: $500

83815   Gilda (Columbia, 1946). Argentinean Poster (29" X 43"). Very Fine on Linen.
Estimate: $2,000-up Starting Bid: $1,000

83817   You Were Never Lovelier (Columbia, 1942). Insert (14" X 36"). Rolled, Fine-.
Estimate: $500-up Starting Bid: $250

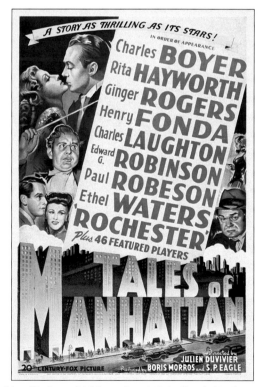

83816   Tales of Manhattan (20th Century Fox, 1942). One Sheet (27" X 41"). Fine/Very Fine
on Linen.
Estimate: $1,000-up Starting Bid: $500

83818   You Were Never Lovelier (Columbia, 1942). Title Lobby Card (11" X 14"). Fine/Very Fine.
Estimate: $400-up Starting Bid: $200

83820 Rita Hayworth Royal Crown Cola Advertisement (1943). Promotional Poster (26.5" X 39"). Very Fine-.
Estimate: $800-up Starting Bid: $600

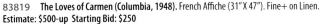

83819 The Loves of Carmen (Columbia, 1948). French Affiche (31" X 47"). Fine+ on Linen.
Estimate: $500-up Starting Bid: $250

83821 Mexicali Rose (Columbia, 1929). Half Sheet (22" X 28"). Erle C. Kenton directs Barbara Stanwyck and Sam Hardy in this early drama set in a seedy bordertown. Stanwyck shines as the title character, in this, only her second credited screen role. In this Pre-Code gem, Rose is kicked out of town by a jealous saloon owner for promiscuity, and seeks revenge by marrying his brother, which leads to tragedy. A stunning early portrait of the top actress, this half sheet is a spectacular item for the many Stanwyck fans. It has been professionally restored to address an area of paper loss at the top right edge border only, a minor corner chip in the lower right, small tack holes in the right and left borders, and a few in the image. All has been expertly repaired, and this colorful poster is ready for prominent display. Fine+ on Paper.
Estimate: $1,800-up Starting Bid: $900

83822   Golden Boy (Columbia, 1939). One Sheet (27" X 41"). This fine dramatization of the Clifford Odet play stars a very young William Holden with Barbara Stanwyck, as a promising violinist who wants to be a boxer. The film made him a star! Columbia pictures was initially unhappy with Holden's work, and tried to dismiss him, but Stanwyck insisted that he be retained. Some thirty-nine years later, when Holden and Stanwyck were joint presenters at the Academy Awards, he interrupted their reading of the nominees to publicly thank her for saving his career. The posters from this classic film are extraordinarily tough to find and this is the first time we have offered a one sheet, much less anything larger than a window card from this film. This is a top Morgan Lithograph using special gold ink to print the title. The poster had fold and crossfold wear. There was general handling and soiling. Excellent conservation work has been performed to return this poster to what appears near mint condition. Fine on Linen.
Estimate: $3,000-up Starting Bid: $1,500

83823   Be Yourself (United Artists, 1930). One Sheet (28" X 41"). Vaudeville and radio star Fannie Brice made very few screen appearances, but this musical comedy uses all her many talents with performance highlights of "When a Woman Loves a Man" and "Cookin' Breakfast for the One I Love," which she co-wrote with her then-husband, producer Billy Rose. Brice stars as the much put-upon girlfriend of boxer Jerry Moore (Robert Armstrong) who takes matters into her own hands when Jerry decides to dump her for "another woman" Lillian Thorpe (Gertrude Astor). The title of the film could be the motto for Brice's life— and after a long and successful career in entertainment, Brice's comedic genius was portrayed in Barbra Streisand's hit Broadway play and film, *Funny Girl*. Prior to professional restoration, this sheet had tears in the right and left borders, three minor tack holes in the white background and one in the artwork, and a tear in Armstrong's hat. All of these issues have been restored and this colorful and rare stone litho shines in all its intended glory. Fine+ on Linen.
Estimate: $1,000-up Starting Bid: $500

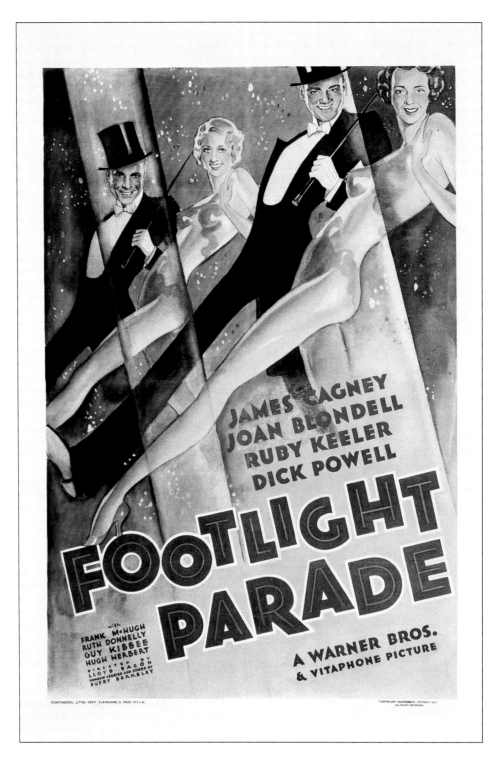

83824   Footlight Parade (Warner Brothers, 1933). One Sheet (27" X 41"). The early 1930s were the heyday years of the early sound musical films and Warner Brothers was at the forefront of this movement with the genius of Busby Berkeley, and three hit films in this year alone: *42nd Street, Gold Diggers of 1933,* and *Footlight Parade.* This energetic classic boasts a line-up of talent that includes Joan Blondell, Ruby Keeler, Dick Powell, and James Cagney, who stars as Broadway producer Chester Kent. Cagney must put on a series of "prologues" in order to raise money for his next show. The chaotic rehearsals, sabotage, and back stage dramas culminate in one sensational climax featuring the unforgettable Harry Warren and Al Dubin hit numbers "By a Waterfall", "Honeymoon Hotel," and "Shanghai Lil." Blondell, who had worked with Cagney in five previous films, is terrific as the wise-cracking His-Girl-Friday, Nan, with character actors Frank McHugh, Guy Kibbee, and Hugh Herbert adding to the fun. Presented here for the first time in a Heritage auction is the extremely rare and very special one sheet for this beloved title. It has been professionally restored to address slight edge wear with some chipping in the borders, crossfold separations with some minor paper loss, and creases in the top left. There was a top right corner chip in the border only. All of these issues have been restored and are no longer apparent. Excellent restoration work has restored this fine poster of art deco design of all four musical stars and it will surely be a long time before another pre-Code item of this rarity appears again. Fine+ on Linen.
Estimate: $25,000-up Starting Bid: $18,000

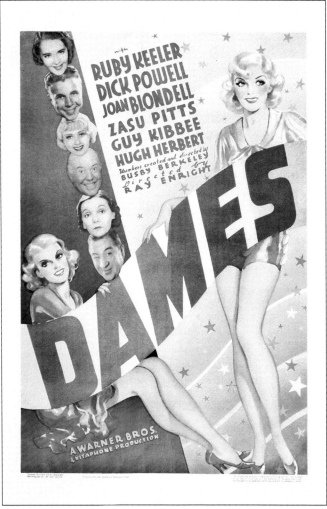

83825 **Dames (Warner Brothers, 1934).** One Sheet (27" X 41"). When trying to explain to a 20-something what life was like before CGI, it's fun to put on a Busby Berkeley film and watch their eyes pop and their jaws drop as you calmly explain that everything they're watching was done with just people and a regular camera. Berkeley's mastery in using human kaleidoscopes and fun shooting angles still holds up visually to this day, and this film is one of his best. This delightful poster features two leggy blonde chorus girls holding the title between them with portraits of all six of the spot-on stars at the top left, including a winking Hugh Herbert who must have known even before the film wrapped that he was giving the performance of his fine career. There were pinholes in the corners in the image and one in the center at the crossfold. With expert linenbacking and minimal touchup this is a real beauty. Very Fine+ on Linen.
Estimate: $3,500-up Starting Bid: $3,000

83826 **Dames (Warner Brothers, 1934).** CGC Graded Lobby Card (11" X 14"). Very Fine.
Estimate: $500-up Starting Bid: $250

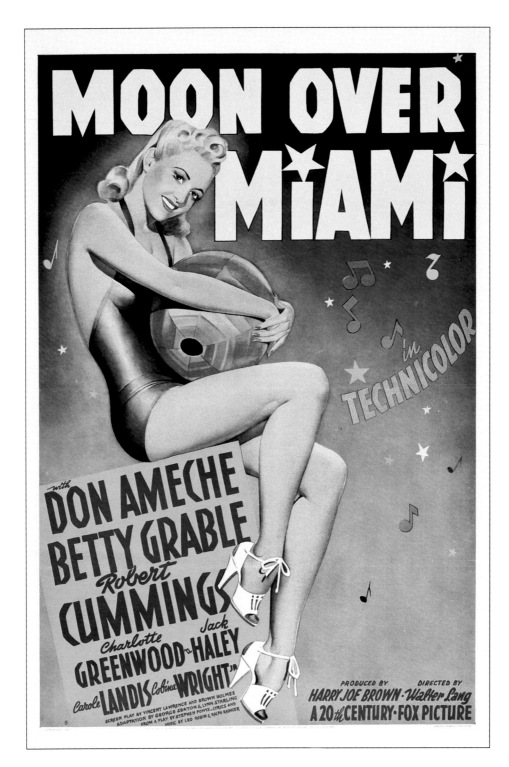

83827 **Moon Over Miami (20th Century Fox, 1941).** One Sheet (27" X 41") Style B. After the success of *Down Argentine Way*, Don Ameche and pin-up star Betty Grable reteam for another fun romantic musical, which was much needed at the time, as America was heading into war. Grable was on her way to becoming 20th Century-Fox's biggest star, a position she would enjoy for a decade, along with being the highest paid actress in Hollywood, and having her legs insured for a million dollars. This gorgeous and always rare one sheet features Grable in one of her most iconic pin-up shots, fashioned after artist Alberto Vargas. It is in excellent condition, and has had professional restoration to address light edge wear at the left, a small chip and tear in the lower left corner, and a minor tear in the top border. This poster is the cleanest copy we have offered and is dazzling to behold. We sold another copy of this poster for $38,850 over two years ago! Very Fine on Linen.
Estimate: $25,000-up Starting Bid: $12,500

83828 42nd Street (Warner Brothers, 1933). Lobby Card (11" X 14"). Very Fine-.
Estimate: $500-up Starting Bid: $250

83829 42nd Street (Warner Brothers, 1933). Lobby Card (11" X 14"). Fine+.
Estimate: $600-up Starting Bid: $300

83830 Moulin Rouge
(United Artists, 1934). Window
Card (14" X 22"). Very Fine-.
Estimate: $500-up
Starting Bid: $250

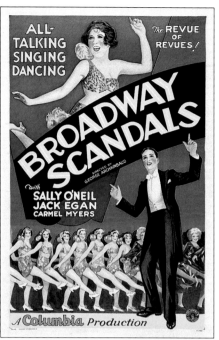

83831 Broadway Scandals
(Columbia, 1929). One Sheet
(27" X 41") Sound Style. Very Fine
on Linen.
Estimate: $800-up
Starting Bid: $400

83832 Broadway Scandals (Columbia, 1929). Lobby Card (11" X 14"). Very Fine.
Estimate: $300-up Starting Bid: $150

83833 Gold Diggers of
Broadway (Warner Brothers,
1929). Window Card (14" X 22").
Very Fine.
Estimate: $500-up
Starting Bid: $250

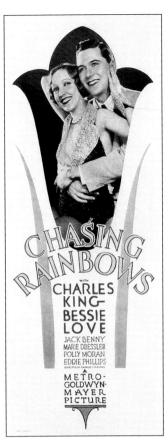

83834   **Chasing Rainbows (MGM, 1930).**
Insert (14" X 36"). Fine+ on Paper.
Estimate: $700-up Starting Bid: $350

83835   **Hollywood Revue of 1929 (MGM, 1929).** Insert (14" X 36"). Hosted by Conrad Nagel and Jack Benny, MGM rolls out their top talent for this all-talking, all-dancing, and all-singing extravaganza. Stars featured include Norma Shearer, John Gilbert, Joan Crawford, Laurel and Hardy, Bessie Love, Marion Davies, etc. This film is also an important landmark as the first film performance of "Singin' in the Rain," sung in the wonderful two-strip Technicolor finale, and which would inspire the classic 1952 film. Posters from this prestigious studio musical are rare indeed, and this is a beauty. Prior to professional restoration it had a diagonal cut at both the bottom and top image areas, pinholes in the field, and a minor tear at the right edge. It now displays wonderfully and will be an important addition to any collection of early musicals. Fine on Paper.
Estimate: $1,500-up Starting Bid: $750

83836   **Love Me Forever (Columbia, 1935).** One Sheet (27" X 41"). Fine+ on Linen.
Estimate: $1,500-up Starting Bid: $750

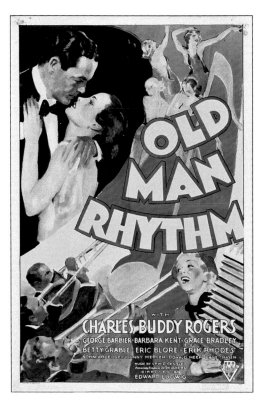

83837   Old Man Rhythm (RKO, 1935). One Sheet (27" X 41"). Fine.
Estimate: $1,000-up Starting Bid: $500

83839   White Christmas (Paramount, 1954). One Sheet (27" X 41"). Very Fine on Linen.
Estimate: $800-up Starting Bid: $400

83838   The Big Broadcast (Paramount, 1932). Lobby Card Set of 8 (11" X 14"). Fine/Very Fine.
Estimate: $600-up Starting Bid: $300

83840   Holiday Inn (Paramount, 1942). One Sheet (27" X 41"). Irving Berlin provides some of his best numbers for this beloved classic, including the debut of "White Christmas." Bing Crosby and Fred Astaire star as musical partners who part ways over the love of the fickle Lila Dixon (Virginia Dale). When Jim Hardy (Crosby) makes a success of his rural Inn/ nightclub that is only open on holidays, with the help of a new love (Marjorie Reynolds) it isn't long before Ted Hanover (Astaire) shows up to spoil things once again. With Astaire dancing, Crosby singing, and Mark Sandrich directing, this picture was an instant box office hit and is as popular today as ever. This rarely seen beauty shows a pinhole in each corner, crossfold separations, light stains in the lower right border, and minor wear at the left edge. Very Fine.
Estimate: $2,500-up Starting Bid: $2,000

83841   **Flying Down to Rio (RKO, 1933).** Window Card (14" X 22"). The plot of this superb RKO musical involves a love triangle between Dolores del Rio, Gene Raymond, and Raul Roulien, but this pales in comparison with the scenes that are most memorable and that make this a classic for the ages involving the dynamic team of Fred Astaire and Ginger Rogers. Marking the first pairing of the dancing duo, this film features some spectacular numbers, including their performance of "The Carioca," and an over-the-top performance of dancing ladies on the wings of a plane for the title song. The film was a huge hit for the studio, and Rogers and Astaire soon became musical legends. Offered here for the first time is the dramatic window card, which has been professionally conserved to address a small hole in Raymond's face, a small tear at the top edge, a small surface abrasion in the title, and pinholes in the imprint area and bottom corners. Opportunities to own a piece of this cinematic gem are few, so do not miss out on this top poster. Fine+ on Cardstock.
Estimate: $2,000-up Starting Bid: $1,000

83842   **Flying Down to Rio (RKO, 1933).** Lobby Card (11" X 14"). Fine/Very Fine.
Estimate: $1,000-up Starting Bid: $800

83843   Follow the Fleet (RKO, 1936). Three Sheet (41" X 81"). Few cinematic pairings are as perfect, enduring, and beloved as the dancing duo Fred Astaire and Ginger Rogers, and when they are combined with a score by the incomparable Irving Berlin, nothing could be finer. Astaire is Navy man Bake Baker, who is on shore leave in San Francisco and determined to rekindle a romance with former girlfriend Sherry Martin (Rogers). He is soon helping her re-vamp an old ship into a nightclub and aiding in Martin's sister's (Harriet Hilliard) relationship with a naval officer played by Randolph Scott. Rogers and Astaire are in top form performing some of their most cherished numbers such as: "Let Yourself Go," "I'm Putting All My Eggs in One Basket," and "Let's Face the Music and Dance." This film is notable as well for two small players on their way to stardom in Hollywood— Betty Grable and Lucille Ball. A magnificent large format poster, this beauty features sumptuous color, one of the best portraits of the dancing stars, and has never before been offered by Heritage. Other than being mounted on linen, little restoration work has been done, and is in excellent condition, with only a few slight surface abrasions in the borders, a small tear in the lower left corner, and very minor fold wear. Do not let this very rare gem from Hollywood's musical heyday pass you by! Very Fine on Linen.
Estimate: $14,000-up Starting Bid: $7,000

83844 Follow the Fleet (RKO, 1936). Lobby Card (11" X 14"). Fine/Very Fine.
Estimate: $600-up Starting Bid: $500

83846 Shall We Dance (RKO, 1937). Window Card (14" X 22"). Fine/Very Fine on Cardstock.
Estimate: $700-up
Starting Bid: $350

83845 Top Hat (RKO, 1935). Insert (14" X 36"). Set at a posh hotel in a very Hollywood-envisioned Venice, Fred Astaire and Ginger Rogers dance the nights away to "The Piccolino," "Cheek to Cheek," "Isn't it a Lovely Day?," and the title song. The fun plot has Rogers mistaking Astaire for her best friend's husband and trying to fend off his attentions. In terrific fashion, Edward Everett Horton, Erik Rhodes, and the irrepressible Eric Blore as Bates, provide comic support. This is one of the dancing pair's finest films and has remained a beloved classic for generations. Original paper for this title rarely turns up, and this is the first time we have been lucky enough to offer this gorgeous format. Prior to professional restoration, it had edge wear, two tears at the right edge, a smaller one at the top border, and one at the left border. There was a minor hole in the left border and a chip in the top right corner. The image area is in excellent condition and the bright colors of the superb artwork are remarkable. Rolled, Fine+ on Paper.
Estimate: $4,500-up
Starting Bid: $2,250

83847 Ziegfeld Follies (MGM, 1945). Title Lobby Card and Lobby Cards (2) (11" X 14"). Near Mint.
Estimate: $700-up Starting Bid: $350

83849   The Big Street (RKO, Late 1940s). First Post War Italian Locandina (13" X 27"). Fine+ on Linen.
Estimate: $400-up
Starting Bid: $200

83848   Ziegfeld Follies (MGM, 1945). Lobby Cards (5) (11" X 14"). Near Mint/Mint.
Estimate: $700-up Starting Bid: $350

83850   The Singing Fool (Warner Brothers, 1927). Italian Billboard (79" X 81"). This large stone litho Italian poster from the fourth Al Jolson film (and his first film after the landmark *The Jazz Singer*) is quite impressive, with magnificent art by one of the greatest of the Italian posters artists, Mario Gros. These large sized posters from the late 1920s are nearly impossible to find. *The Singing Fool* was a tour de force for Jolson who sang some of his best songs in the film, the most famous of which was "Sonny Boy" performed during the finale. There were small tears in the borders and a few in the artwork along with fold wear and crossfold separations. But following a very nice restoration, this incredibly rare poster now displays remarkably well. Very Fine on Linen.
Estimate: $5,000-up Starting Bid: $2,500

83851   Big Boy (Warner Brothers, 1930). Lobby Card (11" X 14"). Near Mint.
Estimate: $500-up Starting Bid: $300

83852   The Wizard of Oz (MGM, 1939). Insert (14" X 36"). The definitive film adaptation of L. Frank Baum's children's fantasy, MGM's 1939 version of *Oz* was done as a lavish musical adventure. It stars Judy Garland as Dorothy, an orphan unhappy with her drab black-and-white existence on a Kansas farm. She soon finds herself traveling "over the rainbow" to the Technicolor land of Oz to begin her wonderful adventures there. The Cowardly Lion (Bert Lahr), the Scarecrow (Ray Bolger) and the Tin Man (Jack Haley) soon join her. Offered here is the very rare and highly desirable insert poster for this film classic, which prominently shows all the main characters. The poster had fold wear with a small hole at the bottom, several tears along the edges that run into the artwork, extra horizontal folds, and a bend in the lower left corner; these have all been addressed with profession restoration, and there has also been some color touch-up as well. Very Good on Paper.
Estimate: $15,000-up Starting Bid: $7,500

83853 **The Wizard of Oz (MGM, 1939).** Lobby Card (11" X 14"). Considered by many to be the best scene card from this classic film, the "crying" card, as it is often referred to, is sought due to the wonderful medium shot of the four stars in a tender moment from the film. This is the ultimate cast card from this film! This lovely copy, which we have not offered before had pinholes in the corners and some slight wear to the corners. The professional conservation work done to it has returned it to a near mint appearance. Fine/Very Fine.
Estimate: $3,000-up Starting Bid: $2,500

83854 **Girl Crazy (MGM, 1943).** Half Sheet (22" X 28") Style A. Rolled, Fine+.
Estimate: $500-up Starting Bid: $250

83855 **Meet Me in St. Louis (MGM, 1944).** Half Sheet (22" X 28") Style B. Rolled, Fine-.
Estimate: $800-up Starting Bid: $400

83856 **Andy Hardy Meets Debutante (MGM, 1940).** Three Sheet (41" X 81") Style A. Fine+ on Linen.
Estimate: $800-up Starting Bid: $400

83857   Judy Garland Promotional Poster (CBS/Capitol,). Television and Record Album poster (21" X 28"). Folded, Very Fine.
Estimate: $500-up Starting Bid: $250

83859   Judy Garland Lobby Card Lot (MGM, 1937-1938). Lobby Cards (5) (11" X 14"). Fine/Very Fine.
Estimate: $400-up Starting Bid: $200

83860   Love Finds Andy Hardy (MGM, 1938). Lobby Cards (2) (11" X 14"). Fine/Very Fine.
Estimate: $400-up Starting Bid: $200

83858   A Star Is Born (Warner Brothers, 1954). One Sheet (27" X 41").
From the collection of Wade Williams. Very Fine.
Estimate: $400-up Starting Bid: $200

83861   Judy Garland and Mickey Rooney Lot (MGM, 1940-1941). Lobby Cards (5) (11" X 14"). Very Fine+.
Estimate: $400-up Starting Bid: $200

83862   Bright Eyes (Fox, 1934). Title Lobby Card (11" X 14"). Fine/Very Fine.
Estimate: $400-up Starting Bid: $200

83863   Now and Forever (Paramount, 1934). Lobby Cards (6) (11" X 14"). Very Good+.
Estimate: $800-up Starting Bid: $400

83865   Susannah of the Mounties (20th Century Fox, 1939). Lobby Card Set of 8 (11" X 14").
Near Mint/Mint.
Estimate: $600-up Starting Bid: $300

83864   Susannah of the Mounties (20th Century Fox, 1939). One Sheet (27" X 41"). Very Good on Linen.
Estimate: $600-up Starting Bid: $300

83866   Wee Willie Winkie (20th Century Fox, 1937). Lobby Card Set of 8 (11" X 14"). Fine/Very Fine.
Estimate: $800-up Starting Bid: $400

83867   Stowaway (20th Century Fox, 1936). Standee
(19.5" X 37.5). Fine/Very Fine.
Estimate: $400-up Starting Bid: $200

**83869   Breakfast At
Tiffany's (Paramount, 1961).**
One Sheet (27" X 41"). Very
Fine+ on Linen.
**Estimate: $4,000-up
Starting Bid: $2,000**

83868   Stowaway (20th Century Fox, 1936). Pre-War
Belgian (24" X 33"). Rolled, Very Fine.
Estimate: $400-up Starting Bid: $200

83870   Breakfast At Tiffany's (Paramount, 1961). Three
Sheet (41" X 81"). Fine- on Linen.
Estimate: $3,000-up Starting Bid: $1,500

83871   Roman Holiday (Paramount, 1953). Belgian
(14" X 22"). Folded, Very Fine+.
Estimate: $600-up Starting Bid: $300

83873   Funny Face (Paramount, 1957). French Grande
(47" X 63"). Fine/Very Fine.
Estimate: $800-up Starting Bid: $400

83874   Funny Face (Paramount, 1957). One Sheet
(27" X 41"). Fine/Very Fine.
Estimate: $600-up Starting Bid: $300

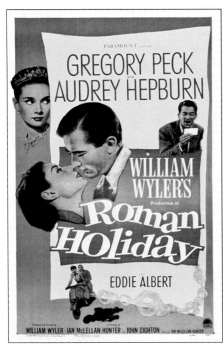

83872   Roman Holiday (Paramount, 1953). One Sheet
(27" X 41"). Very Fine- on Linen.
Estimate: $1,500-up Starting Bid: $750

83875   Funny Face (Paramount, 1957). Half
Sheet (22" X 28") Style B. Folded, Very Fine-.
Estimate: $500-up Starting Bid: $250

83876   My Fair Lady (Warner Brothers, 1964). Italian
Photobusta Set of 10 (13"X 16"). *From the collection of Wade
Williams*. Very Fine.
Estimate: $400-up Starting Bid: $200

83877　**My Fair Lady (Warner Brothers, 1964).** Half Sheet (22" X 28"). Folded, Fine/Very Fine.
Estimate: $400-up
Starting Bid: $200

83878　**An Affair to Remember (20th Century Fox, 1957).** French Grande (47" X 63"). Folded, Very Fine+.
Estimate: $600-up　Starting Bid: $300

83880　**Ladies of the Chorus (Columbia, 1948).** Insert (14" X 36").
Fine+ on Paper.
Estimate: $500-up　Starting Bid: $250

83879　**An Affair to Remember (20th Century Fox, 1957).** Lobby Card Set of 8 (11" X 14"). Fine/Very Fine.
Estimate: $400-up　Starting Bid: $200

83881　**Ladies of the Chorus (Columbia, 1948).** One Sheet (27" X 41").
Fine/Very Fine.
Estimate: $400-up　Starting Bid: $200

83882   The Asphalt Jungle
(MGM, 1950). Half Sheet
(22" X 28") Style B. Fine/Very Fine
on Linen.
Estimate: $600-up
Starting Bid: $300

83883   Don't Bother to Knock (20th Century Fox, 1952). Insert
(14" X 36"). Folded, Very Fine-.
Estimate: $500-up Starting Bid: $250

83885   How to Marry a Millionaire (20th Century Fox, 1953).
One Sheet (27" X 41"). Fine- on Linen.
Estimate: $1,000-up Starting Bid: $500

83884   Niagara (20th Century Fox, 1953). Three Sheet
(41" X 81"). Very Fine+ on Linen.
Estimate: $1,200-up Starting Bid: $600

83886   How to Marry a Millionaire (20th Century Fox, 1953).
Three Sheet (41" X 81"). Very Fine on Linen.
Estimate: $800-up Starting Bid: $400

83887 Gentlemen Prefer Blondes (20th Century Fox, 1953). One Sheet (27" X 41"). Very Fine- on Linen.
Estimate: $800-up Starting Bid: $400

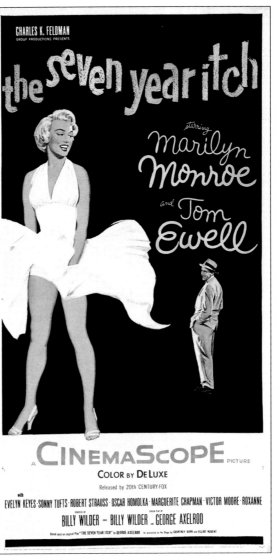

83889 **The Seven Year Itch (20th Century Fox, 1955).** Three Sheet (41" X 81"). Ranking as one of the most iconic and memorable screen moments in all of cinema history, Marilyn Monroe stands over a subway grate, in her unforgettable white gown designed by Bill Travilla, and comments "Isn't it delicious?" as the air lifts her skirt. Tom Ewell can only stand there and watch and dream, as does the star-struck audience. Billy Wilder shot this scene multiple times to get it right, with a growing New York crowd watching, and all involved knowing it would be the key scene of the film. Unfortunately Monroe's husband, Joe DiMaggio, was not happy with the very public gawking at his wife. This poster has had some restoration to address pinholes in the corners, small tears in the top border and at the join of the two sheets, a crease in the image, and some edge wear at the bottom. There are a few light stains at the bottom edge that are still visible, and the linen is trimmed to the edge of the poster. To own this large format image of Monroe at the height of her fame, will be a real prize for any serious fan. Fine/Very Fine on Linen.
Estimate: $2,500-up Starting Bid: $1,250

83888 Gentlemen Prefer Blondes (20th Century Fox, 1953). Japanese B2 (20" X 29"). Folded, Fine/Very Fine.
Estimate: $950-up Starting Bid: $900

83890 **The Seven Year Itch (20th Century Fox, 1955).** Insert (14" X 36"). Rolled, Fine/Very Fine.
Estimate: $800-up Starting Bid: $400

83891 **The Seven Year Itch (20th Century Fox, 1955).** Half Sheet (22" X 28"). Very Fine on Paper.
Estimate: $1,500-up Starting Bid: $750

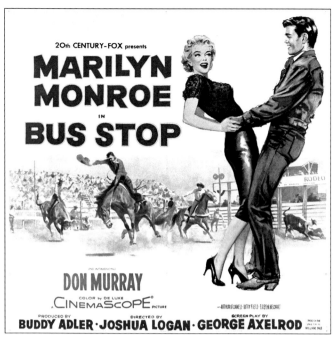

83894 **Some Like It Hot** (United Artists, 1959). Japanese B2 (20" X 29"). Folded, Fine/Very Fine.
Estimate: $700-up
Starting Bid: $600

83892 **Bus Stop (20th Century Fox, 1956).** Six Sheet (81" X 81"). A classic performance by Marilyn Monroe punctuates this light hearted romantic comedy about a girl who longs to find a real man and escape her small town life. This scarce six sheet is unique in that it is the only size done in artwork rather than photo style. Murray was nominated for an Oscar for Best Supporting Actor. This very nice poster has undergone a bit restoration to address minor chips and tears at the edges, and some registration issues. Very Fine on Linen.
Estimate: $1,500-up Starting Bid: $750

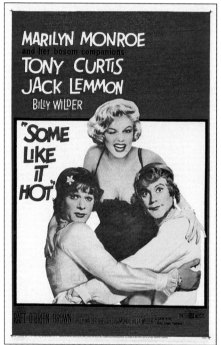

83895 **Some Like It Hot** (United Artists, 1959). One Sheet (27" X 41"). Very Fine+ on Linen.
Estimate: $1,000-up
Starting Bid: $500

83893 **The Prince and the Showgirl (Warner Brothers, 1957).** Three Sheet (41" X 81"). Fine+.
Estimate: $1,200-up Starting Bid: $600

83896 **Some Like It Hot** (United Artists, 1959). CGC Graded Title Lobby Card and Lobby Cards (3) (11" X 14"). Near Mint+.
Estimate: $600-up
Starting Bid: $300

83897   Some Like It Hot (United Artists, 1959). CGC Graded Lobby Cards (4) (11" X 14"). Near Mint+.
Estimate: $600-up Starting Bid: $300

83898   There's No Business Like Show Business (20th Century Fox, 1954). Lobby Card Set of 8 (11" X 14"). *From the collection of Wade Williams.* Fine/Very Fine.
Estimate: $300-up Starting Bid: $150

For full lot descriptions, enlargeable images and online bidding, visit HA.com/7025

83899   The Bronze Venus (Toddy Pictures, R-1943). One Sheet (27" X 41"). Folded, Fine.
Estimate: $400-up Starting Bid: $200

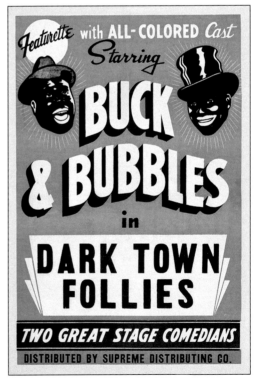

83900   Dark Town Follies (Supreme Distributing, 1930). One Sheet (27" X 41"). Fine- on Linen.
Estimate: $500-up Starting Bid: $250

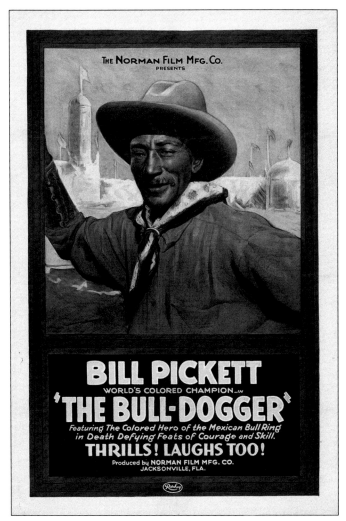

83901   The Bull-Dogger (Norman Film Manufacturing, 1921). One Sheet (27" X 41"). Bill Pickett, a world champion rodeo stuntman, was cast by the Norman Film Manufacturing Company in two feature films during the early 1920s: this title and *The Crimson Skull* the following year. Not much is known about these films except that the production studio was based in Florida and produced films featuring all-black casts tailored for black audiences. Pickett is acknowledged as the originator of the bull-dogging technique, which is wrestling a steer to the ground by grabbing its horns. He was inducted into the National Rodeo Hall of Fame in 1972. This scarce stone litho sheet has a great image of Pickett. Condition included minor fold wear with crossfold separations, small chips in the left border, and a very small tear in Pickett's face. Fine/Very Fine on Linen.
Estimate: $3,000-up Starting Bid: $2,750

83902   The Flying Ace (Norman, 1926). One Sheet (27" X 41"). Fine on Linen.
Estimate: $800-up Starting Bid: $400

83903   Girls Demand Excitement (Fox, 1931). Lobby Cards (5) (11" X 14"). We were really excited when we learned of this title arriving. We got even more excited when we saw the condition of these five cards. This was John Wayne's first film after *The Big Trail*. He plays basketball in college! "Rare" doesn't even begin to describe how hard these cards are to find. Wayne is in two cards, including the rarest, the portrait card. That's Virginia Cherrill in the card with him. She was Chaplin's "blind flower girl" in *City Lights* and Cary Grant's first wife. This is the only original paper on the title we've ever offered. Just a hint of light foxing in a few borders keeps these from grading even higher! Near Mint.
Estimate: $800-up Starting Bid: $400

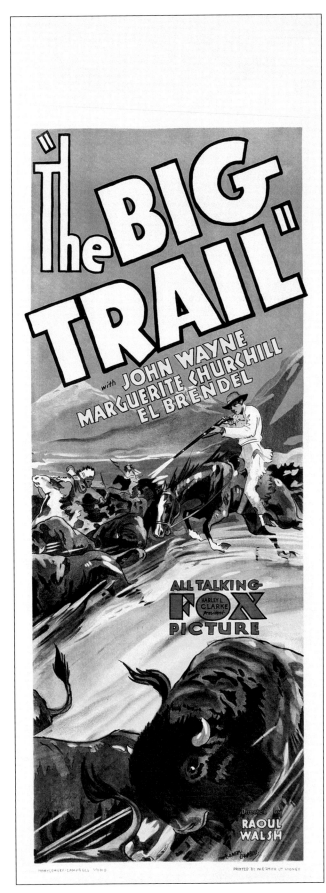

83904 **The Big Trail (Fox, 1930).** Australian Daybill (15" X 40"). Shot in both wide screen 70mm and in standard format 35mm, this was intended to be the epic of all epic Westerns and certainly achieves much for the time period. John Wayne was given his real break in this film, as Gary Cooper, who wanted the role, would not be loaned by Paramount. He displays the raw talents and mannerisms that would latter become his trademark. The expensive shot-on-location movie was financially unsuccessful as a result of being the first widescreen release during a time when theatres would not change over due to the encroachments of the Great Depression. After making *The Big Trail*, Wayne found stardom only in low-budget serials and features, mostly B-Westerns. It would take another nine years, and the film *Stagecoach*, to return Wayne to mainstream movies. Offered in this lot is a very rare prize, a large format poster from this early classic. The gorgeous buffalo hunt artwork is by Australian artist Montgomery Campbell. There was a small tack hole next to the title and small chips and tears along the left border. The poster had wear and small tears to the upper imprint area of the day bill and has now been restored to its former glory. Fine+ on Linen.
Estimate: $6,500-up Starting Bid: $5,000

83905 **Ride Him, Cowboy (Warner Brothers, 1932).** One Sheet (27" X 41"). In the first of his B-westerns for Warners, John Wayne stars as cowpoke who is blamed for a series of barn burnings. Finally cleared of suspicion, Wayne sets out after the real bad guys on his horse Duke. A terrific portrait of JW dominates this dramatic stone litho one sheet. Condition issues included pinholes in the corners and left border, which have been smoothed over with professional restoration. Very Fine+ on Linen.
Estimate: $2,000-up Starting Bid: $1,000

83906 **Stagecoach (United Artists, 1939).** Title Lobby Card (11" X 14"). This seminal Western, directed by John Ford, stars John Wayne in his breakout role as the Ringo Kid, and Claire Trevor as Dallas, a woman with a past. The stars are joined on their fateful stagecoach journey by a grand cast of characters including Thomas Mitchell, John Carradine, Andy Devine, and George Bancroft. A superb film, paper for this title is always popular and this gorgeous title card is a rare find. It has a few minor issues including three pinholes in the top border, one at the bottom, a few small tears in the borders, and a faint crease in the center. These do not detract from this striking artwork of this rare card. Fine/Very Fine.
Estimate: $2,500-up Starting Bid: $1,250

83907 **Stagecoach (United Artists, 1939).** Lobby Card (11" X 14"). After years of toiling in B-Westerns and serials, John Wayne finally hit the big time with John Ford's sagebrush classic. Offered here is the highly desirable dinner table scene, which features most of the main cast, including Wayne, leading lady Claire Trevor, and John Carradine in the back. This excellent unrestored card has a soft crease in the lower left corner, crease in the bottom right corner, a small tear in the bottom border, and some very small stains in the top border. This is one of only two of the scene cards from this set to feature Wayne! Very Fine.
Estimate: $2,000-up Starting Bid: $1,000

83908 **Stagecoach (United Artists, 1939).** Lobby Card (11" X 14"). This terrific lobby card from John Ford's legendary Western has a great image of John Wayne glowering in the background. Original release lobby cards for *Stagecoach* are always highly coveted by collectors, and since Wayne is pictured on only two of the eight this one is is highly regarded! This superb example has minor creasing in three corners, but is otherwise pristine. Very Fine/Near Mint.
Estimate: $2,000-up Starting Bid: $1,000

83909 **Stagecoach (United Artists, 1939).** Lobby Card (11" X 14"). Fine/Very Fine.
Estimate: $700-up Starting Bid: $350

83911 **Stagecoach (United Artists, 1939).** Lobby Cards (2) (11" X 14"). Fine/Very Fine.
Estimate: $1,000-up Starting Bid: $500

83910 **Stagecoach (United Artists, 1939).** Lobby Cards (2) (11" X 14"). Fine/Very Fine.
Estimate: $1,000-up Starting Bid: $500

83912 Stagecoach
(R-1960). Italian 2 - Foglio
(39" X 55"). Fine+.
Estimate: $600-up
Starting Bid: $300

83915   The Trail Beyond (Monogram, 1934). Title Lobby Card (11" X 14"). Very Fine/Near Mint.
Estimate: $800-up Starting Bid: $400

83913   Texas Terror (Monogram, 1935). Title Lobby Card (11" X 14"). Fine+.
Estimate: $700-up Starting Bid: $350

83916   The Trail Beyond (Monogram, 1934). Lobby Cards (2) (11" X 14"). Fine/Very Fine.
Estimate: $600-up Starting Bid: $300

83914   Texas Terror
(Monogram, 1935). Lobby
Cards (2) (11" X 14"). Fine/
Very Fine.
Estimate: $600-up
Starting Bid: $300

83917   Somewhere in Sonora (Warner Brothers - First National, 1933). Title Lobby Card
(11" X 14"). Fine+.
Estimate: $800-up Starting Bid: $400

83918 **Somewhere in Sonora (Warner Brothers - First National, 1933).** Lobby Card (11"X 14"). Very Fine-.
Estimate: $600-up Starting Bid: $300

83919 **'Neath the Arizona Skies (Monogram, 1934).** Lobby Cards (2) (11"X 14"). Fine/Very Fine.
Estimate: $500-up Starting Bid: $250

83920 **The Searchers (Warner Brothers, 1956).** Japanese B2 (20"X 29"). Folded, Fine+.
Estimate: $600-up Starting Bid: $300

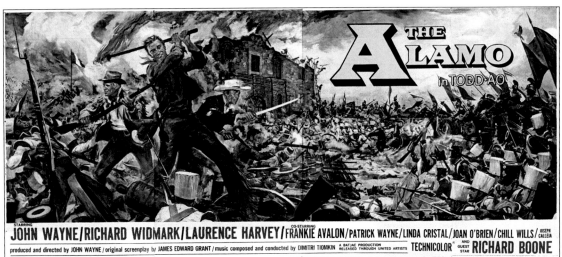

83921 **The Alamo (United Artists, 1960).** Roadshow Todd-AO 24 Sheet (104"X 232"). Okay, for all of you 24 sheet collectors, here it is! Perhaps this is the Holy Grail of the billboard poster collector's circle! Yup, the elusive billboard to the John Wayne epic, *The Alamo!* THAT is the entire Reynold Brown artwork printed in a grand size for you who want to proudly display this on the wall of your Texas hunting lodge (mansion) or perhaps the grand foyer in the John Wayne airport in Santa Ana, California! The poster has a small bit, relatively speaking, of water-staining within the image but nothing that distracts from this stirring depiction of the famous battle for independence of 1836! Completely unrestored, Folded, Fine/Very Fine.
Estimate: $1,600-up Starting Bid: $1,200

83922   Westfront 1918 (Cine-Studio, 1930). Pre-War Belgian (24" X 30.5"). Very Fine on Linen.
Estimate: $3,000-up Starting Bid: $1,500

83923   Captured! (Warner Brothers, 1933). One Sheet (27" X 41"). Very Fine on Linen.
Estimate: $800-up Starting Bid: $500

83924   The Dawn Patrol (Warner Brothers, 1938). CGC Graded Lobby Card (11" X 14"). Very
Fine+.
Estimate: $500-up Starting Bid: $250

83925   The Lost Patrol (RKO, 1934). Lobby Card (11" X 14"). Fine/Very Fine.
Estimate: $400-up Starting Bid: $200

83926   Spartacus (Universal International, R-1964). Italian 2 - Foglio (39" X 55"). Very Fine-.
Estimate: $500-up Starting Bid: $250

83927 The Great Escape (United Artists, 1963). Lobby Card Set of 8 (11" X 14"). Fine+.
Estimate: $700-up Starting Bid: $350

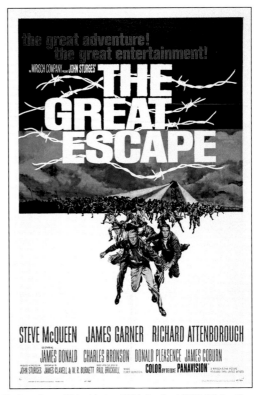

83929 The Great Escape (United Artists, 1963). One Sheet (27" X 41"). Very Fine+.
Estimate: $500-up Starting Bid: $250

83928 The Great Escape (United Artists, 1963). Three Sheet (41" X 81"). Fine- on Linen.
Estimate: $600-up Starting Bid: $300

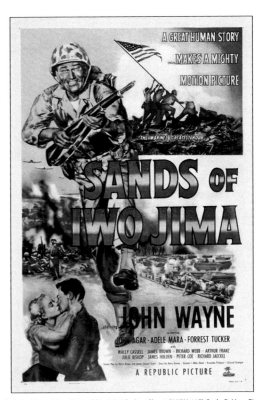

83930 Sands of Iwo Jima (Republic, 1950). One Sheet (27" X 41") Style B. Very Fine- on Linen.
Estimate: $800-up Starting Bid: $400

83931   **Reach for the Sky (Rank, 1956).** British Three Sheet
(40" X 78.5"). Fine/Very Fine on Linen.
Estimate: $300-up Starting Bid: $150

83932   **Tarzan Finds a Son (MGM, 1939).** Insert (14" X 36").
Folded, Fine+.
Estimate: $800-up Starting Bid: $400

83933   **Her Jungle Love (Paramount, 1938).** Australian
Daybill (15" X 40"). Fine/Very Fine on Linen.
Estimate: $600-up Starting Bid: $300

83934   **Paramount Exhibitor Book (Paramount, 1933).** Softbound Book (Multiple Pages, 12" X 17"). Fine/Very Fine.
Estimate: $400-up Starting Bid: $200

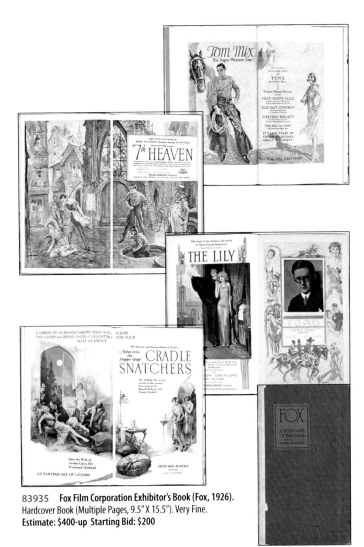

83937   **Audrey Hepburn in "Sabrina" (Paramount, 1954).** Photo (8" X 10"). Very Fine-.
Estimate: $200-up

83935   **Fox Film Corporation Exhibitor's Book (Fox, 1926).**
Hardcover Book (Multiple Pages, 9.5" X 15.5"). Very Fine.
Estimate: $400-up Starting Bid: $200

83938   **Audrey Hepburn (Paramount, Early 1950s).** Photo (8" X 10"). Very Fine-.
Estimate: $200-up

83936   **United Artists Exhibitor Book (United Artists, 1930).**
Hardcover Book (Multiple Pages, 11" X 14"). Very Fine.
Estimate: $300-up Starting Bid: $150

83939   **Audrey Hepburn (Paramount, 1954).** Photo (8" X 10"). Fine/Very Fine.
Estimate: $200-up

83940   Marilyn Monroe
(20th Century Fox, 1950s). Photo
(8" X 10"). Fine/Very Fine.
Estimate: $200-up

83941   Marilyn Monroe (1950s). Keybook Photos (3) (8" X 10"). Fine/Very Fine.
Estimate: $200-up

83942   Marilyn Monroe in "The Asphalt Jungle" (MGM, 1950). Photo (8" X 10"). Very Fine+.
Estimate: $200-up

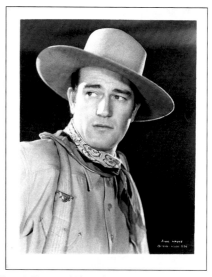

83943   John Wayne in "Stagecoach" (United Artists, 1939). Photo (8" X 10"). Near Mint.
Estimate: $200-up

83944   Clara Bow (Fox, 1932). Portrait Photo (8" X 10"). Very Fine.
Estimate: $200-up

83945   Clara Bow in "Her Wedding Night" by Eugene Robert Richee (Paramount, 1930).
Portrait Photo (8" X 10"). Fine/Very Fine.
Estimate: $200-up

83946   Clara Bow (Paramount, 1920s). Portrait Photo (8" X 10"). Very Fine-.
Estimate: $200-up

83947   Joan Crawford by George Hurrell (MGM, 1930s). Signed Artist's Proof Photo
(14" X 18"). Near Mint.
Estimate: $400-up Starting Bid: $200

83948   Joan Crawford in "Humoresque" by Eugene Robert Richee (Warner Brothers, 1946).
Photo (11" X 14"). Fine/Very Fine.
Estimate: $200-up

83949   Joan Crawford in "Rose-Marie" by Ruth Harriet Louise (MGM, 1928). Portrait Photo
(10" X 13"). Very Fine.
Estimate: $200-up

83950   Joan Crawford in "The Women" by Laszlo Willinger (MGM, 1939). Photo (10" X 13").
Very Fine-.
Estimate: $200-up

83951   Joan Crawford by Ruth Harriet Louise (MGM, Late 1920s). Portrait Photo (10" X 13").
Near Mint.
Estimate: $200-up

83952 **Joan Crawford by Edwin Bower Hesser (1920s).** Portrait Photo (11" X 13"). Very Good/Fine.
Estimate: $200-up

83953 **Veronica Lake (Paramount, 1941).** Portrait Photo (8" X 10"). Fine/Very Fine.
Estimate: $200-up

83954 **Veronica Lake (Paramount, 1940s).** Portrait Photo (11" X 14"). Very Fine+.
Estimate: $200-up

83955 **Veronica Lake (Paramount, 1940s).** Photo (11" X 14"). Very Fine+.
Estimate: $200-up

83956 **Veronica Lake by A.L. Whitey Schafer (Paramount, 1942).** Keybook Photo (8" X 10").
Very Fine+.
Estimate: $200-up

83957 **Nancy Carroll by Eugene Robert Richee (Paramount, 1929).** Portrait Photo
(11" X 14"). Very Fine-.
Estimate: $200-up

83958   Nancy Carroll by Eugene Robert Richee (Paramount, Late 1920s). Portrait Photo (8" X 10"). Near Mint.
Estimate: $200-up

83961   Myrna Loy in "Bride of the Regiment" by Elmer Fryer (First National, 1930). Photo (11" X 14"). Fine+.
Estimate: $200-up

83959   Myrna Loy by Preston Duncan (Warner Brothers, 1920s). Portrait Photo (11" X 14"). Fine-.
Estimate: $200-up

83962   Myrna Loy in "Bride of the Regiment" by Elmer Fryer (First National, 1930). Portrait Photo (11" X 14"). Fine.
Estimate: $200-up

83960   Myrna Loy in "Emma" by George Hurrell (MGM, 1932). Portrait Photo (10" X 13"). Near Mint-.
Estimate: $200-up

83963   Grace Kelly (1955). Portrait Photo (7" X 9"). Fine/Very Fine.
Estimate: $200-up

83964   Constance Bennett by Edwin Bower Hesser (RKO, 1920s). Portrait Photo(10.25" X 13.25"). Fine/Very Fine.
Estimate: $400-up Starting Bid: $200

83967   Barbara Stanwyck by Elmer Fryer (Warner Brothers, 1930s). Portrait Photo (8" X 10"). Fine/Very Fine.
Estimate: $200-up

83965   Constance Bennett in "After Office Hours" by Stephen McNulty (MGM, 1935). Photo (8" X 10"). Very Fine-.
Estimate: $200-up

83968   Rita Hayworth in "Gilda" by Robert Coburn (Columbia, 1946). Photo (8" X 10"). Near Mint+.
Estimate: $200-up

83966   Barbara Stanwyck (Warner Brothers, 1940s). Portrait Photo (11" X 14"). Very Fine+.
Estimate: $200-up

83969   Rita Hayworth in "My Gal Sal" (20th Century Fox, 1942). Photo (11" X 14"). Fine.
Estimate: $200-up

83970   Rita Hayworth in "Susan and God" by Laszlo Willinger (MGM, 1940). Portrait Photo (10" X 12.25"). Fine+.
Estimate: $200-up

83972   Jane Russell in "The Outlaw" (United Artists, 1946). Photo (10.75" X 13.75"). Fine+.
Estimate: $200-up

83971   Lauren Bacall (1940s). Photo (10" X 13"). Very Fine.
Estimate: $200-up

83973   Loretta Young by Melbourne Spurr (1933). Portrait (11" X 14"). Very Fine.
Estimate: $200-up

83974   **Loretta Young by Fred R. Archer (First National, 1929).** Portrait Photo (11" X 14"). Very Fine/Near Mint.
Estimate: $200-up

83977   **Sylvia Sidney by Eugene Robert Richee (Paramount, 1930s).** Portrait Photo (10.75" X 14"). Very Fine+.
Estimate: $200-up

83975   **Loretta Young by Elmer Fryer (Warner Brothers-First National, Early 1930s).** Portrait Photo (11" X 14"). Very Fine+.
Estimate: $200-up

83978   **Sylvia Sidney by Eugene Robert Richee (Paramount, 1937).** Portrait Photo(10" X 13"). Fine+.
Estimate: $200-up

83976   **Loretta Young by Elmer Fryer (First National, Early 1930s).** Portrait Photo (9.5" X 13"). Very Fine+.
Estimate: $200-up

83979   **Marion Davies by James Manatt (MGM, 1930s).** Portrait Photo (10" X 13"). Near Mint+.
Estimate: $200-up

83980   Marion Davies by Elmer Fryer (Warner Brothers, Late 1930s). Portrait Photo (10" X 13"). Near Mint-.
Estimate: $200-up

83983   Ginger Rogers by Elmer Fryer (Warner Brothers, 1932). Portrait Photo (11" X 14"). Fine/Very Fine.
Estimate: $200-up

83981   Jeanette MacDonald by Edwin Bower Hesser (1920s). Portrait Photo (10" X 13"). Very Fine.
Estimate: $200-up

83984   Paul Robeson in "Show Boat" by Freulich (Universal, 1936). Portrait Photo (8" X 10"). Very Fine+.
Estimate: $200-up

83982   Clark Gable and Jeanette MacDonald in "San Francisco" by Clarence Sinclair Bull (MGM, 1936). Portrait Photo (10" X 13"). Very Fine+.
Estimate: $200-up

83985   Anita Page by George Hurrell (MGM, 1930s). Portrait Photo (10" X 13"). Very Fine+.
Estimate: $200-up

83986 Louise Brooks by Eugene Robert Richee (Paramount, 1920s). Portrait Photo (8" X 10"). Very Fine/Near Mint.
Estimate: $200-up

83987 Louise Brooks (Paramount, 1920s). Portrait Photo (8" X 10"). Fine+.
Estimate: $200-up

83988 Louise Brooks and Richard Arlen in "Beggars of Life" (Paramount, 1928). Photo (8" X 10"). Very Fine+.
Estimate: $200-up

83989 Norma Shearer by George Hurrell (MGM, 1930s). Portrait Photo (10" X 13"). Fine.
Estimate: $200-up

83990 Norma Shearer in "Romeo and Juliet" by George Hurrell (MGM, 1936). Portrait Photo (10" X 13"). Very Fine-.
Estimate: $200-up

83991 Norma Shearer by George Hurrell (MGM, 1936). Portrait Photo (10" X 13"). Very Fine-.
Estimate: $200-up

83992   Jean Harlow by Ted Allen (MGM, 1930s). Portrait Photo (10" X 13"). Near Mint-.
Estimate: $200-up

83995   Jean Harlow by George Hurrell (MGM, 1930s). Portrait Photo (9" X 12"). Fine+.
Estimate: $200-up

83993   Jean Harlow and Clark Gable in "Saratoga" by Clarence Sinclair Bull (MGM, 1937).
Photo (10" X 13"). Very Fine+.
Estimate: $200-up

83996   Jean Harlow by George Hurrell (MGM, 1930s). Portrait Photo (10" X 13"). Very Fine/
Near Mint.
Estimate: $200-up

83994   Jean Harlow by Preston Duncan (1930s). Portrait Photo (10.75" X 13.75"). Fine/Very
Fine.
Estimate: $200-up

83997   Jean Harlow by George Hurrell (MGM, 1930s). Portrait Photo (11" X 14"). Very Fine/
Near Mint.
Estimate: $200-up

83998   Jean Harlow by Ted Allan (MGM, 1930s). Portrait Photo (10" X 13"). Very Fine-.
Estimate: $200-up

84001   Anna May Wong in "On the Spot" (Forrest Theatre, 1930). Theater Photo (11" X 14").
Fine.
Estimate: $200-up

83999   Anna May Wong by Edwin Bower Hesser (1920s). Portrait Photo (9.5" X 12") Mounted
to (14" X 18"). Very Fine.
Estimate: $200-up

84002   Anna May Wong by Eugene Robert Richee (Paramount, 1930s). Portrait Photo
(10" X 13"). Very Fine/Near Mint.
Estimate: $200-up

84000   Anna May Wong by Paul Tanqueray (1931). Portrait Photo (7.5" X 9.75"). Very Fine+.
Estimate: $200-up

84003   Anna May Wong by Freulich (Early 1930s). Portrait Photo (8" X 10"). Very Fine.
Estimate: $200-up

84004   Ann Sothern by Clarence Sinclair Bull (MGM, Late 1920s). Portrait Photo (10" X 13").
Very Fine-.
Estimate: $200-up

84007   Dorothy Lamour in "Man About Town" by William Walling (Paramount, 1939).
Photo (10" X 13"). Fine+.
Estimate: $200-up

84005   Ann Sothern by Ernest Bachrach (1936). Signed Portrait Photo (9.5" X 12") Mounted
to (15" X 20"). Very Fine-.
Estimate: $300-up Starting Bid: $150

84008   Greta Garbo in "Anna Christie" by Clarence Sinclair Bull (MGM, 1930). Photo
(11" X 14"). Fine/Very Fine.
Estimate: $200-up

84006   Ann Sothern by Ernest Bachrach (1936). Signed Portrait Photo (10" X 12") Mounted to
(15" X 20"). Very Fine.
Estimate: $300-up Starting Bid: $150

84009   Greta Garbo in "Anna Christie" by Clarence Sinclair Bull (MGM, 1930). Photo
(11" X 14"). Fine+.
Estimate: $200-up

84010   Greta Garbo in "The Painted Veil" by Clarence Sinclair Bull (MGM, 1934). Portrait Photo (10"X 13"). Very Fine/Near Mint.
Estimate: $200-up

84013   Greta Garbo by Ruth Harriet Louise (MGM, Late 1920s). Portrait Photo (10"X 13"). Mint.
Estimate: $200-up

84011   Greta Garbo in "Romance" (MGM, 1930). Photo (10"X 13"). Very Fine+.
Estimate: $200-up

84014   Kay Francis in "Behind the Make-Up" by Otto Dyar (Paramount, 1930). Portrait Photo (11"X 14"). Fine+.
Estimate: $200-up

84012   Greta Garbo in "Conquest" by Clarence Sinclair Bull (MGM, 1937). Portrait Photo (10"X 13"). Very Fine.
Estimate: $200-up

84015   Robert Taylor by George Hurrell (MGM, 1930s). Portrait Photo (10"X 13"). Very Fine/Near Mint.
Estimate: $200-up

84016   Carole Lombard by Edwin Bower Hesser (Fox, 1920s). Portrait Photo (10" X 13.25"). Fine.
Estimate: $400-up Starting Bid: $200

84019   Carole Lombard by William E. Thomas (Pathe, Late 1920s). Portrait Photo (8" X 10"). Very Fine+.
Estimate: $200-up

84017   Carole Lombard and William Powell in "My Man Godfrey" by William Walling Jr. (Universal, 1936). Portrait Photo (10.5" X 13.5"). Very Fine+.
Estimate: $200-up

84020   Carole Lombard (Paramount, 1937). Keybook Photo (8" X 11"). Very Fine+.
Estimate: $200-up

84018   Carole Lombard by Eugene Robert Richee (Paramount, 1930s). Portrait Photo (10.5" X 13.5"). Fine-.
Estimate: $200-up

84021   Carole Lombard (1930s). Keybook Photo (7.5" X 9.5"). Fine/Very Fine.
Estimate: $200-up

84022   Edwina Booth by Ruth Harriet Louise (MGM, 1930). Portrait Photo (10" X 13"). Very Fine.
Estimate: $200-up

84025   Boris Karloff by Jack Freulich (Universal, 1932). Portrait Photo (10.5" X 13.75"). Fine/Very Fine.
Estimate: $200-up

84023   Bela Lugosi by Freulich (Universal, 1930s). Signed Portrait Photo (10.5" X 13.5"). Fine-.
Estimate: $200-up

84026   Boris Karloff by Freulich (Universal, 1930s). Signed Portrait Photo (10.75" X 13.75"). Very Fine.
Estimate: $200-up

84024   Bela Lugosi by Freulich (Universal, 1930s). Signed Portrait Photo (10.5" X 13.5"). Fine+.
Estimate: $200-up

End of Session Three

VINTAGE MOVIE POSTERS

SESSION FOUR – NO FLOOR OR PHONE BIDDING

HERITAGE Live!™, Internet, Fax, and Mail Auction #7025
Saturday, July 17, 2010 • 3:00 PM CT • Lots 84027-84380

A 19.5% Buyer's Premium Will Be Added To All Lots.
To view full descriptions, enlargeable images and bid online, visit HA.com/7025

NEW SPECIAL INTERNET BIDDING FEATURE:

Online proxy bidding ends at HA.com two hours prior to the opening of the live auction. Check the Time Remaining on individual lots for details. After Internet proxy bidding closes, live bidding will take place through Heritage Live™, our bidding software that lets you bid live during the actual auction. Your secret maximum will compete against those bids, and win all ties. To maximize your chances of winning, enter realistic secret maximum bids before live bidding begins. (Important note: Due to software and Internet latency, bids placed through Live Internet Bidding may not register in time and those bidders could lose lots they would otherwise have won, so be sure to place your proxy bids in advance.)

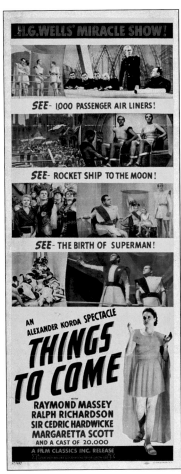

84027 Things to Come (Film Classics, R-1947). Insert (14" X 36"). Fine- on Linen.
Est.: $300-up Start Bid: $150

84028 Rocketship X-M (Lippert, 1950). Insert (14" X 36"). Rolled, Very Fine-.
Est.: $500-up Start Bid: $250

84029 Psycho/ War of the Worlds Combo (Paramount, R-1965). British Quad (30" X 40"). *From the collection of Wade Williams.* Folded, Very Fine+.
Est.: $400-up Start Bid: $200

84030 Forbidden Planet (MGM, 1956). Belgian (14.5" X 22"). Folded, Very Fine-.
Est.: $400-up Start Bid: $200

To view full descriptions, enlargeable images and bid online, visit HA.com/7025

84031 20,000 Leagues Under the Sea (Buena Vista, 1954).
Window Card (14" X 22"). Fine/Very Fine.
Est.: $300-up Start Bid: $150

84033 The Unearthly (Republic, 1957). Lobby Card Set of 8
(11" X 14"). *From the collection of Wade Williams.* Very Fine-.
Est.: $200-up No Min Bid

84035 The Monster that Challenged the World (United
Artists, 1957). Half Sheet (22" X 28"). Folded, Very Fine-.
Est.: $200-up No Min Bid

84032 Killers From Space (RKO, 1954). Lobby Card Set of 8
(11" X 14"). *From the collection of Wade Williams.* Very Fine.
Est.: $500-up Start Bid: $250

84034 It Came from Beneath the Sea (Columbia, 1955).
Insert (14" X 36"). Rolled, Fine+.
Est.: $400-up Start Bid: $200

84036 The Beast with 1,000,000 Eyes! (American Releasing Corp., 1955). Insert (14" X 36"). Rolled, Very Fine-.
Est.: $400-up Start Bid: $200

84037 **The Phantom From 10,000 Leagues (American Releasing Corp., 1955).** Lobby Card Set of 8 (11" X 14"). *From the collection of Wade Williams.* Very Fine-.
Est.: $200-up No Min Bid

84038 **Day the World Ended (American Releasing Corp., 1956).** Half Sheet (22" X 28"). Folded, Fine+.
Est.: $500-up Start Bid: $250

84040 **Teenage Caveman (American International, 1958).** One Sheet (27" X 41"). *From the collection of Wade Williams.* Very Fine.
Est.: $200-up No Min Bid

84041 **It! The Terror from Beyond Space (United Artists, 1958).** One Sheet (27" X 41"). Fine.
Est.: $250-up No Min Bid

84042 **Beginning of the End (Republic, 1957).** Insert (14" X 36"). Rolled, Very Fine.
Est.: $500-up Start Bid: $250

84043 **Invasion of the Saucer-Men (American International, 1957).** Swedish One Sheet (27.5" X 39.5"). Rolled, Fine/Very Fine.
Est.: $300-up Start Bid: $150

The Incredible Shrinking Man (Universal International, 1957). Half Sheet (22" X 28") Style B. Very Fine+ on Paper.
Est.: $400-up Start Bid: $200

84039 **The Incredible Shrinking Man (Universal International, 1957).** Half Sheet (22" X 28") Style B. Very Fine+ on Paper.
Est.: $400-up Start Bid: $200

84044   The Colossus of New York (Paramount, 1958). Italian 4 - Foglio (55" X 78"). Folded, Fine/Very Fine.
Est.: $400-up Start Bid: $200

84045   X - The Man With the X-Ray Eyes (American International, 1963). One Sheet (27" X 41"). Very Fine.
Est.: $300-up Start Bid: $150

For full lot descriptions, enlargeable images and online bidding, visit HA.com/7025

84046   Reptilicus (American International, 1961). Three Sheet (41" X 81"). Near Mint.
Est.: $250-up No Min Bid

84047   King Kong vs. Godzilla (Toho, 1962). Three Sheet (41" X 81"). Very Fine+.
Est.: $250-up No Min Bid

84048   Godzilla vs. the Thing (American International, 1964). One Sheet (27" X 41"). Folded, Very Fine.
Est.: $300-up Start Bid: $150

84049   Destroy All Monsters (American International, 1969). Japanese B2 (20" X 29"). Folded, Very Fine-.
Est.: $400-up Start Bid: $200

84050   The Day of the Triffids (Allied Artists, 1962). Six Sheet (81" X 81"). Near Mint.
Est.: $500-up Start Bid: $250

84051 **One Million Years B.C. (20th Century Fox, 1966).** Insert (14"X 36"). Rolled, Fine/Very Fine.
Est.: $300-up Start Bid: $150

84052 **Fantastic Voyage (20th Century Fox, 1966).** Japanese B2 (20"X 29"). Rolled, Very Fine/Near Mint.
Est.: $200-up No Min Bid

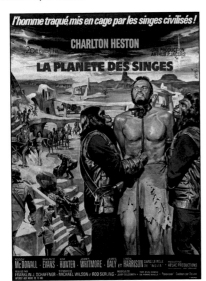

84053 **Planet of the Apes (20th Century Fox, 1968).** French Grande (47"X 63"). Very Fine+.
Est.: $400-up Start Bid: $200

84054 **Planet of the Apes (20th Century Fox, 1968).** One Sheet (27"X 41"). Folded, Very Fine.
Est.: $500-up Start Bid: $250

84055 **Conquest of the Planet of the Apes (20th Century Fox, 1972).** CGC Graded Lobby Card Set of 8 (11"X 14"). Near Mint.
Est.: $125-up No Min Bid

84056 **Star Wars (20th Century Fox, 1977).** One Sheet Style D (27"X 41"). Folded, Near Mint.
Est.: $500-up Start Bid: $250

84057 **Star Wars (20th Century Fox, 1977).** CGC Graded Lobby Card Set of 8 (11"X 14"). Near Mint.
Est.: $300-up Start Bid: $150

84058 **Star Wars (20th Century Fox, 1978).** Japanese B2 (20"X 29") Academy Awards Style. Rolled, Very Fine.
Est.: $200-up No Min Bid

84059 **The Empire Strikes Back (20th Century Fox, 1980).** Advance One Sheet (27"X 41"). Folded, Near Mint/Mint.
Est.: $100-up No Min Bid

84060   The Empire Strikes Back (20th Century Fox, 1980).
Half Sheet (22" X 28") Style A. Rolled, Very Fine.
Est.: $300-up Start Bid: $150

84061   The Empire Strikes Back (20th Century Fox, 1980).
Japanese B2 (20" X 29"). Rolled, Mint.
Est.: $100-up No Min Bid

84062   Escape from New York (Avco Embassy, 1981). Autographed One Sheet (27" X 41") Advance. Very Fine+.
Est.: $250-up No Min Bid

84063   King Kong (RKO, 1933). Advance French Grande (47"
X 63"). Folded, Very Fine-.
Est.: $400-up Start Bid: $200

84064   Night Monster (Realart, R-1949). CGC Graded Lobby
Card Set of 8 (11" X 14"). Very Fine+.
Est.: $200-up No Min Bid

84065   Dr. Jekyll and Mr. Hyde (MGM, Late 1940s). First
Post-War Release Belgian (10.5" X 16.5"). Folded, Fine+.
Est.: $400-up Start Bid: $300

84066   The Unseen (Paramount, 1944). Lobby Card Set of 8
(11" X 14"). Very Fine-.
Est.: $400-up Start Bid: $200

84067   Jungle Captive (Universal, 1945). One Sheet (27" X
41"). Very Fine- on Linen.
Est.: $400-up Start Bid: $200

84068   I Was a Teenage Werewolf (American International,
1957). Half Sheet (22" X 28"). Folded, Very Fine-.
Est.: $200-up No Min Bid

84069 I Was a Teenage Werewolf (American International, R-1961). Belgian (14" X 22"). Folded, Near Mint.
Est.: $200-up No Min Bid

84070 Rodan! The Flying Monster (Toho/ DCA, 1957). Poster (40" X 60"). Rolled, Fine+.
Est.: $300-up Start Bid: $150

84071 How to Make a Monster (American International, 1958). One Sheet (27" X 41"). Very Fine+ on Linen.
Est.: $400-up Start Bid: $200

84072 How to Make a Monster (American International, 1958). Lobby Card Set of 8 (11" X 14"). Near Mint/Mint.
Est.: $300-up Start Bid: $150

84073 How to Make a Monster (American International, 1958). Insert (14" X 36"). Rolled, Very Fine/Near Mint.
Est.: $300-up Start Bid: $150

84074 The Bride and the Beast (Allied Artists, 1958). Poster (40" X 60"). Rolled, Fine.
Est.: $300-up Start Bid: $150

84075 Whatever Happened to Baby Jane? (Warner Brothers, 1962). Lobby Card Set of 8 (11" X 14"). *From the collection of Wade Williams.* Very Fine+.
Est.: $500-up Start Bid: $250

84076 The Beast of Yucca Flats (Cinema Associates, Inc., 1962). One Sheet (27" X 41"). Very Fine+.
Est.: $200-up No Min Bid

84077　Frankenstein Conquers the World (Toho, 1965). Japanese B2 (20" X 28.5") Also known as "Frankenstein vs. Baragon." Rolled, Near Mint/Mint.
Est.: $300-up Start Bid: $150

84078　The Incredibly Strange Creatures Who Stopped Living and Became Mixed-Up Zombies (Fairway International, 1964). One Sheet (27" X 41"). Very Fine.
Est.: $300-up Start Bid: $150

84079　Jaws (Universal, 1975). Insert (14" X 36"). Rolled, Very Fine.
Est.: $300-up Start Bid: $150

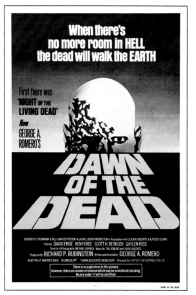

84080　Dawn of the Dead (United Film Distribution, 1978). One Sheet (27" X 41"). Rolled, Near Mint/Mint.
Est.: $500-up Start Bid: $250

84081　The 7th Voyage of Sinbad (Columbia, 1958). Half Sheet (22" X 28") Style B. Folded, Very Fine+.
Est.: $200-up No Min Bid

84082　Willy Wonka & the Chocolate Factory (Paramount, 1971). British Quad (30" X 40"). Very Fine+ on Linen.
Est.: $300-up Start Bid: $150

84083　The Lord of the Rings (United Artists, 1978). CGC Graded Lobby Card Set of 8 (11" X 14"). Near Mint/Mint.
Est.: $150-up No Min Bid

84084　Snow White and the Seven Dwarfs (RKO, 1937). Color-Glos Photos (2) (8" X 10"). Fine/Very Fine.
Est.: $200-up No Min Bid

84085　Terry-Toons Stock Lobby Card (20th Century Fox, 1946). Lobby Card (11" X 14"). Near Mint/Mint.
Est.: $400-up Start Bid: $200

84086   MGM Animation Stock Poster (MGM, 1953). One Sheet (27" X 41") "T.V. of Tomorrow." *From the collection of Wade Williams.* Near Mint+.
Est.: $300-up Start Bid: $150

84087   Lady and the Tramp (Buena Vista, 1955). Half Sheet (22" X 28"). Rolled, Very Fine-.
Est.: $300-up Start Bid: $150

84088   Sleeping Beauty (Buena Vista, 1959). Insert (14" X 36"). Rolled, Fine/Very Fine.
Est.: $300-up Start Bid: $150

84089   Saboteur (Universal, Late 1940s). First Post-War Belgian (15" X 22"). Folded, Fine.
Est.: $300-up Start Bid: $150

84090   Saboteur (Universal, late 1940s). First Post-War French Affiche (23.5" X 31.5"). Rolled, Very Fine-.
Est.: $300-up Start Bid: $150

84091   Strangers on a Train (Warner Brothers, 1951). Half Sheet (22" X 28"). Folded, Fine/Very Fine.
Est.: $350-up Start Bid: $175

84092   Rear Window (Paramount, R-1962). Lobby Card Set of 8 (11" X 14"). *From the collection of Wade Williams.* Fine/Very Fine.
Est.: $400-up Start Bid: $200

84093   Rear Window (Paramount, 1954). Belgian (14" X 21"). Folded, Fine/Very Fine.
Est.: $500-up Start Bid: $250

84094   Vertigo (Paramount, 1958). French Affiche (23.5" X 31.5"). Folded, Very Fine.
Est.: $400-up Start Bid: $350

84095   Vertigo (Paramount, R-1963). Lobby Card Set of 8 (11" X 14"). *From the collection of Wade Williams.* Fine/Very Fine.
Est.: $300-up Start Bid: $150

84096   Diamonds Are Forever (United Artists, 1971). Japanese STB (20" X 58"). Rolled, Very Fine-.
Est.: $200-up No Min Bid

84097   On Her Majesty's Secret Service (United Artists, 1970). Insert (14" X 36"). Very Fine- on Paper.
Est.: $300-up Start Bid: $150

84098   On Her Majesty's Secret Service (United Artists, 1970). Japanese B2 (20" X 28.5") Artwork Style. Folded, Very Fine.
Est.: $175-up No Min Bid

84099   On Her Majesty's Secret Service (United Artists, 1970). Japanese B2 (20" X 28.5"). Folded, Near Mint.
Est.: $200-up No Min Bid

84100   The Man With the Golden Gun (United Artists, 1974). Japanese B2 (20" X 28.5"). Rolled, Very Fine.
Est.: $150-up No Min Bid

84101   The Man With the Golden Gun (United Artists, 1974). CGC Graded Lobby Card Set of 8 (11" X 14"). Near Mint+.
Est.: $200-up No Min Bid

84102   Moonraker (United Artists, 1979). CGC Graded Lobby Card Set of 8 (11" X 14"). Near Mint/Mint.
Est.: $150-up No Min Bid

84103 **Octopussy (MGM/UA, 1983).** Japanese Large Posters (2) (28.5" X 40.5"). Folded, Fine/Very Fine.
Est.: $250-up No Min Bid

84104 **The Crime Doctor (RKO, 1934).** CGC Graded Midget Window Card (8" X 14"). Near Mint.
Est.: $200-up No Min Bid

84105 **Framed (First National, 1927).** One Sheet (27" X 41") Style A. Very Fine-.
Est.: $750-up Start Bid: $375

84106 **Lawyer Man (Warner Brothers, 1933).** Lobby Card (11" X 14"). Very Fine/Near Mint.
Est.: $400-up Start Bid: $200

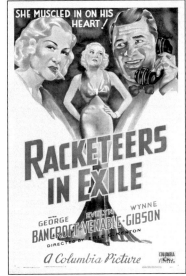

84107 **Racketeers in Exile (Columbia, 1937).** One Sheet (27" X 41"). Fine+ on Linen.
Est.: $300-up Start Bid: $150

84108 **She's Dangerous! (Universal, 1937).** One Sheet (27" X 41"). Fine+.
Est.: $300-up Start Bid: $150

84109 **Hell's Kitchen (Warner Brothers, 1939).** One Sheet (27" X 41"). Folded, Fine/Very Fine.
Est.: $300-up Start Bid: $150

84110 **The Little Giant (First National, 1933).** Lobby Card (11" X 14"). Fine/Very Fine.
Est.: $200-up No Min Bid

84111   Pepe le Moko (DisCina, R-1940s). Belgian (14.5" X 22"). Folded, Fine/Very Fine.
Est.: $400-up Start Bid: $200

84112   The Gay Falcon (RKO, 1941). One Sheet (27" X 41"). Fine.
Est.: $300-up Start Bid: $150

84113   Charlie Chan Carries On (Fox, 1931). Trolley Card (21" X 27"). Fine/Very Fine.
Est.: $300-up Start Bid: $150

84114   Sky Dragon (Monogram, 1949). One Sheet (27" X 41"). Very Fine-.
Est.: $300-up Start Bid: $150

84115   The Red Dragon (Monogram, 1945). Belgian (14" X 21.5"). Folded, Fine.
Est.: $200-up No Min Bid

84117   Saigon (Paramount, 1948). CGC Graded Lobby Card (11" X 14"). Very Fine+.
Est.: $100-up No Min Bid

84118   Force of Evil (MGM, 1948). Insert (14" X 36"). Folded, Fine+.
Est.: $500-up Start Bid: $250

84116   East of the River (Warner Brothers, 1940). Midget Window Card (8" X 14"). Very Fine+.
Est.: $100-up No Min Bid

84119   Criss Cross (Universal International, 1949). One Sheet (27" X 41"). Folded, Very Good+.
Est.: $400-up Start Bid: $200

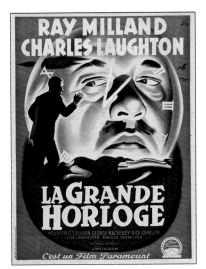

84120   The Big Clock (Paramount, 1948). French Affiche (23.5" X 31.5"). Fine+ on Linen.
Est.: $500-up Start Bid: $250

84121   The Great O'Malley (Warner Brothers, 1937). One Sheet (27" X 41"). Fine/Very Fine.
Est.: $400-up Start Bid: $200

84122   Brother Orchid (Warner Brothers, 1940). One Sheet (27" X 41"). Folded, Fine.
Est.: $300-up Start Bid: $150

84123   The Wagons Roll at Night (Warner Brothers, 1941). One Sheet (27" X 41"). Fine.
Est.: $300-up Start Bid: $150

84124   The Big Sleep (Warner Brothers, 1946). Lobby Card (11" X 14"). Very Fine.
Est.: $400-up Start Bid: $200

84125   The Two Mrs. Carrolls (Warner Brothers, 1947). One Sheet (27" X 41"). Fine-.
Est.: $500-up Start Bid: $250

84126   Sorry, Wrong Number (Paramount, 1948). One Sheet (27" X 41"). Fine/Very Fine on Linen.
Est.: $400-up Start Bid: $200

84127   The St. Louis Kid (Warner Brothers, 1934). CGC Graded Lobby Card (11" X 14"). Very Fine/Near Mint.
Est.: $200-up No Min Bid

84128   The Mayor of Hell (Warner Brothers, 1933). Lobby Card (11" X 14"). Very Fine-.
Est.: $300-up Start Bid: $150

84129　White Heat (Warner Brothers, 1949). Belgian (14" X 22"). Folded, Very Fine-.
Est.: $400-up Start Bid: $200

84132　Affair with a Stranger (RKO, 1953). One Sheet (27" X 41"). Very Fine- on Linen.
Est.: $300-up Start Bid: $150

84135　Johnny O'clock (Columbia, R-1956). One Sheet (27" X 41"). Fine/Very Fine.
Est.: $300-up Start Bid: $150

84130　The Asphalt Jungle (MGM, R-1954). Three Sheet (41" X 81"). Fine/Very Fine on Linen.
Est.: $300-up Start Bid: $150

84133　While the City Sleeps (RKO, 1956). Three Sheet (41" X 81"). Fine/Very Fine.
Est.: $150-up No Min Bid

84136　Laura (20th Century Fox, 1944). Lobby Card (11" X 14"). Fine-.
Est.: $300-up Start Bid: $150

84137　Niagara (20th Century Fox, 1953). Belgian (14" X 22"). Folded, Fine/Very Fine.
Est.: $400-up Start Bid: $200

84131　The Narrow Margin (RKO, 1952). Half Sheet (22" X 28") Style B. *From the collection of Wade Williams.* Rolled, Fine+.
Est.: $400-up Start Bid: $200

84134　Confidential Agent (Warner Brothers, 1945). CGC Graded Lobby Card (11" X 14"). Near Mint-.
Est.: $200-up No Min Bid

84138 Bullitt (Warner Brothers, 1968). Lobby Card Set of 8 (11" X 14"). Very Fine/Near Mint.
Est.: $500-up Start Bid: $250

84139 Bullitt (Warner Brothers, 1968). German A0 (33" X 46"). Folded, Very Fine/Near Mint.
Est.: $500-up Start Bid: $250

84140 The Thomas Crown Affair (United Artists, 1968). Three Sheet (41" X 81"). Fine/Very Fine.
Est.: $300-up Start Bid: $150

84141 The Bride Wore Black (United Artists, 1968). Japanese STB (20" X 58"). Folded, Very Fine-.
Est.: $350-up Start Bid: $175

84142 Point Blank (MGM, 1967). One Sheet (27" X 41"). Fine/Very Fine on Linen.
Est.: $250-up No Min Bid

84143 Dirty Harry (Warner Brothers, 1971). Italian 4 - Foglio (55" X 78"). Very Fine/Near Mint.
Est.: $300-up Start Bid: $150

84144 Goodfellas (Warner Brothers, 1990). CGC Graded Lobby Card Set of 8 (11" X 14"). Near Mint/Mint.
Est.: $300-up Start Bid: $150

For full lot descriptions, enlargeable images and online bidding, visit HA.com/7025

84145   Road to Perdition (DreamWorks, 2002). Lobby Card Set of 11 (11" X 14"). Mint.
Est.: $250-up No Min Bid

84146   The Flower of No Man's Land (Columbia, 1916). One Sheet (27" X 41"). Very Fine.
Est.: $500-up Start Bid: $250

84147   Screen Snapshots (Screen Snapshots, Inc., 1920s). One Sheet (27" X 41"). Fine+ on Linen.
Est.: $300-up Start Bid: $150

84148   Whispering Devils (Equity, 1920). Half Sheet (22" X 28"). Rolled, Very Fine-.
Est.: $200-up No Min Bid

84149   Beyond the Rocks (Paramount, 1922). Lobby Card (11" X 14"). Very Fine-.
Est.: $500-up Start Bid: $250

84150   The Ruling Passion (United Artists, 1922). Half Sheets (2) (22" X 28") Styles A and B. Folded, Fine/Very Fine.
Est.: $300-up Start Bid: $150

84151   Big Dan (Fox, 1923). One Sheet (27" X 41"). Fine on Linen.
Est.: $500-up Start Bid: $250

84152   Broken Barriers (Metro, 1924). Lobby Cards (3) (11" X 14"). Very Fine-.
Est.: $300-up Start Bid: $150

84153 My Son (First National, 1925). Title Lobby Card and Lobby Card (11" X 14"). Very Fine.
Est.: $400-up Start Bid: $200

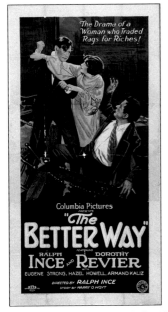

84154 The Better Way (Columbia, 1926). Three Sheet (41" X 81"). Fine.
Est.: $400-up Start Bid: $200

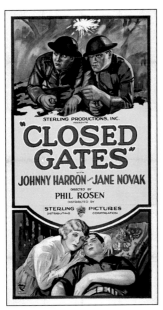

84155 Closed Gates (Sterling Pictures, 1927). Three Sheet (41" X 78"). Fine/Very Fine.
Est.: $900-up Start Bid: $450

84156 Weary River (First National, 1929). One Sheet (27" X 41") Style A. Fine/Very Fine on Linen.
Est.: $700-up Start Bid: $350

84157 What Wives Want (Universal, 1923). One Sheet (27" X 41"). Very Good+ on Linen.
Est.: $600-up Start Bid: $300

84158 Night After Night (Paramount, 1932). Lobby Card (11" X 14"). Fine+.
Est.: $200-up No Min Bid

84159 Uptown New York (World Wide, 1932). CGC Graded Lobby Card (11" X 14"). Very Fine+.
Est.: $200-up No Min Bid

84160 The House on 56th Street (Warner Brothers, 1933). Midget Window Card (8" X 14"). Very Fine.
Est.: $250-up No Min Bid

84161 Riffraff (MGM, 1936). Lobby Card (11" X 14"). Very Fine-.
Est.: $400-up Start Bid: $200

84162　**Mannequin (MGM, 1937).** CGC Graded Lobby Card (11" X 14"). Near Mint.
Est.: $100-up No Min Bid

84165　**The Sign of the Cross (Paramount, 1932).** Lobby Card (11" X 14"). Fine/Very Fine.
Est.: $400-up Start Bid: $350

84168　**Four Frightened People (Paramount, 1934).** CGC Graded Lobby Card (11" X 14"). Very Fine.
Est.: $200-up No Min Bid

84163　**Another Dawn (Warner Brothers, 1937).** CGC Graded Lobby Card (11" X 14"). Very Fine+.
Est.: $200-up No Min Bid

84166　**The Sign of the Cross (Paramount, 1932).** Lobby Cards (2) (11" X 14"). Fine/Very Fine.
Est.: $500-up Start Bid: $250

84169　**A Tale of Two Cities (MGM, 1935).** CGC Graded Lobby Card (11" X 14"). Very Fine+.
Est.: $200-up No Min Bid

84164　**Juarez (Warner Brothers, 1939).** One Sheet (27" X 41"). Fine on Linen.
Est.: $400-up Start Bid: $200

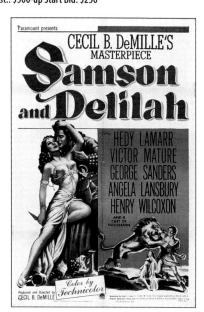

84167　**Samson and Delilah (Paramount, 1949).** One Sheet (27" X 41"). Fine.
Est.: $400-up Start Bid: $200

84170　**Citizen Kane (Titanus, R-1966).** Italian 2 - Foglio (39" X 55"). Fine/Very Fine on Linen.
Est.: $400-up Start Bid: $200

84171 White Cargo (MGM, 1942). One Sheet (27" X 41") Style D. Fine/Very Fine.
Est.: $400-up Start Bid: $200

84172 A Letter to Three Wives (20th Century Fox, 1949). One Sheet (27" X 41"). Fine+.
Est.: $200-up No Min Bid

84173 Salty O'Rourke (Paramount, 1945). One Sheet (27" X 41"). Fine/Very Fine on Linen.
Est.: $300-up Start Bid: $150

84174 Bus Stop (20th Century Fox, 1956). One Sheet (27" X 41"). Folded, Very Fine.
Est.: $500-up Start Bid: $250

84175 Bus Stop (20th Century Fox, 1956). Color Photo Set of 10 (8" X 10"). *From the collection of Wade Williams.* Very Fine/ Near Mint.
Est.: $500-up Start Bid: $250

84176 Bus Stop (20th Century Fox, 1956). Belgian (15" X 22"). Very Fine-.
Est.: $400-up Start Bid: $200

84177 Clash By Night (RKO, 1952). Three Sheet (41" X 81"). Fine/Very Fine.
Est.: $500-up Start Bid: $250

84178 The Misfits (United Artists, 1961). Three Sheet (41" X 81"). Very Fine on Linen.
Est.: $300-up Start Bid: $150

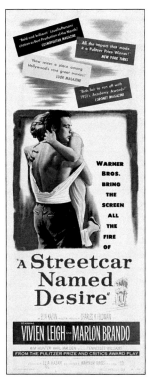

84179   A Streetcar Named Desire (Warner Brothers, 1951).
Insert (14" X 36"). Rolled, Fine/Very Fine.
Est.: $500-up Start Bid: $250

84180   The Wild One (Columbia, 1953). Lobby Card (11" X
14"). *From the collection of Wade Williams.* Fine.
Est.: $200-up No Min Bid

84181   The Wild One (Columbia, 1953). Window Card (14" X
22"). Folded, Fine/Very Fine.
Est.: $300-up Start Bid: $150

84182   Giant (Warner Brothers, 1956). Insert (14" X 36").
Folded, Fine/Very Fine.
Est.: $400-up Start Bid: $200

84183   Written on the Wind/ All That Heaven Allows Lot
(Universal International, 1955-1956). One Sheets (2) (27" X
41"). Fine/Very Fine.
Est.: $400-up Start Bid: $200

84184   Magnificent Obsession (Universal International,
1954). Three Sheet (41" X 81"). Fine/Very Fine on Linen.
Est.: $200-up No Min Bid

84185   Playgirl (Universal International, 1954). CGC Graded Lobby Card Set of 8 (11" X 14"). Near Mint+.
Est.: $125-up No Min Bid

84186   To Kill a Mockingbird (Universal, 1963). Half Sheet
(22" X 28"). Rolled, Very Fine-.
Est.: $400-up Start Bid: $200

84187 Cool Hand Luke (Warner Brothers, 1967). Italian 4 - Foglio (55" X 78"). Very Fine+.
Est.: $400-up Start Bid: $200

84188 Cool Hand Luke (Warner Brothers, 1967). Half Sheet (22" X 28"). Folded, Very Fine+.
Est.: $600-up Start Bid: $300

84189 The Graduate (Embassy, 1968). Japanese B2 (20" X 29"). Rolled, Very Fine+.
Est.: $300-up Start Bid: $150

84190 One Flew Over the Cuckoo's Nest (United Artists, 1975). Half Sheet (22" X 28"). Rolled, Very Fine-.
Est.: $400-up Start Bid: $200

84191 Darling (Cocinor, 1966). French Grande (47" X 63"). Folded, Near Mint.
Est.: $300-up Start Bid: $150

84192 La Loi (Les Films Corona, 1959). French Affiche (23.5" X 31.5"). Folded, Very Fine-.
Est.: $300-up Start Bid: $300

84193 Repulsion (Towa, 1965). Japanese B2 (20" X 29"). Rolled, Mint.
Est.: $300-up Start Bid: $150

84194 Love in the Afternoon (Allied Artists, 1957). One Sheet (27" X 41"). Very Fine-.
Est.: $300-up Start Bid: $150

84195 Green Mansions (MGM, 1959). CGC Graded Lobby Card (11" X 14"). Near Mint+.
Est.: $200-up No Min Bid

84196   Whoopee! (United Artists, 1930). Lobby Card (11" X 14"). Very Fine.
Est.: $400-up Start Bid: $200

84197   Shipmates Forever (Warner Brothers - First National, 1935). CGC Graded Lobby Card (11" X 14"). Very Fine+.
Est.: $200-up No Min Bid

84198   Captain January (20th Century Fox, 1936). Pre-War Belgian (24" X 33"). Very Fine+ on Linen.
Est.: $300-up Start Bid: $150

84199   The Poor Little Rich Girl (20th Century Fox, 1936). French Grande (47" X 63"). Very Fine+ on Linen.
Est.: $400-up Start Bid: $200

84200   Show Boat (Universal, 1936). CGC Graded Lobby Card (11" X 14"). Very Fine+.
Est.: $400-up Start Bid: $200

84201   Rose of Washington Square (20th Century Fox, 1939). One Sheet (27" X 41"). *From the collection of Wade Williams.* Fine- on Linen.
Est.: $500-up Start Bid: $250

84202   Two Girls on Broadway (MGM, 1940). Midget Window Card (8" X 14"). Very Fine+.
Est.: $100-up No Min Bid

84203   You'll Never Get Rich (Columbia, 1941). Title Lobby Card (11" X 14"). Very Fine/Near Mint.
Est.: $300-up Start Bid: $150

84204   Yankee Doodle Dandy (Warner Brothers, 1942). Lobby Card (11" X 14"). Fine+.
Est.: $400-up Start Bid: $200

84205   Judy Garland Lobby Card Lot (MGM, 1941-1942). Lobby Cards (4) (11" X 14"). Very Fine-.
Est.: $400-up Start Bid: $200

84206   Easter Parade (MGM, 1948). Lobby Cards (3) (11" X 14"). Very Fine+.
Est.: $300-up Start Bid: $150

84207   A Star Is Born (Warner Brothers, 1954). Three Sheet (41" X 81"). *From the collection of Wade Williams.* Fine+.
Est.: $600-up Start Bid: $300

84208   Gentlemen Prefer Blondes (20th Century Fox, 1953). Insert (14" X 36"). Very Fine-.
Est.: $400-up Start Bid: $200

84209   White Christmas (Paramount, 1954). Insert (14" X 36"). Fine on Paper.
Est.: $400-up Start Bid: $200

84210   Gigi (MGM, 1958). One Sheet (27" X 41"). Fine+ on Linen.
Est.: $200-up No Min Bid

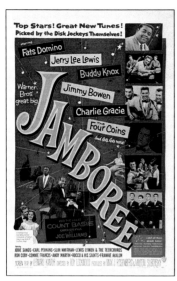

84211 Jamboree (Warner Brothers, 1957). One Sheet (27" X 41"). Very Fine on Linen.
Est.: $200-up No Min Bid

84212 Blue Hawaii (Paramount, 1961). Half Sheet (22" X 28"). Very Fine.
Est.: $300-up Start Bid: $150

84213 Viva Las Vegas (MGM, 1964). One Sheet (27" X 41"). Fine+.
Est.: $300-up Start Bid: $150

84214 Help! (United Artists, 1965). Six Sheet (81" X 81"). Very Fine/Near Mint.
Est.: $600-up Start Bid: $300

84215 Let It Be (United Artists, 1970). Japanese B2 (20" X 28.5"). Rolled, Near Mint+.
Est.: $200-up No Min Bid

84216 The Prisoner of Zenda (United Artists, 1937). Insert (14" X 36"). Rolled, Very Fine+.
Est.: $400-up Start Bid: $200

84217 The Adventures of Robin Hood (Warner Brothers, 1938). Educational Panels (5) (19" X 25"). Fine/Very Fine on Linen.
Est.: $500-up Start Bid: $250

84218 The Sea Hawk (Warner Brothers, 1940). Swedish One Sheet (27.5" X 39.5") Photo Style. Rolled, Fine/Very Fine.
Est.: $500-up Start Bid: $250

84219 Batman (20th Century Fox, 1966). French Grande (47" X 63"). Folded, Very Fine/Near Mint.
Est.: $300-up Start Bid: $150

84220 Le Samouraï (Herald, 1968). Japanese B2 (20" X 29").
Rolled, Mint.
Est.: $300-up Start Bid: $150

84221 The Manchurian Candidate (United Artists, 1962).
British Quad (30" X 40"). Very Fine+.
Est.: $400-up Start Bid: $200

84222 Treasure Island (MGM, 1934). CGC Graded Lobby
Card (11" X 14"). Fine/Very Fine.
Est.: $200-up No Min Bid

84223 The Last Outpost (Paramount, 1935). CGC Graded
Lobby Card (11" X 14"). Very Fine.
Est.: $100-up No Min Bid

84224 Wee Willie Winkie (20th Century Fox, 1937). Pre-
War Belgian (23" X 30"). Fine/Very Fine on Linen.
Est.: $300-up Start Bid: $150

84225 The General Died at Dawn (Paramount, R-1957).
Italian 4 - Foglio (55" X 78"). Very Fine.
Est.: $400-up Start Bid: $200

84226 Beau Geste (Paramount, 1939). Lobby Cards (2) (11"
X 14"). Fine.
Est.: $500-up Start Bid: $250

84227 The New Adventures of Tarzan (Burroughs-Tarzan-
Enterprise, 1935). One Sheet (28" X 41"). From the Theaters of Old
Detroit Collection. Very Good+.
Est.: $400-up Start Bid: $200

84228 Two Years Before the Mast (Paramount, 1946).
Three Sheet (41" X 81"). Very Fine on Linen.
Est.: $400-up Start Bid: $200

84229   Wake of the Red Witch (Republic, 1949). Three Sheet (41" X 81"). Very Fine+.
Est.: $250-up No Min Bid

84230   The African Queen (United Artists, 1952). Belgian (14" X 18.5"). Folded, Fine/Very Fine.
Est.: $400-up Start Bid: $200

84231   Hercules (Embassy, 1959). CGC Graded Lobby Card Set of 8 (11" X 14"). Near Mint+.
Est.: $250-up No Min Bid

84232   Raiders of the Lost Ark (Paramount, 1981). Half Sheet (22" X 28"). Rolled, Very Fine-.
Est.: $250-up No Min Bid

84233   Brewster's Millions (Paramount, 1921). Lobby Cards (2) (11" X 14"). Very Fine-.
Est.: $300-up Start Bid: $150

84234   Painted People (First National, 1924). Title Lobby Card and Lobby Card (11" X 14"). Fine/Very Fine.
Est.: $300-up Start Bid: $150

84235   Crazy That Way (Fox, 1930). Three Sheet (41" X 81"). Fine.
Est.: $1,200-up Start Bid: $600

84236   The Cohens and Kellys in Africa (Universal, 1930). Half Sheet (22" X 28"). Rolled, Fine.
Est.: $400-up Start Bid: $200

84237   Many Happy Returns (Paramount, 1934). CGC Graded Lobby Card (11" X 14"). Near Mint/Mint.
Est.: $300-up Start Bid: $150

84238   Many Happy Returns (Paramount, 1934). CGC Graded Lobby Cards (2) (11" X 14"). Near Mint-.
Est.: $300-up Start Bid: $150

84239   Son of a Sailor (Warner Brothers - First National, 1933). Title Lobby Card (11" X 14"). Fine+.
Est.: $350-up Start Bid: $300

84240   Mrs. Wiggs of the Cabbage Patch (Paramount, 1934). Lobby Cards (2) (11" X 14"). Very Fine-.
Est.: $400-up Start Bid: $200

84241   Break of Hearts (RKO, 1935). Lobby Cards (2) (11" X 14"). Fine/Very Fine.
Est.: $300-up Start Bid: $150

84242   The Princess Comes Across (Paramount, 1936). Lobby Card (11" X 14"). Fine/Very Fine.
Est.: $300-up Start Bid: $150

84243   Four's a Crowd (Warner Brothers, 1938). CGC Graded Lobby Card (11" X 14"). Very Fine.
Est.: $200-up No Min Bid

84244   No Time for Comedy (Warner Brothers, 1940). Lobby Card (11" X 14"). Near Mint-.
Est.: $300-up Start Bid: $150

84245   A Chump at Oxford (United Artists, late 1940s). First Post-War Belgian (11" X 17"). Fine/Very Fine.
Est.: $400-up Start Bid: $200

84246   Laurel and Hardy Stock Poster (MGM, 1947). One Sheet (27" X 41"). Fine on Linen.
Est.: $400-up Start Bid: $200

84247   Forty Little Mothers (MGM, 1940). Midget Window Card (8" X 14"). Fine/Very Fine.
Est.: $100-up No Min Bid

84248   Love Finds Andy Hardy (MGM, 1938). Lobby Card (11" X 14"). Very Fine-.
Est.: $200-up No Min Bid

84249   Andy Hardy's Double Life (MGM, 1942). CGC Graded Lobby Card (11" X 14"). Very Fine.
Est.: $100-up No Min Bid

84250   Topper (Film Classics, R-1944). Half Sheet (22" X 28"). Rolled, Fine-.
Est.: $500-up Start Bid: $250

84251   The Bachelor and the Bobby Soxer (RKO, 1947). Lobby Card Set of 8 (11" X 14"). Fine+.
Est.: $400-up Start Bid: $200

84252   The Adventures of Baron Munchausen (UFA, 1943). Italian Foglio (20" X 28"). Folded, Very Fine.
Est.: $400-up Start Bid: $200

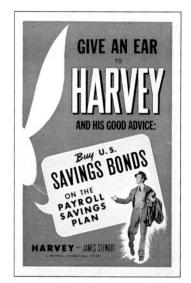

84253   Harvey (Universal International, 1950). Savings Bond Poster (12.5" X 19"). Folded, Fine+.
Est.: $400-up Start Bid: $200

84254   The Long, Long Trailer (MGM, 1954). One Sheet (27" X 41"). Fine+ on Linen.
Est.: $400-up Start Bid: $200

84255　O. Henry's Full House (20th Century Fox, 1952). Three Sheet (41" X 81"). Fine/Very Fine on Linen.
Est.: $200-up No Min Bid

84256　The Seven Year Itch (20th Century Fox, 1955). Title Lobby Card (11" X 14"). *From the collection of Wade Williams.* Fine/Very Fine.
Est.: $500-up Start Bid: $250

84257　The Seven Year Itch (20th Century Fox, 1955). Italian Photobusta (19.5" X 27.5"). Folded, Very Fine.
Est.: $400-up Start Bid: $200

84258　Monkey Business (20th Century Fox, 1952). Three Sheet (41" X 81"). Very Fine on Linen.
Est.: $300-up Start Bid: $150

84259　Let's Make Love (20th Century Fox, 1960). Three Sheet (41" X 81"). Fine+ on Linen.
Est.: $300-up Start Bid: $150

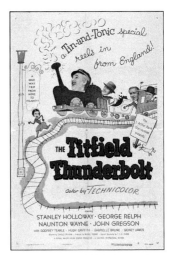

84260　The Titfield Thunderbolt (Universal, 1953). One Sheet (27" X 41"). *From the collection of Wade Williams.* Folded, Fine/Very Fine.
Est.: $300-up Start Bid: $150

84261　Pillow Talk (Universal International, 1959). One Sheet (27" X 41"). Very Fine- on Linen.
Est.: $500-up Start Bid: $250

84262　Pillow Talk (Universal International, 1959). Lobby Card Set of 8 (11" X 14"). Fine/Very Fine.
Est.: $300-up Start Bid: $150

84263 Cat Ballou (Columbia, 1965). Japanese B2 (20" X 28.5"). Folded, Near Mint-.
Est.: $300-up Start Bid: $150

84266 Harold and Maude (Paramount, 1971). Italian 4 - Foglio (55" X 78"). Folded, Very Fine-.
Est.: $350-up Start Bid: $300

84269 Sex and the Single Sailor (William Mishkin Motion Pictures Inc., 1967). One Sheet (27" X 41"). Rolled, Very Fine.
Est.: $300-up Start Bid: $150

84264 Beach Party (American International, 1963). One Sheet (27" X 41"). Fine/Very Fine.
Est.: $250-up No Min Bid

84267 Why Girls Leave Home (PRC, 1945). One Sheet (27" X 41"). *From the collection of Wade Williams.* Very Fine.
Est.: $300-up Start Bid: $150

84270 New Frontier (Republic, 1939). One Sheet (27" X 41"). Very Good on Linen.
Est.: $500-up Start Bid: $250

84265 Carry On Screaming! (Anglo Amalgamated, 1966). British One Sheet (27" X 40"). Very Fine+ on Linen.
Est.: $200-up No Min Bid

84268 Hot Rod Rumble (Allied Artists, 1957). One Sheet (27" X 41"). Good/Very Good on Linen.
Est.: $600-up Start Bid: $500

84271 Red River (United Artists, 1948). Belgian (14" X 22"). Folded, Fine.
Est.: $300-up Start Bid: $150

84272   Three Godfathers (MGM, 1936). One Sheet (27" X 41"). Fine/Very Fine on Linen.
Est.: $400-up Start Bid: $200

84274   Jesse James (20th Century Fox, R-1946). Lobby Card Set of 8 (11" X 14"). Very Fine+.
Est.: $400-up Start Bid: $200

84277   No Man's Gold (Fox, 1926). Lobby Cards (4) (11" X 14"). Very Fine.
Est.: $400-up Start Bid: $200

84273   3 Godfathers (MGM, 1948). Insert (14" X 36"). Folded, Fine/Very Fine.
Est.: $300-up Start Bid: $150

84275   They Died With Their Boots On (Warner Brothers, 1947). First Post-War Belgian (15" X 22.5"). Folded, Very Fine.
Est.: $400-up Start Bid: $200

84276   Blood on the Moon (RKO, 1948). One Sheet (27" X 41"). Fine-.
Est.: $500-up Start Bid: $250

84278   Bar 20 Rides Again (Paramount, 1935). One Sheet (27" X 41"). Very Good on Linen.
Est.: $400-up Start Bid: $200

84279   Stagecoach War (Paramount, 1940). One Sheet (27" X 41"). Fine on Linen.
Est.: $400-up Start Bid: $200

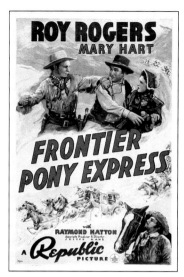

84282   Frontier Pony Express (Republic, 1939). One Sheet (27" X 41"). Fine/Very Fine on Linen.
Est.: $400-up Start Bid: $200

84285   Dodge City Trail (Columbia, 1936). One Sheet (27" X 41"). Fine+ on Linen.
Est.: $300-up Start Bid: $150

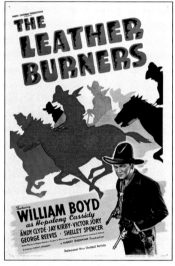

84280   The Leather Burners (United Artists, 1943). One Sheet (27" X 41"). Very Fine+ on Linen.
Est.: $400-up Start Bid: $200

84283   Song of Nevada (Republic, 1944). One Sheet (27" X 41"). Very Good- on Linen.
Est.: $200-up No Min Bid

84281   Rhythm of the Saddle (Republic, 1938). One Sheet (27" X 41"). Fine on Linen.
Est.: $600-up Start Bid: $300

84284   Gordon of Ghost City Lot (Universal, 1933). Title Lobby Cards (2) (11" X 14") Stock Title Card and Ch. 3 — "Trapped". Very Fine-.
Est.: $400-up Start Bid: $200

84286   The Revenge Rider (Columbia, 1935). Title Lobby Card and Lobby Cards (3) (11" X 14"). Fine/Very Fine.
Est.: $500-up Start Bid: $250

84287 Lone Hand Saunders (FBO, 1926). Lobby Cards (6) (11" X 14"). Fine/Very Fine.
Est.: $300-up Start Bid: $150

84288 Fred Thomson Lot (FBO, 1926). Lobby Cards (5) (11" X 14"). Fine/Very Fine.
Est.: $300-up Start Bid: $150

84289 Cheyenne Rides Again (Victory, 1937). One Sheet (27" X 41"). Fine/Very Fine on Linen.
Est.: $400-up Start Bid: $200

84290 A Fistful of Dollars (Adria Film, 1968). Yugoslavian Poster (19" X 27"). Folded, Fine+.
Est.: $100-up No Min Bid

84291 High Plains Drifter (Universal, 1973). Half Sheet (22" X 28"). Rolled, Very Fine/Near Mint.
Est.: $300-up Start Bid: $150

84292 Once Upon a Time in the West (Paramount, 1969). Lobby Card Set of 8 (11" X 14"). Very Fine-.
Est.: $200-up No Min Bid

84293 Butch Cassidy and the Sundance Kid (20th Century Fox, 1969). Three Sheet (41" X 81"). Very Fine.
Est.: $400-up Start Bid: $200

84294 Butch Cassidy and the Sundance Kid (20th Century Fox, 1969). Japanese STB (20" X 58"). Rolled, Very Fine.
Est.: $400-up Start Bid: $200

84295   Tombstone (Buena Vista, 1993). Lobby Card Set of 8 (11" X 14"). Mint.
Est.: $200-up No Min Bid

84296   Hell's Angels (United Artists, R-1937). Lobby Card (11" X 14"). Very Fine-.
Est.: $300-up Start Bid: $150

84297   Four Men and a Prayer (20th Century Fox, 1938). CGC Graded Lobby Card Set of 8 (11" X 14"). Very Fine+.
Est.: $500-up Start Bid: $250

84298   British Intelligence (Warner Brothers, 1940). One Sheet (27" X 41"). Folded, Very Fine+.
Est.: $300-up Start Bid: $150

84299   Sundown (United Artists, 1941). Insert (14" X 36"). Folded, Very Fine-.
Est.: $300-up Start Bid: $150

84300   I Wanted Wings (Paramount, 1941). Lobby Card (11" X 14"). Fine+.
Est.: $350-up Start Bid: $300

84301   I Wanted Wings (Paramount, 1941). Lobby Card (11" X 14"). Very Fine-.
Est.: $200-up No Min Bid

84302   Keep Your Powder Dry (MGM, 1945). Lobby Card Set of 8 (11" X 14"). Very Fine-.
Est.: $400-up Start Bid: $200

84303   Kanal (P.P. Film, 1957). Japanese B2 (20" X 29"). Folded, Very Fine-.
Est.: $200-up No Min Bid

84304   Lawrence of Arabia (Columbia, 1962). Still Set of 10 (8" X 10"). Very Fine.
Est.: $200-up No Min Bid

84305   Elmer, the Great (Warner Brothers-First National, 1933). Title Lobby Card (11" X 14"). Fine/Very Fine.
Est.: $350-up Start Bid: $300

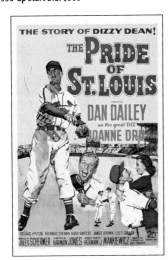

84306   The Pride of St. Louis (20th Century Fox, 1952). One Sheet (27" X 41"). Very Fine+.
Est.: $300-up Start Bid: $150

84307   The Hustler (20th Century Fox, 1961). One Sheet (27" X 41"). Fine+.
Est.: $500-up Start Bid: $250

84308   The Hustler (20th Century Fox, 1961). German A1 (23" X 33"). Folded, Fine/Very Fine.
Est.: $350-up Start Bid: $300

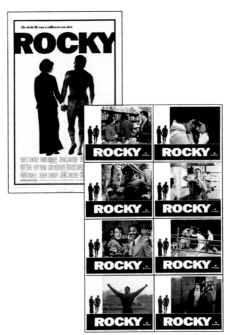

84309   Rocky (United Artists, 1977). One Sheet (27" X 41") and Lobby Card Set of 8 (11" X 14"). Near Mint/Mint.
Est.: $300-up Start Bid: $150

84310   RKO   Exhibitor Book (RKO, 1934). Hardcover Book (50 Pages, 12" X 12"). Very Fine.
Est.: $300-up Start Bid: $150

84311   Monogram   Exhibitor Book (Monogram, 1932). Book (Multiple Pages, 13" X 18"). Fine+.
Est.: $300-up Start Bid: $150

84312   Clara Bow in "No Limit" by Eugene Robert Richee (Paramount, 1931). Portrait Photo (11" X 14"). Very Fine. Est.: $200-up

84315   Clara Bow (Fox, 1932). Portrait Photo (8" X 10"). Very Fine. Est.: $200-up

84318   Greta Garbo in "Inspiration" (MGM, 1931). Photo (10" X 13"). Fine. Est.: $200-up

84313   Clara Bow in "Call Her Savage" by Hal Phyfe (Fox, 1932). Portrait Photo (11" X 14"). Very Fine. Est.: $200-up

84316   Greta Garbo in "Susan Lenox (Her Fall and Rise)" by Clarence Sinclair Bull (MGM, 1931). Photo (8" X 10"). Very Fine. Est.: $200-up

84319   Carole Lombard (Paramount, 1930s). Photo (8" X 10"). Very Fine. Est.: $200-up

84314   Clara Bow in "Call Her Savage" by Hal Phyfe (Fox, 1932). Portrait Photo(11" X 14"). Very Fine. Est.: $200-up

84317   Greta Garbo in "Romance" by George Hurrell (MGM, 1930). Portrait Photo(10" X 13"). Fine. Est.: $200-up

84320   Carole Lombard by Scotty Welbourne (1938). Portrait Photo (10.5" X 13.5"). Fine/Very Fine. Est.: $200-up

84321   Carole Lombard and James Stewart in "Made for Each Other" (United Artists, 1939). Portrait Photo (10.5" X 14"). Very Fine-.
Est.: $200-up

84324   Myrna Loy (MGM, 1930s). Portrait Photo (10.5" X 13"). Fine+.
Est.: $200-up

84327   Ruth Roland by Lansing Brown (1920s). Hand-Painted Photo (10.5" X 13.5"). Very Good+.
Est.: $200-up

84322   William Powell and Myrna Loy in "The Great Ziegfeld" by Clarence Sinclair Bull (MGM, 1936). Photo (10" X 13"). Very Fine.
Est.: $200-up

84325   Myrna Loy by Clarence Sinclair Bull (MGM, 1933). Portrait Photo (10" X 13"). Very Fine.
Est.: $200-up

84328   Ruth Roland by Edwin Bower Hesser (1920s). Hand-Painted Photo (11" X 14"). Fine/Very Fine.
Est.: $200-up

84323   Myrna Loy in "Parnell" by Clarence Sinclair Bull (MGM, 1937). Portrait Photo (10.25" X 13"). Fine/Very Fine.
Est.: $200-up

84326   Ruth Roland by Strauss Peyton (1922). Hand-Painted Photo (11" X 14"). Fine.
Est.: $200-up

84329   Veronica Lake (Paramount, 1940). Portrait Photo (8" X 10"). Very Fine.
Est.: $200-up

84330   Veronica Lake (Paramount, 1940). Portrait Photo (8"
X 10"). Very Fine.
Est.: $200-up

84331   Veronica Lake (Paramount, 1940s). Portrait Photo
(11" X 14"). Very Fine.
Est.: $200-up

84332   Veronica Lake by A.L. Whitey Schafer (Paramount,
1944). Photo (8" X 10"). Fine-.
Est.: $200-up

84333   Rita Hayworth (Columbia, 1941). Portrait Photo (11"
X 14"). Fine.
Est.: $200-up

84334   Joan Crawford in "A Woman's Face" (MGM, 1941).
Autographed Photo (10" X 13"). Fine+.
Est.: $200-up

84335   Joan Crawford by Clarence Sinclair Bull (MGM,
1930s). Portrait Photo (10" X 13"). Very Fine/Near Mint.
Est.: $200-up

84336   Joan Crawford and Robert Montgomery in "Letty
Lynton" By George Hurrell (MGM, 1932). Portrait (10" X 13").
Very Fine.
Est.: $200-up

84337   Marlene Dietrich in "The Devil is a Woman" by Don
English (Paramount, 1935). Portrait Photo (10" X 13"). Fine.
Est.: $200-up

84338   Jean Harlow by Clarence Sinclair Bull (MGM, 1930s).
Photo (8" X 10"). Near Mint.
Est.: $200-up

84339   Jean Harlow (MGM, 1930s). Portrait Photo (8" X 10"). Very Fine.
Est.: $200-up

84342   Jean Harlow in "The Secret Six" by Clarence Sinclair Bull (MGM, 1931). Portrait Photo (8" X 10"). Fine/Very Fine.
Est.: $200-up

84345   Anna May Wong in "Daughter of Shanghai" (Paramount, 1937). Photo (8" X 10"). Very Fine+.
Est.: $200-up

84340   Jean Harlow (MGM, 1930s). Portrait photo (8" X 10"). Fine+.
Est.: $200-up

84343   Jean Harlow in "Reckless" by William Grimes (MGM, 1935). Photo (10" X 13"). Near Mint.
Est.: $200-up

84346   Anna May Wong in "Daughter of the Dragon" (Paramount, 1931). Keybook Photo (7.5" X 9.5"). Very Fine.
Est.: $200-up

84341   Jean Harlow (MGM, 1930s). Portrait Photo (8" X 10"). Very Fine+.
Est.: $200-up

84344   Anna May Wong in "Daughter of Shanghai" (Paramount, 1937). Photo (8" X 10"). Very Fine+.
Est.: $200-up

84347   Norma Shearer and Johnny Mack Brown in "A Lady of Chance" (MGM, 1928). Photo (8" X 10"). Fine/Very Fine.
Est.: $200-up

84348   **Hedy Lamarr by Ned Scott (1938).** Portrait Photo (9.75" X 13"). Fine/Very Fine.
Est.: $200-up

84349   **Hedy Lamarr and William Powell in "The Heavenly Body" (MGM, 1943).** Portrait (10" X 13"). Very Fine.
Est.: $200-up

84350   **Mary Pickford by Melbourne Spurr (1920s).** Portrait Photo (9" X 11.75"). Fine/Very Fine.
Est.: $200-up

84351   **Colleen Moore by George Hurrell (MGM, 1930s).** Portrait Photo (10" X 13"). Very Fine+.
Est.: $200-up

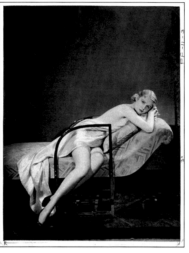

84352   **Gloria Stuart by Ray Jones (Universal, 1932).** Portrait Photo (11" X 14"). Fine+.
Est.: $200-up

84353   **Bette Davis by Elmer Fryer (Warner Brothers, 1930s).** Portrait Photo (8" X 10"). Very Fine.
Est.: $200-up

84354   **Bette Davis by Elmer Fryer (Warner Brothers, 1930s).** Portrait Photo (8" X 10"). Very Fine.
Est.: $200-up

84355   **Claudette Colbert by Otto Dyar (Paramount, 1932).** Portrait Photo (11" X 14"). Fine/Very Fine.
Est.: $200-up

84356   **Claudette Colbert in "I Met Him in Paris" by Eugene Robert Richee (Paramount, 1937).** Portrait Photo (10" X 13"). Very Fine-.
Est.: $200-up

84357   Claudette Colbert by Eugene Robert Richee (Paramount, 1937). Portrait (10" X 13.25"). Fine/Very Fine.
Est.: $200-up

84360   Lucille Ball in "Stage Door" by Ernest A. Bachrach (RKO, 1937). Photo (8" X 10"). Very Fine.
Est.: $200-up

84363   Stepin Fetchit (1930). Photo (8" X 10"). Very Fine-.
Est.: $200-up

84358   Lucille Ball (RKO, 1941). Portrait Photo (10.5" X 13"). Very Fine-.
Est.: $200-up

84361   Bessie Love in "They Learned About Women" by William Grimes (MGM, 1930). Photos (2) (11" X 14"). Fine/Very Fine.
Est.: $200-up

84364   Erich von Stroheim in "Sunset Boulevard" (Paramount, 1950). Photo (7.5" X 9.25"). Very Fine+.
Est.: $200-up

84359   Loretta Young by Elmer Fryer (Warner Brothers/First National, 1930s). Portrait Photo (11" X 14"). Very Fine.
Est.: $200-up

84362   Dale Evans (Republic, 1944). Portrait Photo (11" X 14"). Fine.
Est.: $200-up

84365   Van Johnson and Gloria DeHaven in "Scene of the Crime" (MGM, 1949). Photo (10" X 13"). Very Fine.
Est.: $200-up

84366   Frank Sinatra in "Till the Clouds Roll By" (MGM, 1946). Photo (10.25" X 13"). Very Fine.
Est.: $200-up

84367   Elvis Presley in "Love Me Tender" (20th Century Fox, 1956). Portrait Photos (2) (8" X 10"). Very Fine/Near Mint.
Est.: $200-up

84368   Elvis Presley (Paramount, 1957). Portrait Photo (8" X 10"). Fine/Very Fine.
Est.: $200-up

84369   Elvis Presley in "King Creole" (Paramount, 1958). Photo (8" X 10"). Very Fine.
Est.: $200-up

84370   Elvis Presley in "King Creole" (Paramount, 1958). Keybook Photos (5) (8" X 11"). Very Fine.
Est.: $200-up

84371   Ginger Rogers by George DeBarron (1930). Theater Portrait (11" X 14"). Fine/Very Fine.
Est.: $200-up

84372   Ginger Rogers by George DeBarron (1930). Theater Photo (11" X 14"). Fine/Very Fine.
Est.: $200-up

84373   Mickey Rooney and Judy Garland in "Babes on Broadway" by Clarence Sinclair Bull (MGM, 1941). Photo (10" X 13"). Very Fine-.
Est.: $200-up

84374   Tallulah Bankhead by George Maillard Kesslere (1930s). Portrait Photo (10.5" X 13.5"). Fine.
Est.: $200-up

84376   Lauren Bacall (Warner Brothers, 1940s). Portrait Photo (8" X 10"). Fine/Very Fine.
Est.: $200-up

84378   Cary Grant and Grace Kelly in "To Catch a Thief" (Paramount, 1955). Photo (8" X 10"). Very Fine-.
Est.: $200-up

84379   Grace Kelly in "To Catch a Thief" (Paramount, 1955). Photo (8" X 10"). Very Fine.
Est.: $200-up

84375   Mae West and Randolph Scott in "Go West Young Man" by Eugene Robert Richee (Paramount, 1936). Photo (10" X 13"). Very Fine-.
Est.: $200-up

84377   Mae West in "Every Day's a Holiday" by Eugene Robert Richee (Paramount, 1937). Photo (10" X 13"). Fine+.
Est.: $200-up

84380   Bela Lugosi and Anne Nagel (Universal, 1940). Photo (8" X 10"). Fine+.
Est.: $200-up

End of Auction

Heritage Auction Galleries Staff

Steve Ivy - Co-Chairman and CEO

Steve Ivy began collecting and studying rare coins as a youth, and as a teenager began advertising coins for sale in national publications in 1963. Seven years later, at the age of 20, he opened for business in downtown Dallas, and in 1976, incorporated as an auction company. Steve managed the business as well as serving as chief buyer, buying and selling hundreds of millions of dollars of coins during the 1970s and early 1980s. In early 1983, James Halperin became a full partner, and the name of the corporation was changed to Heritage Auctions. Steve's primary responsibilities now include management of the marketing and selling efforts of the company, the formation of corporate policy for long-term growth, and corporate relations with financial institutions. He remains intimately involved in all the various categories Heritage Auctions deals in today. Steve engages in daily discourse with industry leaders on all aspects of the fine art and collectibles business, and his views on market trends and developments are respected throughout the industry. He previously served on both the Board of Directors of the Professional Numismatists Guild (past president), and The Industry Council for Tangible Assets (past Chairman). Steve's keen appreciation of history is reflected in his active participation in other organizations, including past board positions on the Texas Historical Foundation and the Dallas Historical Society (where he also served as Exhibits Chairman). Steve is an avid collector of Texas books, manuscripts, and national currency, and he owns one of the largest and finest collections in private hands. He is also a past Board Chair of Dallas Challenge, and is currently the Finance Chair of the Phoenix House of Texas.

James Halperin - Co-Chairman

Born in Boston in 1952, Jim formed a part-time rare coin business at age 15 after discovering he had a knack (along with a nearly photographic memory) for coins. Jim scored a perfect 800 on his math SATs and received early acceptance to Harvard College, but after attending three semesters took a permanent leave of absence to pursue his full-time numismatic career. In 1975, Jim supervised the protocols for the first mainframe computer system in the numismatic business, which would catapult New England Rare Coin Galleries to the top of the industry in less than four years. In 1982, Jim's business merged with that of his friend and former archrival Steve Ivy. Their partnership has become Heritage Auctions, the third-largest auction house in the world. Jim is also a well-known futurist, an active collector of EC comics and early 20th-century American art (visit www.jhalpe.com), venture capital investor, philanthropist (he endows a multimillion-dollar health education foundation), and part-time novelist. His first fiction book, *The Truth Machine*, was published in 1996, became an international science fiction bestseller, and was optioned for movie development by Warner Brothers and Lions Gate. Jim's second novel, *The First Immortal*, was published in early 1998 and immediately optioned as a Hallmark Hall of Fame television miniseries.

Greg Rohan - President

At the age of eight, Greg Rohan started collecting coins as well as buying them for resale to his schoolmates. By 1971, at the age of 10, he was already buying and selling coins from a dealer's table at trade shows in his hometown of Seattle. His business grew rapidly, and by 1985 he had offices in both Seattle and Minneapolis. He joined Heritage in 1987 as Executive Vice-President. Today, as a partner and as President of Heritage, his responsibilities include overseeing the firm's private client group and working with top collectors in every field in which Heritage is active. Greg has been involved with many of the rarest items and most important collections handled by the firm, including the purchase and/or sale of the Ed Trompeter Collection (the world's largest numismatic purchase according to the Guinness Book of World Records). During his career, Greg has handled more than $1 billion of rare coins, collectibles and art. He has provided expert testimony for the United States Attorneys in San Francisco, Dallas, and Philadelphia, and for the Federal Trade Commission (FTC). He has worked with collectors, consignors, and their advisors regarding significant collections of books, manuscripts, comics, currency, jewelry, vintage movie posters, sports and entertainment memorabilia, decorative arts, and fine art. Greg is a past Chapter Chairman for North Texas of the Young Presidents' Organization (YPO), and is an active supporter of the arts. Greg co-authored "The Collectors Estate Handbook," winner of the NLG's Robert Friedberg Award for numismatic book of the year. He previously served on the seven-person Advisory Board to the Federal Reserve Bank of Dallas, in his second appointed term.

Paul Minshull - Chief Operating Officer

As Chief Operating Officer, Paul Minshull's managerial responsibilities include integrating sales, personnel, inventory, security and MIS for Heritage. His major accomplishments include overseeing the hardware migration from mainframe to PC, the software migration of all inventory and sales systems, and implementation of a major Internet presence. Heritage's successful employee-suggestion program has generated 200 or more ideas each month since 1995, and has helped increase employee productivity, expand business, and improve employee retention. Paul oversees the company's highly-regarded IT department, and has been one of the driving force behind Heritage's Web development, now a significant portion of Heritage's future plans. As the first auction house that combined traditional floor bidding with active Internet bidding, the totally interactive systems have catapulted Heritage to the top collectible and Fine Art website (Forbes Magazine's "Best of the Web"). Paul came to Heritage in 1984. Since 1994 Paul has been the Chief Operating Officer for all Heritage companies and affiliates.

Todd Imhof - Executive Vice President

Unlike most of his contemporaries, Todd Imhof did not start collecting in his teens. Shortly after graduating college, Todd declined offers from prestigious Wall Street banks to join a former classmate at a small rare coin firm in the Seattle area. In the mid-1980s, the rare coin industry was rapidly changing, with the advent of third-party grading and growing computer technologies. As a newcomer, Todd more easily embraced these new dynamics and quickly emerged as a highly respected dealer. In 1991, he co-founded Pinnacle Rarities, a firm specialized in servicing the savviest and most preeminent collectors in numismatics. At only 25, he was accepted into the PNG, and currently serves on its Consumer Protection Committee and its Legislation/Taxation Issues Committee. In 1992, he was invited to join the Board of Directors for the Industry Council for Tangible Assets, later serving as its Chairman (2002-2005). Since joining Heritage in 2006, Todd continues to advise most of Heritage's largest and most prominent clients.

Leo Frese - Managing Director, Beverly Hills

Leo has been involved in the business of collectibles and rare coins for four decades, starting as a professional numismatist in 1971. He has been with Heritage for more than 20 years, literally working his way up the Heritage ladder before becoming Director of Consignments. Leo has been actively involved in assisting clients sell nearly $500,000,000 of material at auction, and recently relocated to Los Angeles to head up Heritage Auction Galleries Beverly Hills, the West Coast branch of Heritage Auctions. Leo was recently accepted as a member of PNG, is a life member of the ANA, and holds membership in FUN, CSNS among other organizations.

Jim Stoutjesdyk - Vice President

Jim Stoutjesdyk was named Vice President of Heritage Rare Coin Galleries in 2004. He was named ANA's Outstanding Young Numismatist of the Year in 1987. A University of Michigan graduate, he was first employed by Superior Galleries, eventually becoming their Director of Collector Sales. Since joining Heritage in 1993, Jim has served in many capacities. Jim's duties now include buying and selling, pricing all new purchases, assisting with auction estimates and reserves, and overseeing the daily operations of the rare coin department.

Norma L. Gonzalez - VP of Auction Operations

Norma Gonzalez joined the U.S. Navy in August of 1993 and received her Bachelor's Degree in Resource Management. She joined Heritage in 1998 and was promoted to Vice President in 2003. She currently manages the operations departments, including Coins, Currency, World & Ancient Coins, Sportscards & Memorabilia, Comics, Movie Posters, Pop Culture and Political Memorabilia.

Debbie Rexing - VP - Marketing

Debbie Rexing joined the Heritage team in 2001 and her marketing credentials include degrees in Business Administration and Human Resources from The Ohio State University. Debbie has worked across many categories within the company leading to her comprehensive and integrative approach to the job. She guides all aspects of Heritage's print marketing strategies – advertisements, brochures, direct mail campaigns, coordination of print buying, catalog design and production, The Heritage Magazine, and media and press relations.

Ron Brackemyre - Vice President

Ron Brackemyre began his career at Heritage Auction Galleries in 1998 as the Manager of the Shipping Department, was promoted to Consignment Operations Manager for Numismatics in 2004 and in 2009 added oversight of the entire photography operation at Heritage, wherein his department coordinates all photography, scanning and photoshopping. He is also responsible for the security of all of Heritage's coin and currency consignments, both at the Dallas world headquarters and at shows, as well as cataloging of coins for upcoming auctions, coordination of auction planning, security and transportation logistics, lot-view, auction prep and oversight for the entire shipping department.

Marti Korver - Manager - Credit/Collections

Marti Korver was recruited out of the banking profession by Jim Ruddy, and she worked with Paul Rynearson, Karl Stephens, and Judy Cahn on ancients and world coins at Bowers & Ruddy Galleries, in Hollywood, CA. She migrated into the coin auction business, and represented bidders as agent at B&R auctions for 10 years. She also worked as a research assistant for Q. David Bowers for several years.

Mark Prendergast - Director, Trusts & Estates

Mark Prendergast earned his degree in Art History from Vanderbilt University and began his career in the arts working with a national dealer in private sales of 20th Century American Art. Joining Christie's in 1998 and advancing during a 10 year tenure to the position of Vice President, he was instrumental in bringing to market many important and prominent works of art, collections and estates. Having established a Houston office for Heritage, he serves as Director of Business Development, Trusts & Estates, providing assistance to fiduciary professionals and private clients with appraisals, collection assessments and auction consignments in all areas of art and collectibles.

Jared Green - Vice President of Corporate & Institutional Client Development

Jared Green primarily works on developing institutional clients, including corporations and non-profits, and championing new ventures for Heritage's collectibles and art businesses. He maintains relationships with a number of Fortune 500 companies that have collections of rarities and fine art. Prior to joining Heritage, Mr. Green worked for several years as a business analyst with Cap Gemini-Ernst & Young in its Strategic Advisory Services group. He is a native of North Carolina and graduated with honors from Duke University with a degree in Public Policy. He completed his MBA at Emory University, where he focused on Strategy and Entrepreneurship.

Movie Poster Department

Grey Smith – Director of Vintage Movie Posters
Grey Smith studied film and received a degree in Communications from the University of Texas at Austin, after which he pursued a career in the motion picture industry, traveling the globe as a Set Decorator and Prop Master from the late 1970s through the late 1990s. As an Art Director, he worked on more than 35 feature films, with many famous directors and always searched for, collected and sold movie posters and studied the market. In 2001 he began as Heritage's first Movie Poster Expert and now heads the world's #1 Vintage Poster Auction venue.

Bruce Carteron – Auction Coordinator
Bruce Carteron opened the first movie poster shop in Denver, Colorado, more than 29 years ago, and began attending film conventions to expand his business. He eventually started a mail order catalog and Internet business devoted to posters, which he ran until 2004. Bruce joined Heritage in early 2006, where he helps coordinate the Signature and Weekly Auctions.

Cataloged by: Grey Smith, Bruce Carteron, Donna Walker, Isaiah Evans, Ed Neal, Jeff Smith

Edited by: Grey Smith and Bruce Carteron

Operations Support by: Joel Lopez

Catalog and Internet Imaging by: Kristin Bazan, Brenna Wilson, Linsey Johnson, Greg Kopriva, Josh Ray, Colleen McInerney

Production and Design by: Michael Puttonen, Mark Masat, Mary Hermann, Debbie Rexing, Carl Watson

Terms and Conditions of Auction

Auctioneer and Auction:

1. This Auction is presented by Heritage Auction Galleries, a d/b/a/ of Heritage Auctions, Inc., or its affiliates Heritage Numismatic Auctions, Inc., or Heritage Vintage Sports Auctions, Inc., or Currency Auctions of America, Inc., as identified with the applicable licensing information on the title page of the catalog or on the HA.com Internet site (the "Auctioneer"). The Auction is conducted under these Terms and Conditions of Auction and applicable state and local law. Announcements and corrections from the podium and those made through the Terms and Conditions of Auctions appearing on the Internet at HA.com supersede those in the printed catalog.

Buyer's Premium:

2. On bids placed through Auctioneer, a Buyer's Premium of fifteen percent (15%) will be added to the successful hammer price bid on lots in Coin, Currency, and Philatelic auctions or nineteen and one-half percent (19.5%) on lots in all other auctions. There is a minimum Buyer's Premium of $14.00 per lot. In Gallery Auctions (sealed bid auctions of mostly bulk numismatic material), the Buyer's Premium is 19.5%.

Auction Venues:

3. The following Auctions are conducted solely on the Internet: Heritage Weekly Internet Auctions (Coin, Currency, Comics, and Vintage Movie Poster); Heritage Monthly Internet Auctions (Sports, and Stamps). Signature* Auctions and Grand Format Auctions accept bids from the Internet, telephone, fax, or mail first, followed by a floor bidding session; Heritage Live and real-time telephone bidding are available to registered clients during these auctions.

Bidders:

4. Any person participating or registering for the Auction agrees to be bound by and accepts these Terms and Conditions of Auction ("Bidder(s)").

5. All Bidders must meet Auctioneer's qualifications to bid. Any Bidder who is not a client in good standing of the Auctioneer may be disqualified at Auctioneer's sole option and will not be awarded lots. Such determination may be made by Auctioneer in its sole and unlimited discretion, at any time prior to, during, or even after the close of the Auction. Auctioneer reserves the right to exclude any person from the auction.

6. If an entity places a bid, then the person executing the bid on behalf of the entity agrees to personally guarantee payment for any successful bid.

Credit:

7. Bidders who have not established credit with the Auctioneer must either furnish satisfactory credit information (including two collectibles-related business references) well in advance of the Auction or supply valid credit card information. Bids placed through our Interactive Internet program will only be accepted from pre-registered Bidders; Bidders who are not members of HA.com or affiliates should pre-register at least 48 hours before the start of the first session (exclusive of holidays or weekends) to allow adequate time to contact references. Credit may be granted at the discretion of Auctioneer. Additionally Bidders who have not previously established credit or who wish to bid in excess of their established credit history may be required to provide their social security number or the last four digits thereof to us so a credit check may be performed prior to Auctioneer's acceptance of a bid.

Bidding Options:

8. Bids in Signature**.** Auctions or Grand Format Auctions may be placed as set forth in the printed catalog section entitled "Choose your bidding method." For auctions held solely on the Internet, see the alternatives on HA.com. Review at HA.com/common/howtobid.php.

9. Presentment of Bids: Non-Internet bids (including but not limited to podium, fax, phone and mail bids) are treated similar to floor bids in that they must be on-increment or at a half increment (called a cut bid). Any podium, fax, phone, or mail bids that do not conform to a full or half increment will be rounded up or down to the nearest full or half increment and this revised amount will be considered your high bid.

10. Auctioneer's Execution of Certain Bids. Auctioneer cannot be responsible for your errors in bidding, so carefully check that every bid is entered correctly. When identical mail or FAX bids are submitted, preference is given to the first received. To ensure the greatest accuracy, your written bids should be entered on the standard printed bid sheet and be received at Auctioneer's place of business at least two business days before the Auction start. Auctioneer is not responsible for executing mail bids or FAX bids received on or after the day the first lot is sold, nor Internet bids submitted after the published closing time; nor is Auctioneer responsible for proper execution of bids submitted by telephone, mail, FAX, e-mail, Internet, or in person once the Auction begins. Internet bids may not be withdrawn until your written request is received and acknowledged by Auctioneer (FAX: 214-4438425); such requests must state the reason, and may constitute grounds for withdrawal of bidding privileges. Lots won by mail Bidders will not be delivered at the Auction unless prearranged.

11. Caveat as to Bid Increments. Bid increments (over the current bid level) determine the lowest amount you may bid on a particular lot. Bids greater than one increment over the current bid can be any whole dollar amount. It is possible under several circumstances for winning bids to be between increments, sometimes only $1 above the previous increment. Please see: "How can I lose by less than an increment?" on our website. Bids will be accepted in whole dollar amounts only. No "buy" or "unlimited" bids will be accepted.

The following chart governs current bidding increments.

Current Bid	Bid Increment	Current Bid	Bid Increment
<$10	$1	$20,000 - $29,999	$2,000
$10 - $29	$2	$30,000 - $49,999	$2,500
$30 - $49	$3	$50,000 - $99,999	$5,000
$50 - $99	$5	$100,000 - $199,999	$10,000
$100 - $199	$10	$200,000 - $299,999	$20,000
$200 - $299	$20	$300,000 - $499,999	$25,000
$300 - $499	$25	$500,000 - $999,999	$50,000
$500 - $999	$50	$1,000,000 - $1,999,999	$100,000
$1,000 - $1,999	$100	$2,000,000 - $2,999,999	$200,000
$2,000 - $2,999	$200	$3,000,000 - $4,999,999	$250,000
$3,000 - $4,999	$250	$5,000,000 - $9,999,999	$500,000
$5,000 - $9,999	$500	>$10,000,000	$1,000,000
$10,000 - $19,999	$1,000		

12. If Auctioneer calls for a full increment, a bidder may request Auctioneer to accept a bid at half of the increment ("Cut Bid") only once per lot. After offering a Cut Bid, bidders may continue to participate only at full increments. Off-increment bids may be accepted by the Auctioneer at Signature* Auctions and Grand Format Auctions. If the Auctioneer solicits bids other than the expected increment, these bids will not be considered Cut Bids.

Conducting the Auction:

13. Notice of the consignor's liberty to place bids on his lots in the Auction is hereby made in accordance with Article 2 of the Texas Business and Commercial Code. A "Minimum Bid" is an amount below which the lot will not sell. THE CONSIGNOR OF PROPERTY MAY PLACE WRITTEN "Minimum Bids" ON HIS LOTS IN ADVANCE OF THE AUCTION; ON SUCH LOTS, IF THE HAMMER PRICE DOES NOT MEET THE "Minimum Bid", THE CONSIGNOR MAY PAY A REDUCED COMMISSION ON THOSE LOTS. "Minimum Bids" are generally posted online several days prior to the Auction closing. For any successful bid placed by a consignor on his Property on the Auction floor, or by any means during the live session, or after the "Minimum Bid" for an Auction have been posted, we will require the consignor to pay full Buyer's Premium and Seller's Commissions on such lot.

14. The highest qualified Bidder recognized by the Auctioneer shall be the buyer. In the event of a tie bid, the earliest bid received or recognized wins. In the event of any dispute between any Bidders at an auction, Auctioneer may at his sole discretion reoffer the lot. Auctioneer's decision and declaration of the winning Bidder shall be final and binding upon all Bidders. Bids properly offered, whether by floor Bidder or other means of bidding, may on occasion be missed or go unrecognized; in such cases, the Auctioneer may declare the recognized bid accepted as the winning bid, regardless of whether a competing bid may have been higher.

15. Auctioneer reserves the right to refuse to honor any bid or to limit the amount of any bid, in its sole discretion. A bid is considered not made in "Good Faith" when made by an insolvent or irresponsible person, a person under the age of eighteen, or is not supported by satisfactory credit, collectibles references, or otherwise. Regardless of the disclosure of his identity, any bid by a consignor or his agent on a lot consigned by him is deemed to be made in "Good Faith." Any person apparently appearing on the OFAC list is not eligible to bid.

16. Nominal Bids. The Auctioneer in its sole discretion may reject nominal bids, small opening bids, or very nominal advances. If a lot bearing estimates fails to open for 40–60% of the low estimate, the Auctioneer may pass the item or may place a protective bid on behalf of the consignor.

17. Lots bearing bidding estimates shall open at Auctioneer's discretion (approximately 50%-60% of the low estimate). In the event that no bid meets or exceeds that opening amount, the lot shall pass as unsold.

18. All items are to be purchased per lot as numerically indicated and no lots will be broken. Auctioneer reserves the right to withdraw, prior to the close, any lots from the Auction.

19. Auctioneer reserves the right to rescind the sale in the event of nonpayment, breach of a warranty, disputed ownership, auctioneer's clerical error or omission in exercising bids and reserves, or for any other reason and in Auctioneer's sole discretion. In cases of nonpayment, Auctioneer's election to void a sale does not relieve the Bidder from their obligation to pay Auctioneer its fees (seller's and buyer's premium) and any other damages or expenses pertaining to the lot.

20. Auctioneer occasionally experiences Internet and/or Server service outages, and Auctioneer periodically schedules system downtime for maintenance and other purposes, during which Bidders cannot participate or place bids. If such outages occur, we may at our discretion extend bidding for the Auction. Bidders unable to place their Bids through the Internet are directed to contact Client Services at 1-800-872-6467.

21. The Auctioneer, its affiliates, or their employees consign items to be sold in the Auction, and may bid on those lots or any other lots. Auctioneer or affiliates expressly reserve the right to modify any such bids at any time prior to the hammer based upon data made known to the Auctioneer or its affiliates. The Auctioneer may extend advances, guarantees, or loans to certain consignors.

22. The Auctioneer has the right to sell certain unsold items after the close of the Auction. Such lots shall be considered sold during the Auction and all these Terms and Conditions shall apply to such sales including but not limited to the Buyer's Premium, return rights, and disclaimers.

Payment:

23. All sales are strictly for cash in United States dollars (including U.S. currency, bank wire, cashier checks, travelers checks, eChecks, and bank money orders, all subject to reporting requirements). All are subject to clearing and funds being received In Auctioneer's account before delivery of the purchases. Auctioneer reserves the right to determine if a check constitutes "good funds" when drawn on a U.S. bank for ten days, and thirty days when drawn on an international bank. Credit Card (Visa or Master Card only) and PayPal payments may be accepted up to $10,000 from non-dealers at the sole discretion of the Auctioneer, subject to the following limitations: a) sales are only to the cardholder, b) purchases are shipped to the cardholder's registered and verified address, c) Auctioneer may pre-approve the cardholder's credit line, d) a credit card transaction may not be used in conjunction with any other financing or extended terms offered by the Auctioneer, and must transact immediately upon invoice presentation, e) rights of return are governed by these Terms and Conditions, which supersede those conditions promulgated by the card issuer, f) floor Bidders must present their card.

24. Payment is due upon closing of the Auction session, or upon presentment of an invoice. Auctioneer reserves the right to void an invoice if payment in full is not received within 7 days after the close of the Auction. In cases of nonpayment, Auctioneer's election to void a sale does not relieve the Bidder from their obligation to pay Auctioneer its fees (seller's and buyer's premium) on the lot and any other damages pertaining to the lot.

25. Lots delivered to you, or your representative in the States of Texas, California, **New York**, or other states where the Auction may be held, are subject to all applicable state and local taxes, unless appropriate permits are on file with Auctioneer. Bidder agrees to pay Auctioneer the actual amount of tax due in the event that sales tax is not properly collected due to: 1) an expired, inaccurate, inappropriate tax certificate or declaration, 2) an incorrect interpretation of the applicable statute, 3) or any other reason. The appropriate form or certificate must be on file at and verified by Auctioneer five days before Auction or tax must be paid; only if such form or certificate is received by Auctioneer within 4 days after the Auction can a refund of tax paid be made. Lots from different Auctions may not be aggregated for sales tax purposes.

26. In the event that a Bidder's payment is dishonored upon presentment(s), Bidder shall pay the maximum statutory processing fee set by applicable state law. If you attempt to pay via eCheck and your financial institution denies this transfer from your bank account, or the payment cannot be completed using the selected funding source, you agree to complete payment using your credit card on file.

27. If any Auction invoice submitted by Auctioneer is not paid in full when due, the unpaid balance will bear interest at the highest rate permitted by law from the date of invoice until paid. Any invoice not paid when due will bear a three percent (3%) late fee on the invoice amount or three percent (3%) of any installment that is past due. If the Auctioneer refers any invoice to an attorney for collection, the buyer agrees to pay attorney's fees, court costs, and other collection costs incurred by Auctioneer. If Auctioneer assigns collection to its in-house legal staff, such attorney's time expended on the matter shall be compensated at a rate comparable to the hourly rate of independent attorneys.

28. In the event a successful Bidder fails to pay any amounts due, Auctioneer reserves the right to sell the lot(s) securing the invoice to any underbidders in the Auction that the lot(s) appeared, or at subsequent private or public sale, or relist the lot(s) in a future auction conducted by Auctioneer. A defaulting Bidder agrees to pay for the reasonable costs of resale (including a 10% seller's commission, if consigned to an auction conducted by Auctioneer). The defaulting Bidder is liable to pay any difference between his total original invoice for the lot(s), plus any applicable interest, and the net proceeds for the lot(s) if sold at private sale or the subsequent hammer price of the lot(s) less the 10% seller's commissions, if sold at an Auctioneer's auction.

29. Auctioneer reserves the right to require payment in full in good funds before delivery of the merchandise.
30. Auctioneer shall have a lien against the merchandise purchased by the buyer to secure payment of the Auction invoice. Auctioneer is further granted a lien and the right to retain possession of any other property of the buyer then held by the Auctioneer or its affiliates to secure payment of any Auction invoice or any other amounts due the Auctioneer or affiliates from the buyer. With respect to these lien rights, Auctioneer shall have all the rights of a secured creditor under Article 9 of the Texas Uniform Commercial Code, including but not limited to the right of sale. In addition, with respect to payment of the Auction invoice(s), the buyer waives any and all rights of offset he might otherwise have against the Auctioneer and the consignor of the merchandise included on the invoice. If a Bidder owes Auctioneer or its affiliates on any account, Auctioneer and its affiliates shall have the right to offset such unpaid account by any credit balance due Bidder, and it may secure by possessory lien any unpaid amount by any of the Bidder's property in their possession.
31. Title shall not pass to the successful Bidder until all invoices are paid in full. It is the responsibility of the buyer to provide adequate insurance coverage for the items once they have been delivered to a common carrier or third-party shipper.

Delivery; Shipping; and Handling Charges:

32. Buyer is liable for shipping and handling. Please refer to Auctioneer's website www.HA.com/common/shipping.php for the latest charges or call Auctioneer. Auctioneer is unable to combine purchases from other auctions or affiliates into one package for shipping purposes. Lots won will be shipped in a commercially reasonable time after payment in good funds for the merchandise and the shipping fees is received or credit extended, except when third-party shipment occurs.
33. Successful international Bidders shall provide written shipping instructions, including specified customs declarations, to the Auctioneer for any lots to be delivered outside of the United States. NOTE: Declaration value shall be the item'(s) hammer price together with its buyer's premium and Auctioneer shall use the correct harmonized code for the lot. Domestic Buyers on lots designated for third-party shipment must designate the common carrier, accept risk of loss, and prepay shipping costs.
34. All shipping charges will be borne by the successful Bidder. Any risk of loss during shipment will be borne by the buyer following Auctioneer's delivery to the designated common carrier or third-party shipper, regardless of domestic or foreign shipment.
35. Due to the nature of some items sold, it shall be the responsibility for the successful bidder to arrange pick-up and shipping through third-parties; as to such items Auctioneer shall have no liability. Failure to pick-up or arrange shipping in a timely fashion (within ten days) shall subject Lots to storage and moving charges, including a $100 administration fee plus $10 daily storage for larger items and $5.00 daily for smaller items (storage fee per item) after 35 days. In the event the Lot is not removed within ninety days, the Lot may be offered for sale to recover any past due storage or moving fees, including a 10% Seller's Commission.
36. The laws of various countries regulate the import or export of certain plant and animal properties, including (but not limited to) items made of (or including) ivory, whalebone, turtleshell, coral, crocodile, or other wildlife. Transport of such lots may require special licenses for export, import, or both. Bidder is responsible for: 1) obtaining all information on such restricted items for both export and import; 2) obtaining all such licenses and/or permits. Delay or failure to obtain any such license or permit does not relieve the buyer of timely compliance with standard payment terms. For further information, please contact Ron Brackemyre at 800-872-6467 ext. 1312.
37. Any request for shipping verification for undelivered packages must be made within 30 days of shipment by Auctioneer.

Cataloging, Warranties and Disclaimers:

38. NO WARRANTY, WHETHER EXPRESSED OR IMPLIED, IS MADE WITH RESPECT TO ANY DESCRIPTION CONTAINED IN THIS AUCTION OR ANY SECOND OPINE. Any description of the items or second opine contained in this Auction is for the sole purpose of identifying the items for those Bidders who do not have the opportunity to view the lots prior to bidding, and no description of items has been made part of the basis of the bargain or has created any express warranty that the goods would conform to any description made by Auctioneer. Color variations can be expected in any electronic or printed imaging, and are not grounds for the return of any lot. NOTE: Auctioneer, in specified auction venues, for example, Fine Art, may have express written warranties and you are referred to those specific terms and conditions. .
39. Auctioneer is selling only such right or title to the items being sold as Auctioneer may have by virtue of consignment agreements on the date of auction and disclaims any warranty of title to the Property. Auctioneer disclaims any warranty of merchantability or fitness for any particular purposes. All images, descriptions, sales data, and archival records are the exclusive property of Auctioneer, and may be used by Auctioneer for advertising, promotion, archival records, and any other uses deemed appropriate.
40. Translations of foreign language documents may be provided as a convenience to interested parties. Auctioneer makes no representation as to the accuracy of those translations and will not be held responsible for errors in bidding arising from inaccuracies in translation.
41. Auctioneer disclaims all liability for damages, consequential or otherwise, arising out of or in connection with the sale of any Property by Auctioneer to Bidder. No third party may rely on any benefit of these Terms and Conditions and any rights, if any, established hereunder are personal to the Bidder and may not be assigned. Any statement made by the Auctioneer is an opinion and does not constitute a warranty or representation. No employee of Auctioneer may alter these Terms and Conditions, and, unless signed by a principal of Auctioneer, any such alteration is null and void.
42. Auctioneer shall not be liable for breakage of glass or damage to frames (patent or latent); such defects, in any event, shall not be a basis for any claim for return or reduction in purchase price.

Release:

43. In consideration of participation in the Auction and the placing of a bid, Bidder expressly releases Auctioneer, its officers, directors and employees, its affiliates, and its outside experts that provide second opines, from any and all claims, cause of action, chose of action, whether at law or equity or any arbitration or mediation rights existing under the rules of any professional society or affiliation based upon the assigned description, or a derivative theory, breach of warranty express or implied, representation or other matter set forth within these Terms and Conditions of Auction or otherwise. In the event of a claim, Bidder agrees that such rights and privileges conferred therein are strictly construed as specifically declared herein; e.g., authenticity, typographical error, etc. and are the exclusive remedy. Bidder, by non-compliance to these express terms of a granted remedy, shall waive any claim against Auctioneer.
44. Notice: Some Property sold by Auctioneer are inherently dangerous e.g. firearms, cannons, and small items that may be swallowed or ingested or may have latent defects all of which may cause harm to a person. Purchaser accepts all risk of loss or damage from its purchase of these items and Auctioneer disclaims any liability whether under contract or tort for damages and losses, direct or inconsequential, and expressly disclaims any warranty as to safety or usage of any lot sold.

Dispute Resolution and Arbitration Provision:

45. By placing a bid or otherwise participating in the auction, Bidder accepts these Terms and Conditions of Auction, and specifically agrees to the dispute resolution provided herein. Consumer disputes shall be resolved through court litigation which has an exclusive Dallas, Texas venue clause and jury waiver. Non-consumer dispute shall be determined in binding arbitration which arbitration replaces the right to go to court, including the right to a jury trial.
46. Auctioneer in no event shall be responsible for consequential damages, incidental damages, compensatory damages, or any other damages arising or claimed to be arising from the auction of any lot. In the event that Auctioneer cannot deliver the lot or subsequently it is established that the lot lacks title, or other transfer or condition issue is claimed, In such cases the sole remedy shall be limited to rescission of sale and refund of the amount paid by Bidder; in no case shall Auctioneer's maximum liability exceed the high bid on that lot, which bid shall be deemed for all purposes the value of the lot. After one year has elapsed, Auctioneer's maximum liability shall be limited to any commissions and fees Auctioneer earned on that lot.
47. In the event of an attribution error, Auctioneer may at its sole discretion, correct the error on the Internet, or, if discovered at a later date, to refund the buyer's purchase price without further obligation.
48. Dispute Resolution for Consumers and Non-Consumers: Any claim, dispute, or controversy in connection with, relating to and /or arising out of the Auction, participation in the Auction. Award of lots, damages of claims to lots, descriptions, condition reports, provenance, estimates, return and warranty rights, any interpretation of these Terms and Conditions, any alleged verbal modification of these Terms and Conditions and/or any purported settlement whether asserted in contract, tort, under Federal or State statute or regulation shall or any other matter: a) if presented by a consumer, be exclusively heard by, and the parties consent to, exclusive in personam jurisdiction in the State District Courts of Dallas County, Texas. THE PARTIES EXPRESSLY WAIVE ANY RIGHT TO TRIAL BY JURY. Any appeals shall be solely pursued in the appellate courts of the State of Texas; or b) for any claimant other than a consumer, the claim shall be presented in confidential binding arbitration before a single arbitrator, that the parties may agree upon, selected from the JAMS list of Texas arbitrators. The case is not to be administrated by JAMS; however, if the parties cannot agree on an arbitrator, then JAMS shall appoint the arbitrator and it shall be conducted under JAMS rules. The locale shall be Dallas Texas. The arbitrator's award may be enforced in any court of competent jurisdiction. Any party on any claim involving the purchase or sale of numismatic or related items may elect arbitration through binding PNG arbitration. Any claim must be brought within one (1) year of the alleged breach, default or misrepresentation or the claim is waived. This agreement and any claims shall be determined and construed under Texas law. The prevailing party (party that is awarded substantial and material relief on its claim or defense) may be awarded its reasonable attorneys' fees and costs.
49. No claims of any kind can be considered after the settlements have been made with the consignors. Any dispute after the settlement date is strictly between the Bidder and consignor without involvement or responsibility of the Auctioneer.
50. In consideration of their participation in or application for the Auction, a person or entity (whether the successful Bidder, a Bidder, a purchaser and/or other Auction participant or registrant) agrees that all disputes in any way relating to, arising under, connected with, or incidental to these Terms and Conditions and purchases, or default in payment thereof, shall be arbitrated pursuant to the arbitration provision. In the event that any matter including actions to compel arbitration, construe the agreement, actions in aid or arbitration or otherwise needs to be litigated, such litigation shall be exclusively in the Courts of the State of Texas, in Dallas County, Texas, and if necessary the corresponding appellate courts. For such actions, the successful Bidder, purchaser, or Auction participant also expressly submits himself to the personal jurisdiction of the State of Texas.
51. These Terms & Conditions provide specific remedies for occurrences in the auction and delivery process. Where such remedies are afforded, they shall be interpreted strictly. Bidder agrees that any claim shall utilize such remedies; Bidder making a claim in excess of those remedies provided in these Terms and Conditions agrees that in no case whatsoever shall Auctioneer's maximum liability exceed the high bid on that lot, which bid shall be deemed for all purposes the value of the lot.

Miscellaneous:

52. Agreements between Bidders and consignors to effectuate a non-sale of an item at Auction, inhibit bidding on a consigned item to enter into a private sale agreement for said item, or to utilize the Auctioneer's Auction to obtain sales for non-selling consigned items subsequent to the Auction, are strictly prohibited. If a subsequent sale of a previously consigned item occurs in violation of this provision, Auctioneer reserves the right to charge Bidder the applicable Buyer's Premium and consignor a Seller's Commission as determined for each auction venue and by the terms of the seller's agreement.
53. Acceptance of these Terms and Conditions qualifies Bidder as a client who has consented to be contacted by Heritage in the future. In conformity with "do-not-call" regulations promulgated by the Federal or State regulatory agencies, participation by the Bidder is affirmative consent to being contacted at the phone number shown in his application and this consent shall remain in effect until it is revoked in writing. Heritage may from time to time contact Bidder concerning sale, purchase, and auction opportunities available through Heritage and its affiliates and subsidiaries.
54. Rules of Construction: Auctioneer presents properties in a number of collectible fields, and as such, specific venues have promulgated supplemental Terms and Conditions. Nothing herein shall be construed to waive the general Terms and Conditions of Auction by these additional rules and shall be construed to give force and effect to the rules in their entirety.

State Notices:

Notice as to an Auction in California. Auctioneer has in compliance with Title 2.95 of the California Civil Code as amended October 11, 1993 Sec. 1812.600, posted with the California Secretary of State its bonds for it and its employees, and the auction is being conducted in compliance with Sec. 2338 of the Commercial Code and Sec. 535 of the Penal Code.

Notice as to an Auction in New York City. These Terms and Conditions are designed to conform to the applicable sections of the New York City Department of Consumer Affairs Rules and Regulations as Amended. This is a Public Auction Sale conducted by Auctioneer. The New York City licensed Auctioneer is Samuel W. Foose, No.0952360, who will conduct the Auction on behalf of Heritage Auctions, Inc. ("Auctioneer"). All lots are subject to: the consignor's right to bid thereon in accord with these Terms and Conditions of Auction, consignor's option to receive advances on their consignments, and Auctioneer, in its sole discretion, may offer limited extended financing to registered bidders, in accord with Auctioneer's internal credit standards. A registered bidder may inquire whether a lot is subject to an advance or reserve. Auctioneer has made advances to various consignors in this sale.

Notice as to an Auction in Texas. In compliance with TDLR rule 67.100(c)(1), notice is hereby provided that this auction is covered by a Recovery Fund administered by the Texas Department of Licensing and Regulation, P.O. Box 12157, Austin, Texas 78711 (512) 463-6599. Any complaints may be directed to the same address.

Notice as to an Auction in Ohio: Auction firm and Auctioneer are licensed by the Dept. of Agriculture, and either the licensee is bonded in favor of the state or an aggrieved person may initiate a claim against the auction recovery fund created in Section 4707.25 of the Revised Code as a result of the licensee's actions, whichever is applicable.

Additional Terms & Conditions:
MEMORABILIA & HISTORICAL AUCTIONS

MEMORABILIA & HISTORICAL TERM A: Signature. and Grand Format Auctions of Autographs, Sports Collectibles, Music, Entertainment, Political, Americana, Vintage Movie Posters and Pop Culture memorabilia are not on approval. When the lot is accompanied by a Certificate of Authenticity (or its equivalent) from an third-party authentication provider, buyer has no right of return. On lots not accompanied by third-party authentication or under extremely limited circumstances not including authenticity (e.g. gross cataloging error), a purchaser who did not bid from the floor may request Auctioneer to evaluate voiding a sale; such request must be made in writing detailing the alleged gross error, and submission of the lot to Auctioneer must be pre-approved by Auctioneer. A Bidder must notify the appropriate department head (check the inside front cover of the catalog or our website for a listing of department heads) in writing of the Bidder's request within three (3) days of the non-floor bidder's receipt of the lot. Any lot that is to be evaluated for return must be received in our offices within 35 days after Auction. AFTER THAT 35 DAY PERIOD, NO LOT MAY BE RETURNED FOR ANY REASONS. Lots returned must be in the same condition as when sold and must include any Certificate of Authenticity. No lots purchased by floor bidders (including those bidders acting as agents for others) may be returned. Late remittance for purchases may be considered just cause to revoke all return privileges.

MEMORABILIA & HISTORICAL TERM B: When a memorabilia lot is accompanied by a Certificate of Authenticity (or its equivalent) from an independent third-party authentication provider, Auctioneer does not warrant authenticity of that lot. Bidder shall solely rely upon warranties of the authentication provider issuing the Certificate or opinion. For information as to such authentication providers' warranties the bidder is directed to: SCD Authentic, 4034 West National Ave., Milwaukee, WI 53215 (800) 345-3168; JO Sports, Inc., P.O. Box 607 Brookhaven, NY 11719 (631) 286-0970; PSA/DNA; 130 Brookshire Lane, Orwigsburg, Pa. 17961; Mike Gutierrez Autographs, 8150 Raintree Drive Suite A, Scottsdale, AZ. 85260; or as otherwise noted on the Certificate.

MEMORABILIA & HISTORICAL TERM C: As authenticity and provenance are not warranted, if a Bidder intends to challenge, authenticity or provenance of a lot he must notify Auctioneer in writing within thirty-five (35) days of the Auction's conclusion. Any claim as to provenance or authenticity must be first transmitted to Auctioneer by credible and definitive evidence or the opine of a qualified third party expert and there is no assurance after such presentment that Auctioneer will validate the claim. Authentication is not an exact science and contrary opinions may not be recognized by Auctioneer. Even if Auctioneer agrees with the contrary opinion of such authentication and validates the claim, Auctioneer's liability for reimbursement for any opine by Bidder's expert shall not exceed $500. Acceptance of a claim under this provision shall be limited to rescission of the sale and refund of purchase price; in no case shall Auctioneer's maximum liability exceed the high bid on that lot, which bid shall be deemed for all purposes the value of the lot. While every effort is made to determine provenance and authenticity, it is the responsibility of the Bidder to arrive at their own conclusion prior to bidding.

MEMORABILIA & HISTORICAL TERM D: In the event Auctioneer cannot deliver the lot or subsequently it is established that the lot lacks title, or other transfer or condition issue is claimed, Auctioneer's liability shall be limited to rescission of sale and refund of purchase price; in no case shall Auctioneer's maximum liability exceed the high bid on that lot, which bid shall be deemed for all purposes the value of the lot. After one year has elapsed from the close of the Auction, Auctioneer's maximum liability shall be limited to any commissions and fees Auctioneer earned on that lot.

MEMORABILIA & HISTORICAL TERM E: On the fall of Auctioneer's hammer, buyer assumes full risk and responsibility for lot, including shipment by common carrier, and must provide their own insurance coverage for shipments.

MEMORABILIA & HISTORICAL TERM F: Auctioneer complies with all Federal and State rules and regulations relating to the purchasing, registration and shipping of firearms. A purchaser is required to provide appropriate documents and the payment of associated fees, if any. Purchaser is responsible for providing a shipping address that is suitable for the receipt of a firearm.

MEMORABILIA AND HISTORICAL TERM G -SCREEN SHOT. Screen shots included in the catalog or on the Heritage Internet are provided for reference only. Important Notice: Many identical versions of props and costumes are created for film and television productions in the normal course of a production. Heritage does not warrant or represent that the screen shots referenced are exact images of the offered item (unless specifically noted in the written description). Use of a screen shot does not constitute a warranty or representation of authenticity or provenance. There is not a right of return or refund based upon a claim arising out of or pertaining to any reference to a screen shot.

MEMORABILIA AND HISTORICAL TERM H-Special Limited Warranty of Costumes in July Sale: Items from The Hollywood Studio Collection. Provenance, authenticity, and item descriptions are warranted exclusively by The Hollywood Studio Collection. Any claim as to misattribution shall be made exclusively against The Hollywood Studio Collection.

WIRING INSTRUCTIONS:

BANK INFORMATION:
Wells Fargo Bank
420 Montgomery Street
San Francisco, CA 94104-1207

ACCOUNT NAME: Heritage Auction Galleries

ABA NUMBER: 121000248

ACCOUNT NUMBER: 4121930028

SWIFT CODE: WFBIUS6S

Your five most effective bidding techniques:

❶ Interactive Internet™ Proxy Bidding
(leave your maximum Bid at HA.com before the auction starts)

Heritage's exclusive Interactive Internet™ system is fun and easy! Before you start, you must register online at HA.com and obtain your Username and Password.

1. Login to the HA.com website, using your Username and Password.

2. Chose the specialty you're interested in at the top of the homepage (i.e. coins, currency, comics, movie posters, fine art, etc.).

3. Search or browse for the lots that interest you. Every auction has search features and a 'drop-down' menu list.

4. Select a lot by clicking on the link or the photo icon. Read the description, and view the full-color photography. Note that clicking on the image will enlarge the photo with amazing detail.

5. View the current opening bid. Below the lot description, note the historic pricing information to help you establish price levels. Clicking on a link will take you directly to our Permanent Auction Archives for more information and images.

6. If the current price is within your range, Bid! At the top of the lot page is a box containing the Current Bid and an entry box for your "Secret Maximum Bid" – the maximum amount you are willing to pay for the item before the Buyer's Premium is added. Click the button marked "Place Bid" (if you are not logged in, a login box will open first so you can enter your username (or e-mail address) and password.

7. After you are satisfied that all the information is correct, confirm your "Secret Maximum Bid" by clicking on the "Confirm Absentee Bid" button. You will receive immediate notification letting you know if you are now the top bidder, or if another bidder had previously bid higher than your amount. If you bid your maximum amount and someone has already bid higher, you will immediately know so you can concentrate on other lots.

8. Before the auction, if another bidder surpasses your "Secret Maximum Bid", you will be notified automatically by e-mail containing a link to review the lot and possibly bid higher.

9. Interactive Internet™ bidding closes at 10 P.M. Central Time the night before the session is offered in a floor event. Interactive Internet™ bidding closes two hours before live sessions where there is no floor bidding.

10. The Interactive Internet™ system generally opens the lot at the next increment above the second highest bid. As the high bidder, your "Secret Maximum Bid" will compete for you during the floor auction. Of course, it is possible in a Signature® or Grand Format live auction that you may be outbid on the floor or by a Heritage Live bidder after Internet bidding closes. Bid early, as the earliest bird wins in the event of a tie bid. For more information about bidding and bid increments, please see the section labeled "Bidding Increments" elsewhere in this catalog.

11. After the auction, you will be notified of your success. It's that easy!

6-8-10

❷HERITAGE Live!™ Bidding
(participate in the Live auction via the Internet)

1. Look on each auction's homepage to verify whether that auction is "HA.com/Live Enabled." All Signature® and Grand Format auctions use the HERITAGE Live!™ system, and many feature live audio and/or video. Determine your lots of interest and maximum bids.

2. Note on the auction's homepage the session dates and times (and especially time zones!) so you can plan your participation. You actually have two methods of using HERITAGE Live!™: a) you can leave a proxy bid through this system, much like the Interactive Internet™ (we recommend you do this before the session starts), or b) you can sit in front of your computer much as the audience is sitting in the auction room during the actual auction.

3. Login at HA.com/Live.

4. Until you become experienced (and this happens quickly!) you will want to login well before your lot comes up so you can watch the activity on other lots. It is as intuitive as participating in a live auction.

5. When your lot hits the auction block, you can continue to bid live against the floor and other live bidders by simply clicking the "Bid" button; the amount you are bidding is clearly displayed on the console.

❸ Mail Bidding
(deposit your maximum Bid with the U.S.P.S. well before the auction starts)

Mail bidding at auction is fun and easy, but by eliminating the interactivity of our online systems, some of your bids may be outbid before you lick the stamp, and you will have no idea of your overall chances until the auction is over!

1. Look through the printed catalog, and determine your lots of interest.

2. Research their market value by checking price lists and other price guidelines.

3. Fill out your bid sheet, entering your maximum bid on each lot. Bid using whole dollar amounts only. Verify your bids, because you are responsible for any errors you make! Please consult the Bidding Increments chart in the Terms & Conditions.

4. Please fill out your bid sheet completely! We also need: a) Your name and complete address for mailing invoices and lots; b) Your telephone number if any problems or changes arise; c) Your references; if you have not established credit with Heritage, you must send a 25% deposit, or list dealers with whom you have credit established; d) Total your bid sheet; add up all bids and list that total in the box; e) Sign your bid sheet, thereby agreeing to abide by the Terms & Conditions of Auction printed in the catalog.

5. Mail early, because preference is given to the first bid received in case of a tie.

6. When bidding by mail, you frequently purchase items at less than your maximum bid. Bidding generally opens at the next published increment above the second highest mail or Internet bid previously received; if additional floor, phone, or HERITAGE Live!™ bids are made, we act as your agent, bidding in increments over any additional bid until you win the lot or are outbid. For example, if you submitted a bid of $750, and the second highest bid was $375, bidding would start at $400; if no other bids were placed, you would purchase the lot for $400.

7. You can also Fax your Bid Sheet if time is short. Use our exclusive Fax Hotline: 214-443-8425.

❹ Telephone Bidding (when you are traveling, or do not have access to HERITAGE Live!™)

1. To participate in an auction by telephone, you must make preliminary arrangements with Client Services (Toll Free 866-835-3243) at least three days before the auction.

2. We strongly recommend that you place preliminary bids by mail or Internet if you intend to participate by telephone. On many occasions, this dual approach has reduced disappointments due to telephone (cell) problems, unexpected travel, late night sessions, and time zone differences. Keep a list of your preliminary bids, and we will help you avoid bidding against yourself.

❺ Attend in Person (whenever possible)

Auctions are fun, and we encourage you to attend as many as possible – although our HERITAGE Live!™ system brings all of the action right to your computer screen. Auction dates and session times are printed on the title page of each catalog, and appear on the homepage of each auction at HA.com. Join us if you can!

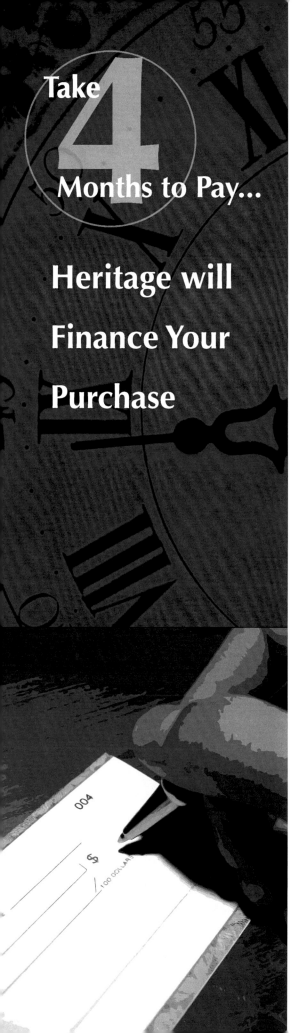

Take 4 Months to Pay...

Heritage will Finance Your Purchase

We're collectors too, and we understand that on occasion there is more to buy than there is cash. Consider Heritage's Extended Payment Plan [EPP] for your purchases totaling $2,500 or more.

Extended Payment Plan [EPP] Conditions

• Minimum invoice total is $2,500.

• Minimum Down Payment is 25% of the total invoice.

• A signed and returned EPP Agreement is required.

• The EPP is subject to a 3% *fully refundable* Set-up Fee (based on the total invoice amount) payable as part of the first monthly payment.

• The 3% Set-up Fee is refundable provided all monthly payments are made by eCheck, bank draft, personal check drawn on good funds, or cash; and if all such payments are made according to the EPP schedule.

• Monthly payments can be automatically processed with an eCheck, Visa, or MasterCard.

• You may take up to four equal monthly payments to pay the balance.

• Interest is calculated at only 1% per month on the unpaid balance.

• Your EPP must be kept current or additional interest may apply.

• There is no penalty for paying off early.

• Shipment will be made when final payment is received.

• All traditional auction and sales policies still apply.

There is no return privilege once you have confirmed your sale, and penalties can be incurred on cancelled invoices. To avoid additional fees, you must make your down payment within 14 days of the auction. All material purchased under the EPP will be physically secured by Heritage until paid in full.

To exercise the EPP option, please notify **Eric Thomas** at **214.409.1241** or email at **EricT@HA.com** upon receipt of your invoice.

We appreciate your business and wish you good luck with your bidding.

HERITAGE AUCTION GALLERIES
ANNOUNCES ITS NEWEST LOCATION

HERITAGE
Beverly Hills

The third largest full service fine art and collectibles auction house in the world, behind Sotheby's and Christie's

Heritage's newest location brings state-of-the-art technology, professional and friendly service and our roster of the most knowledgeable experts in their respective fields – Rare Coins and Currency, Estate & Fine Jewelry, American & European Paintings & Sculpture, Comics & Comic Art, Art of the American West, Furniture & Decorative Arts, Illustration Art, Modern & Contemporary Art, Silver & Vertu,

20th Century Design, Photography, American Indian Art, Americana & Political Memorabilia, Civil War & Arms & Militaria, Historical Manuscripts, Rare Books, Space Exploration, Fine Watches & Timepieces, Music & Entertainment Memorabilia, Natural History, Rare Stamps, Sports Collectibles, Vintage Movie Posters and more!

Whether it's your entire collection or a single valuable piece, we can provide

practical answers and help you decide which of our different auction venues is most appropriate. Heritage Auctions Beverly Hills is dedicated to putting your consignment in front of the right buyers to maximize your prices realized. We provide confidential appraisal and estate services to individuals, corporations, museums and other institutions in our offices, or we can gladly come to you.

Call today to discuss your collection and discover all the possibilities that only Heritage can provide.

Leo Frese
Managing Director
– Beverly Hills
Leo@HA.com
800-872-6467 ext. 1294

Michael Moline
Senior Vice President
– Beverly Hills
MMoline@HA.com
800-872-6467 ext. 1361

Shaunda Fry
Consignment Director
ShaundaF@HA.com
800-872-6467 ext. 1159

Carolyn Mani
Consignment Director
CarolynM@HA.com
800-872-6467 ext. 1677

David Michaels
Director of Ancient Coins
DMichaels@HA.com
800-872-6467 ext. 1606

Map: Santa Monica Blvd. / Wilshire Blvd. / S. Beverly Dr. / W. Olympic Blvd.

9478 W. Olympic Blvd. First Floor
Beverly Hills, California 90212
Monday – Friday 9 AM – 5 PM PT
Saturday 9 AM – 1 PM PT
310-492-8600 | 800-872-6467 | HA.com/BH

Receive a free catalog in any category, online at HA.com/CATF19536
or call 866-835-3243 and reference CATF19536.

VINTAGE MOVIE POSTERS INDEX

TITLE	STUDIO	LOT
Blob	Paramount, 1958	83653
Blob	Paramount, 1958	83160
Blonde Bait	Associated Film, 1956	83198
Blonde Sinner	Allied Artists, 1956	83195
Blonde Sinner	Allied Artists, 1956	83196
Blood on the Moon	RKO, 1948	84276
Blow-Up	MGM, 1967	83609
Blue Dahlia	Paramount, 1946	83076
Blue Dahlia	Paramount, 1946	83075
Blue Dahlia	Paramount, 1946	83074
Blue Dahlia	Paramount, 1946	83077
Blue Hawaii	Paramount, 1961	84212
Blue Hawaii	Paramount, 1961	83587
Bluebeard's Eighth Wife	Paramount, 1923	83702
Body and Soul	Fox, 1931	83446
Bohemian Girl	MGM, 1936	83782
Bohemian Girl	MGM, 1936	83783
Bohemian Girl	MGM, 1936	83784
Bonjour Tristesse	Columbia, 1958	83573
Bonnie Scotland	MGM, 1935	83785
Boris Karloff by Freulich	Universal, 1930s	84025
Boris Karloff by Jack Freulich	Universal, 1932	84024
Bowery	United Artists, 1933	83502
Brain Eaters	American International, 1958	83689
Break of Hearts	RKO, 1935	84241
Breakfast At Tiffany's	Paramount, 1961	83869
Breakfast At Tiffany's	Paramount, 1961	83868
Brewster's Millions	Paramount, 1921	84233
Bride and the Beast	Allied Artists, 1958	84074
Bride of Frankenstein	Realart, R-1953	83287
Bride of Frankenstein	Universal, 1935	83249
Bride of the Monster	Filmmakers Releasing, 1956	83285
Bride Wore Black	Dear, 1968	83617
Bride Wore Black	United Artists, 1968	84141
Bright Eyes	Fox, 1934	83861
British Intelligence	Warner Brothers, 1940	84298
Broadway Scandals	Columbia, 1929	83831
Broadway Scandals	Columbia, 1929	83830
Broken Barriers	Metro, 1924	84152
Broken Blossoms	1919	83692
Bronze Venus	Toddy Pictures, R-1943	83898
Brother Orchid	Warner Brothers, 1940	84122
Buck Privates	Universal, 1941	83762
Bulldog Drummond	United Artists, 1929	83043
Bulldog Drummond	United Artists, 1929	83044
Bull-Dogger	Norman Film Manufacturing, 1921	83900
Bullitt	Warner Brothers, 1968	84138
Bullitt	Warner Brothers, 1968	84139
Bullitt	Warner Brothers, 1968	83122
Bus Stop	20th Century Fox, 1956	83891
Bus Stop	20th Century Fox, 1956	84175
Bus Stop	20th Century Fox, 1956	84176
Bus Stop	20th Century Fox, 1956	84174
Buster Keaton by George Hurrell	MGM, 1931	83768
Busybody Bear	MGM, 1952	83042
Butch Cassidy and the Sundance Kid	20th Century Fox, 1969	83248
Butch Cassidy and the Sundance Kid	20th Century Fox, 1969	83247

TITLE	STUDIO	LOT
Butch Cassidy and the Sundance Kid	20th Century Fox, 1969	84293
Butch Cassidy and the Sundance Kid	20th Century Fox, 1969	83246
Butch Cassidy and the Sundance Kid	20th Century Fox, 1969	84294
Bwana Devil	United Artists, 1953	83560
Cabaret	Allied Artists, 1972	83331
Calcutta	Paramount, 1946	83078
Call Her Savage	Fox, 1932	83555
Call Northside 777	20th Century Fox, 1948	83095
Camille	MGM, 1937	83523
Canary Murder Case	Paramount, 1929	83050
Canary Murder Case	Paramount, 1929	83051
Captain America	Republic, 1944	83404
Captain January	20th Century Fox, 1936	84198
Captive Wild Woman	Universal, 1943	83735
Captured!	Warner Brothers, 1933	83922
Carole Lombard	Paramount, 1937	84019
Carole Lombard	Paramount, 1930s	84319
Carole Lombard	1930s	84020
Carole Lombard and James Stewart in "Made for Each Other"	United Artists, 1939	84321
Carole Lombard and William Powell in "My Man Godfrey" by William Walling Jr.	Universal, 1936	84016
Carole Lombard by Edwin Bower Hesser	Fox, 1920s	84015
Carole Lombard by Eugene Robert Richee	Paramount, 1930s	84017
Carole Lombard by Scotty Welbourne	1938	84320
Carole Lombard by William E. Thomas	Pathe, Late 1920s	84018
Carry On Screaming!	Anglo Amalgamated, 1966	84265
Cary Grant and Grace Kelly in "To Catch a Thief"	Paramount, 1955	84378
Casablanca	Warner Brothers, 1940s	83314
Casablanca	Warner Brothers, Late 1940s	83319
Casablanca	Warner Brothers, 1942	83315
Casablanca	Warner Brothers, 1942	83316
Casablanca	Warner Brothers, 1942	83317
Casablanca	Warner Brothers, 1942	83318
Cat and the Canary	Paramount, 1939	83754
Cat Ballou	Columbia, 1965	84263
Cat Nap Pluto	RKO, 1948	83012
Cat on a Hot Tin Roof	MGM, 1958	83561
Cat on a Hot Tin Roof	MGM, 1958	83562
Cat People	RKO, 1942	83731
Cat People	RKO, R-1952	83733
Cat-Women of the Moon	Astor Pictures, 1954	83683
Central Park	Warner Brothers - First National, 1932	83515
Central Park	Warner Brothers - First National, 1932	83516
Champion	Herald, 1951	83706
Charge of the Light Brigade	Warner Brothers, 1936	83485
Charlie Chan at Monte Carlo	20th Century Fox, 1937	83053
Charlie Chan at the Circus	20th Century Fox, 1936	83054
Charlie Chan Carries On	Fox, 1931	84113
Chasing Rainbows	MGM, 1930	83833
Cheyenne Rides Again	Victory, 1937	84289
China	Paramount, 1943	83100

TITLE	STUDIO	LOT
China	Paramount, 1943	83101
Chump at Oxford	United Artists, late 1940s	84245
Ciao! Manhattan	Constantin Film, 1974	83572
Citizen Kane	RKO, 1941	83472
Citizen Kane	RKO, 1941	83473
Citizen Kane	RKO, 1941	83471
Citizen Kane	Titanus, R-1966	84170
City for Conquest	Warner Brothers, 1940	83440
City of the Dead	British Lion, 1960	83748
Clara Bow	Paramount, 1920s	83945
Clara Bow	Fox, 1932	83943
Clara Bow	Fox, 1932	84315
Clara Bow in "Call Her Savage" by Hal Phyfe	Fox, 1932	84313
Clara Bow in "Call Her Savage" by Hal Phyfe	Fox, 1932	84314
Clara Bow in "Her Wedding Night" by Eugene Robert Richee	Paramount, 1930	83944
Clara Bow in "No Limit" by Eugene Robert Richee	Paramount, 1931	84312
Clark Gable and Jeanette MacDonald in "San Francisco" by Clarence Sinclair Bull	MGM, 1936	83981
Clash By Night	RKO, 1952	84177
Claudette Colbert by Eugene Robert Richee	Paramount, 1937	84357
Claudette Colbert by Otto Dyar	Paramount, 1932	84355
Claudette Colbert in "I Met Him in Paris" by Eugene Robert Richee	Paramount, 1937	84356
Cleopatra	Paramount, 1934	83546
Clockwork Orange	Warner Brothers, 1971	83150
Closed Gates	Sterling Pictures, 1927	84155
Cock of the Air	United Artists, 1932	83497
Cohens and Kellys in Africa	Universal, 1930	84236
Colleen Moore by George Hurrell	MGM, 1930s	84351
College	United Artists, 1929	83766
Colossus of New York	Paramount, 1958	84044
Conan the Barbarian	20th Century Fox, 1982	83399
Confessions of a Nazi Spy	Warner Brothers, 1939	83430
Confidential Agent	Warner Brothers, 1945	84134
Conquest of the Planet of the Apes	20th Century Fox, 1972	84055
Constance Bennett by Edwin Bower Hesser	RKO, 1920s	83963
Constance Bennett in "After Office Hours" by Stephen McNulty	MGM, 1935	83964
Cool Hand Luke	Warner Brothers, 1967	84188
Cool Hand Luke	Warner Brothers, 1967	84187
Cool Hand Luke	Warner Brothers, 1967	83565
Cool Hand Luke	Warner Brothers, 1967	83566
Crack-Up	20th Century Fox, 1936	83114
Crazy That Way	Fox, 1930	84235
Crazy That Way	Fox, 1930	83517
Creature From the Black Lagoon	Universal International, 1954	83297
Creature From the Black Lagoon	Universal International, 1954	83299
Creature From the Black Lagoon	Universal International, 1954	83301
Creature From the Black Lagoon	Universal International, 1954	83302

TITLE	STUDIO	LOT
Creature From the Black Lagoon	Universal International, 1954	83303
Creature From the Black Lagoon	Universal International, 1954	83300
Creature From the Black Lagoon	Universal International, 1954	83296
Creature From the Black Lagoon	Universal International, 1954	83298
Creature Walks Among Us	Universal International, 1956	83310
Creature Walks Among Us	Universal International, 1956	83309
Creature Walks Among Us	Universal International, 1956	83308
Crime Doctor	RKO, 1934	84104
Crime School	Warner Brothers, 1938	83447
Criss Cross	Universal International, 1949	84119
Crossfire	RKO, 1947	83109
Cruise Cat	MGM, 1952	83032
Curse of the Demon	Columbia, 1957	83741
Curse of the Demon	Columbia, 1957	83740
Curse of the Demon	Columbia, 1957	83739
D.O.A.	United Artists, 1950	83110
Dale Evans	Republic, 1944	84362
Dames	Warner Brothers, 1934	83824
Dames	Warner Brothers, 1934	83825
Dangerous Curves	Paramount, 1929	83554
Dante's Inferno	Jawitz Pictures Corp., 1921	83290
Dark Passage	Warner Brothers, 1947	83454
Dark Town Follies	Supreme Distributing, 1930	83899
Darling	Cocinor, 1966	84191
Daughters of Today	Unknown, Early 1930s	83191
Dawn of the Dead	United Film Distribution, 1978	84080
Dawn Patrol	Warner Brothers, 1938	83923
Day At The Races	MGM, 1937	83775
Day At The Races	MGM, 1937	83774
Day of the Triffids	Allied Artists, 1962	84050
Day the Earth Stood Still	20th Century Fox, 1952	83626
Day the Earth Stood Still	20th Century Fox, 1951	83165
Day the Earth Stood Still	20th Century Fox, 1951	83627
Day the Earth Stood Still	20th Century Fox, 1951	83164
Day the World Ended	American Releasing Corp., 1956	83188
Day the World Ended	American Releasing Corp., 1956	84038
Dead of Night	Eagle Lion, 1946	83737
Dead of Night	Universal, 1946	83736
Dead Reckoning	Columbia, 1947	83457
Deadly Mantis	Universal International, 1957	83185
Deadly Mantis	Universal International, 1957	83667
Deadwood Dick	Columbia, 1940	83406
Delicious	Fox, 1931	83547
Destroy All Monsters	American International, 1969	84049
Destry Rides Again	Universal, 1939	83215
Destry Rides Again	Universal, 1932	83213
Devil With Women	Fox, 1930	83444
Dial M For Murder	Warner Brothers, 1954	83356
Diamonds Are Forever	United Artists, 1971	84096
Dirigible	Columbia, 1931	83496

TITLE	STUDIO	LOT
Dirty Harry	Warner Brothers, 1971	84143
Dirty Harry	Warner Brothers, 1971	83119
Dodge City	Warner Brothers, 1938	83483
Dodge City	Warner Brothers, 1938	83484
Dodge City Trail	Columbia, 1936	84285
Donald's Cousin Gus	RKO, 1939	83006
Don't Bother to Knock	20th Century Fox, 1952	83882
Dorothy Lamour in "Man About Town" by William Walling	Paramount, 1939	84006
Double Indemnity	Paramount, 1944	83081
Double Indemnity	Paramount, 1946	83080
Double Indemnity	Paramount, 1944	83079
Double Indemnity	Paramount, 1944	83082
Doughboys	MGM, 1930	83764
Dr. Jekyll and Mr. Hyde	Paramount, 1931	83721
Dr. Jekyll and Mr. Hyde	MGM, Late 1940s	84065
Dr. Jekyll and Mr. Hyde	Paramount, R-1936	83720
Dr. No	United Artists, 1962	83132
Dr. No	United Artists, 1962	83124
Dr. No	United Artists, 1962	83125
Dr. No	United Artists, 1962	83133
Dracula	Universal, 1931	83252
Dracula	Universal, 1931	83253
Dracula's Daughter	Universal, 1936	83280
Dracula's Daughter	Universal, 1936	83281
Dragstrip Girl	American International, 1957	83199
Droopy's Good Deed	MGM, 1951	83034
Duel in the Sun	United Artists, 1947	83244
Dumbo	RKO, 1947	83021
Dynamite	MGM, 1929	83501
Each Dawn I Die	Warner Brothers, 1939	83439
Eagle	United Artists, 1925	83693
Earth vs. the Flying Saucers	Columbia, 1956	83646
East of Eden	Warner Brothers, 1955	83581
East of Eden	Warner Brothers, 1955	83582
East of the River	Warner Brothers, 1940	84116
Easter Parade	MGM, 1948	84206
Easy Rider	Columbia, R-1972	83571
Edgar Bergen and Charlie McCarthy Stock Poster	Warner Brothers, R-1938	83763
Edwina Booth by Ruth Harriet Louise	MGM, 1930	84021
El Gaucho Goofy	RKO, R-1955	83013
El Vampiro	Alemeda Films, 1957	83293
Elmer, the Great	Warner Brothers-First National, 1933	84305
Elvis Presley	Paramount, 1957	84368
Elvis Presley in "King Creole"	Paramount, 1958	84370
Elvis Presley in "King Creole"	Paramount, 1958	84369
Elvis Presley in "Love Me Tender"	20th Century Fox, 1956	84367
Empire Strikes Back	20th Century Fox, 1980	84060
Empire Strikes Back	20th Century Fox, 1980	84059
Empire Strikes Back	20th Century Fox, 1980	83180
Empire Strikes Back	20th Century Fox, 1980	84061
Endless Summer	Cinema 5, 1966	83708
Erich von Stroheim in "Sunset Boulevard"	Paramount, 1950	84364
Escape from New York	Avco Embassy, 1981	84062
Everybody Against James Bond	United Artists, 1972	83141
Fantasia	RKO, 1940	83019
Fantastic Voyage	20th Century Fox, 1966	84052

TITLE	STUDIO	LOT
Fantastic Voyage	20th Century Fox, 1966	83176
Fantastic Voyage	20th Century Fox, 1966	83175
Farm-Hand	Bray Studios, 1927	83035
Farmyard Symphony	RKO, 1938	83008
Faster, Pussycat! Kill! Kill!	Eve Productions, 1965	83203
Faster, Pussycat! Kill! Kill!	Eve Productions, 1965	83201
Faster, Pussycat! Kill! Kill!	Eve Productions, 1965	83202
Feet First	Paramount, 1930	83779
Fistful of Dollars	United Artists, 1967	83411
Fistful of Dollars	Adria Film, 1968	84290
Fistful of Dollars	United Artists, 1967	83416
Fistful of Dollars	United Artists, 1967	83414
Fistful of Dollars	PEA, 1965	83412
Fistful of Dollars	United Artists, 1967	83415
Flagpole Jitters	Columbia, 1956	83791
Flirtation	J.D. Trop, 1934	83204
Flower of No Man's Land	Columbia, 1916	84146
Fly	20th Century Fox, 1958	83177
Fly / Return of the Fly	Grand National Pictures, R-1960's	83178
Flying Ace	Norman, 1926	83901
Flying Cat	MGM, 1952	83031
Flying Down to Rio	RKO, 1933	83841
Flying Down to Rio	RKO, 1933	83840
Follow the Fleet	RKO, 1936	83843
Follow the Fleet	RKO, 1936	83842
Footlight Parade	Warner Brothers, 1933	83823
For a Few Dollars More	PEA, R-1970s	83413
For a Few Dollars More	United Artists, 1967	83417
For a Few Dollars More	PEA, 1965	83410
Forbidden Planet	MGM, 1956	83641
Forbidden Planet	MGM, 1956	84030
Forbidden Planet	MGM, 1956	83162
Forbidden Planet	MGM, 1956	83642
Force of Evil	MGM, 1948	84118
Foreign Correspondent	Sangraf, late 1940s	83343
Forty Little Mothers	MGM, 1940	84247
Fountainhead	Warner Brothers, 1949	83476
Four Frightened People	Paramount, 1934	84168
Four Men and a Prayer	20th Century Fox, 1938	84297
Four's a Crowd	Warner Brothers, 1938	84243
Fox Film Corporation Exhibitor's Book	Fox, 1926	83934
Fraidy Cat	MGM, R-1951	83029
Framed	First National, 1927	84105
Frank Sinatra in "Till the Clouds Roll By"	MGM, 1946	84366
Frankenstein	Universal, 1931	83250
Frankenstein Conquers the World	Toho, 1965	84077
Frankenstein Meets the Wolf Man	Universal, 1943	83268
Frankenstein Meets the Wolf Man	Universal, 1950s	83271
Frankenstein Meets the Wolf Man	Universal, 1943	83269
Frankenstein Meets the Wolf Man	Universal, 1943	83270
Fred Thomson Lot	FBO, 1926	84288
Free and Easy	MGM, 1930	83765
Freshman	Pathé, 1925	83777
From Russia with Love	United Artists, 1964	83129
From Russia with Love	United Artists, 1964	83130
From Russia with Love	United Artists, 1964	83131

TITLE	STUDIO	LOT
Frontier Pony Express	Republic, 1939	84282
Funny Face	Paramount, 1957	83874
Funny Face	Paramount, 1957	83872
Funny Face	Paramount, 1957	83873
Fury	MGM, 1936	83099
G.I. Blues	Paramount, 1960	83589
Gaucho	United Artists, 1927	83494
Gaucho	United Artists, 1927	83495
Gay Deception	Fox, 1935	83543
Gay Falcon	RKO, 1941	84112
General Died at Dawn	Paramount, R-1957	84225
Gentlemen Prefer Blondes	20th Century Fox, 1953	83886
Gentlemen Prefer Blondes	20th Century Fox, 1953	84208
Gentlemen Prefer Blondes	20th Century Fox, 1953	83887
Ghost Breakers	Paramount, 1940	83753
Ghost of Frankenstein	Universal, 1942	83267
Ghost of Frankenstein	Universal, 1942	83266
Giant	Warner Brothers, 1956	84182
Giant Leeches	American International, 1959	83690
Giant Leeches	American International, 1959	83691
Gigi	MGM, 1958	84210
Gigolettes of Paris	Majestic, 1933	83510
Gilda	Columbia, 1946	83814
Gilda	Columbia, R-1959	83813
Ginger Rogers by Elmer Fryer	Warner Brothers, 1932	83982
Ginger Rogers by George DeBarron	1930	84372
Ginger Rogers by George DeBarron	1930	84371
Girl Crazy	MGM, 1943	83853
Girl in Danger	Columbia, 1934	83058
Girl in the Pullman	Pathé, 1927	83698
Girl With An Itch	Howco, 1958	83205
Girls Demand Excitement	Fox, 1931	83902
Give Me Your Heart	Warner Brothers, 1936	83521
Glass Key	Paramount, 1942	83068
Glass Key	Paramount, 1942	83067
Glass Key	Paramount, 1948	83070
Glass Key	Paramount, late 1940s	83069
Gloria Stuart by Ray Jones	Universal, 1932	84352
Gloria's Romance	K-E-S-E Service, 1916	83701
Go West	MGM, 1940	83771
Godfather	Paramount, 1972	83121
Godzilla	Trans World, 1956	83660
Godzilla vs. the Thing	American International, 1964	84048
Gold Diggers of Broadway	Warner Brothers, 1929	83832
Golden Arrow	Warner Brothers - First National, 1936	83421
Golden Boy	Columbia, 1939	83821
Golden Eggs	RKO, 1941	83007
Goldfinger	United Artists, 1964	83127
Goldfinger	United Artists, 1964	83128
Goldfinger	United Artists, 1964	83126
Gone with the Wind	MGM, 1939	83333
Gone with the Wind	MGM, 1939	83335
Gone with the Wind	MGM, 1939	83336
Gone with the Wind	MGM, 1939	83337
Gone with the Wind	MGM, 1939	83334
Good, the Bad and the Ugly	PEA, 1966	83407
Good, the Bad and the Ugly	PEA, 1966	83408
Good, the Bad and the Ugly	PEA, 1966	83409

TITLE	STUDIO	LOT
Goodfellas	Warner Brothers, 1990	84144
Gordon of Ghost City Lot	Universal, 1933	84284
Grace Kelly	1955	83962
Grace Kelly in "To Catch a Thief"	Paramount, 1955	84379
Graduate	Embassy, 1968	84189
Grand Exit	Columbia, 1935	83059
Grapes of Wrath	20th Century Fox, 1940	83467
Grapes of Wrath	20th Century Fox, 1940	83470
Grapes of Wrath	20th Century Fox, 1940	83468
Grapes of Wrath	20th Century Fox, 1940	83469
Great Escape	United Artists, 1963	83927
Great Escape	United Artists, 1963	83926
Great Escape	United Artists, 1963	83928
Great Gatsby	Paramount, 1949	83111
Great O'Malley	Warner Brothers, 1937	84121
Great Ziegfeld	MGM, 1936	83313
Green Mansions	MGM, 1959	84195
Greta Garbo by Ruth Harriet Louise	MGM, Late 1920s	84012
Greta Garbo in "Anna Christie" by Clarence Sinclair Bull	MGM, 1930	84007
Greta Garbo in "Anna Christie" by Clarence Sinclair Bull	MGM, 1930	84008
Greta Garbo in "Conquest" by Clarence Sinclair Bull	MGM, 1937	84011
Greta Garbo in "Inspiration"	MGM, 1931	84318
Greta Garbo in "Romance"	MGM, 1930	84010
Greta Garbo in "Romance" by George Hurrell	MGM, 1930	84317
Greta Garbo in "Susan Lenox"	Her Fall and Rise	84316
Greta Garbo in "The Painted Veil" by Clarence Sinclair Bull	MGM, 1934	84009
Gun Crazy	United Artists, 1949	83113
Half A Sinner	Universal, 1934	83551
Half-Wits Holiday	Columbia, 1947	83787
Harakiri	Euro International, 1962	83624
Hard Day's Night	United Artists, 1964	83592
Hard Day's Night	United Artists, 1964	83594
Hard Day's Night	United Artists, 1964	83595
Hard Luck	Metro, 1921	83767
Harold and Maude	Paramount, 1971	84266
Harvey	Universal International, 1950	83809
Harvey	Universal International, 1950	84253
Harvey	Universal International, 1950	83808
Hatch Up Your Troubles	MGM, 1949	83026
Hate Ship	First National, 1929	83291
Head	Columbia, 1968	83599
Heart Buster	Fox, 1924	83214
Hedy Lamarr and William Powell in "The Heavenly Body"	MGM, 1943	84349
Hedy Lamarr by Ned Scott	1938	84348
Hell's Angels	United Artists, R-1937	84296
Hell's Kitchen	Warner Brothers, 1939	84109
Help!	United Artists, 1965	83593
Help!	United Artists, 1965	84214
Her Jungle Love	Paramount, 1938	83932
Hercules	Embassy, 1959	84231
Hideout in the Sun	Wica Pictures, 1960	83206
High Noon	United Artists, 1952	83240
High Plains Drifter	Universal, 1973	84291

TITLE	STUDIO	LOT
High Sierra	Warner Brothers, R-1947	83453
Hiroshima, mon amour	Cocinor, 1959	83620
Holiday Inn	Paramount, 1942	83839
Hollywood Revue of 1929	MGM, 1929	83834
Hop-a-long Cassidy	Paramount, 1935	83211
Horror of Dracula	Universal International, 1958	83294
Hot Rod Rumble	Allied Artists, 1957	84268
Hot Saturday	Paramount, 1932	83549
Hot Water	Pathé, 1924	83780
Hot Water	Pathé, 1924	83781
House of Frankenstein	Universal, 1944	83265
House of Frankenstein	Universal, 1944	83263
House of Frankenstein	Universal, 1944	83264
House of Frankenstein	Universal, 1944	83262
House on 56th Street	Warner Brothers, 1933	84160
House on Haunted Hill	Allied Artists, 1959	83746
House on Haunted Hill	Allied Artists, 1959	83747
How to Make a Monster	American International, 1958	84071
How to Make a Monster	American International, 1958	84072
How to Make a Monster	American International, 1958	84073
How to Marry a Millionaire	20th Century Fox, 1953	83884
How to Marry a Millionaire	20th Century Fox, 1953	83885
Hula	Paramount, 1927	83552
Human Monster	Monogram, 1939	83282
Hunchback of Notre Dame	RKO, 1939	83727
Hunchback of Notre Dame	Universal, 1923	83726
Hurricane Express	Mascot, 1932	83391
Hustler	20th Century Fox, 1961	83714
Hustler	20th Century Fox, 1961	84308
Hustler	20th Century Fox, R-1964	83713
Hustler	20th Century Fox, 1961	84307
Hustler	20th Century Fox, 1961	83712
I Am a Fugitive From a Chain Gang	Warner Brothers, 1932	83434
I Love Trouble	Columbia, 1948	83112
I Married a Witch	United Artists, 1942	83066
I Wanted Wings	Paramount, 1941	84301
I Wanted Wings	Paramount, 1941	84300
I Was a Teenage Frankenstein	American International, 1957	83744
I Was a Teenage Werewolf	American International, R-1961	84069
I Was a Teenage Werewolf	American International, 1957	84068
I Was a Teenage Werewolf	American International, 1957	83745
In a Lonely Place	Columbia, 1950	83463
In Old Caliente	Republic, 1939	83228
Incredible Shrinking Man	Universal International, 1957	83657
Incredible Shrinking Man	Universal International, 1957	83656
Incredible Shrinking Man	Universal International, 1957	83655
Incredible Shrinking Man	Universal International, 1957	84039
Incredibly Strange Creatures Who Stopped Living and Became Mixed-Up Zombies	Fairway International, 1964	84078
Inside Cackle Corners	MGM, 1951	83038
Invaders from Mars	20th Century Fox, 1953	83634
Invaders from Mars	20th Century Fox, 1953	83635

TITLE	STUDIO	LOT
Invaders from Mars	20th Century Fox, 1953	83170
Invaders from Mars	20th Century Fox, 1955	83633
Invasion of the Body Snatchers	Allied Artists, 1956	83644
Invasion of the Body Snatchers	Allied Artists, 1956	83643
Invasion of the Saucer-Men	American International, 1957	84043
Invasion of the Saucer-Men	American International, 1957	83157
Invisible Boy	MGM, 1957	83163
Invisible Man	Realart, R-1951	83295
Invisible Ray	Universal, 1935	83257
Invisible Ray	Universal, 1935	83258
Invisible Ray	Universal, 1935	83259
Invisible Ray	Realart, R-1948	83260
Iron Claw	Pathé, 1916	83398
Iron Man	Universal, 1931	83530
Island of Lost Souls	Paramount, 1933	83719
Isle of Fury	Warner Brothers, 1936	83448
Isle of the Dead	RKO, 1945	83734
It All Came True	Warner Brothers, 1940	83450
It Came from Beneath the Sea	Columbia, 1955	84034
It Came from Outer Space	Universal International, 1953	83636
It Came from Outer Space	Universal International, 1953	83166
It Came from Outer Space	Universal International, 1953	83147
It Came from Outer Space	Universal International, 1953	83637
It Conquered the World	American International, 1956	83648
It Conquered the World/ The She-Creature Combo	American International, 1956	83649
It Happened One Night	Columbia, 1934	83332
It! The Terror from Beyond Space	United Artists, 1958	84041
Italian Job	Paramount, 1969	83120
It's a Wonderful Life	RKO, 1946	83800
It's a Wonderful Life	RKO, 1946	83801
It's a Wonderful Life	RKO, 1946	83797
It's a Wonderful Life	RKO, 1946	83798
It's a Wonderful Life	RKO, 1946	83799
Jailhouse Rock	MGM, 1957	83586
Jailhouse Rock	MGM, 1957	83583
Jamboree	Warner Brothers, 1957	84211
James Cagney Personality Poster	Warner Brothers, 1934	83441
Jane Russell in "The Outlaw"	United Artists, 1946	83971
Java Head	First Division Pictures, 1934	83536
Jaws	Universal, 1975	84079
Jean Harlow	MGM, 1930s	84339
Jean Harlow	MGM, 1930s	84340
Jean Harlow	MGM, 1930s	84341
Jean Harlow and Clark Gable in "Saratoga" by Clarence Sinclair Bull	MGM, 1937	83992
Jean Harlow by Clarence Sinclair Bull	MGM, 1930s	84338
Jean Harlow by George Hurrell	MGM, 1930s	83994
Jean Harlow by George Hurrell	MGM, 1930s	83996
Jean Harlow by George Hurrell	MGM, 1930s	83995
Jean Harlow by Preston Duncan	1930s	83993

TITLE	STUDIO	LOT
Jean Harlow by Ted Allan	MGM, 1930s	83997
Jean Harlow by Ted Allen	MGM, 1930s	83991
Jean Harlow in "Reckless" by William Grimes	MGM, 1935	84343
Jean Harlow in "The Secret Six" by Clarence Sinclair Bull	MGM, 1931	84342
Jeanette MacDonald by Edwin Bower Hesser	1920s	83980
Jerky Turkey	MGM, 1945	83033
Jerry and the Lion	MGM, 1949	83027
Jesse James	20th Century Fox, 1939	83210
Jesse James	20th Century Fox, R-1946	84274
Jezebel	Warner Brothers, 1939	83424
Jimi Hendrix	Warner Brothers, 1973	83600
Jimmy the Gent	Warner Brothers, 1934	83436
Joan Crawford and Robert Montgomery in "Letty Lynton" By George Hurrell	MGM, 1932	84336
Joan Crawford by Clarence Sinclair Bull	MGM, 1930s	84335
Joan Crawford by Edwin Bower Hesser	1920s	83951
Joan Crawford by George Hurrell	MGM, 1930s	83946
Joan Crawford by Ruth Harriet Louise	MGM, Late 1920s	83950
Joan Crawford in "A Woman's Face"	MGM, 1941	84334
Joan Crawford in "Humoresque" by Eugene Robert Richee	Warner Brothers, 1946	83947
Joan Crawford in "Rose-Marie" by Ruth Harriet Louise	MGM, 1928	83948
Joan Crawford in "The Women" by Laszlo Willinger	MGM, 1939	83949
Joe Louis vs. Max Schmeling Boxing Poster	Empire City, 1937	83707
John Wayne in "Stagecoach"	United Artists, 1939	83942
Johnny O'clock	Columbia, R-1956	84135
Juarez	Warner Brothers, late 1940s	83425
Juarez	Warner Brothers, 1939	84164
Judy Garland and Mickey Rooney Lot	MGM, 1940-1941	83860
Judy Garland Lobby Card Lot	MGM, 1937-1938	83858
Judy Garland Lobby Card Lot	MGM, 1941-1942	84205
Judy Garland Promotional Poster	CBS/Capitol,	83856
Jungle Captive	Universal, 1945	84067
Just Imagine	Fox, 1930	83145
Justice of the Range	Columbia, 1935	83222
Kagemusha	20th Century Fox, 1980	83625
Kanal	P.P. Film, 1957	84303
Kay Francis in "Behind the Make-Up" by Otto Dyar	Paramount, 1930	84013
Keep Your Powder Dry	MGM, 1945	84302
Key Largo	Warner Brothers, 1948	83460
Key Largo	Warner Brothers, 1948	83459
Key Largo	Warner Brothers, 1948	83458
Kid Galahad	Warner Brothers, 1937	83428
Killers From Space	RKO, 1954	84032
King Creole	Paramount, 1958	83584
King Kong	RKO, 1933	84063
King Kong	RKO, 1933	83730
King Kong	RKO, R-1950s	83729
King Kong	RKO, R-1946	83728

TITLE	STUDIO	LOT
King Kong vs. Godzilla	Toho, 1962	84047
King of the Underworld	Warner Brothers, 1939	83449
Kiss of Death	20th Century Fox, 1947	83102
Knickerbocker Buckaroo	Artcraft, 1919	83493
Krazy Kat	Columbia, 1936	83036
Kwaidan	Toho, 1965	83752
La Dolce Vita	Astor, 1961	83604
La Loi	Les Films Corona, 1959	84192
Ladies of the Chorus	Columbia, 1948	83879
Ladies of the Chorus	Columbia, 1948	83880
Lady and the Tramp	Buena Vista, 1955	84087
Lady From Shanghai	Columbia, 1947	83812
Lady in the Lake	MGM, 1947	83093
Last Outpost	Paramount, 1935	84223
Laura	20th Century Fox, 1944	83089
Laura	20th Century Fox, 1944	84136
Laura	20th Century Fox, 1944	83090
Laurel and Hardy Stock Poster	MGM, 1947	84246
Lauren Bacall	1940s	83970
Lauren Bacall	Warner Brothers, 1940s	84376
Lavender Hill Mob	Rank, 1951	83614
L'Avventura	Cino del Duca, 1961	83602
L'Avventura	Cino del Duca, 1961	83601
Law and Order	Universal, 1932	83212
Lawrence of Arabia	Columbia, 1962	83328
Lawrence of Arabia	Columbia, 1962	83329
Lawrence of Arabia	Columbia, 1962	84304
Lawrence of Arabia	Columbia, 1962	83330
Lawyer Man	Warner Brothers, 1933	84106
Le Mans	Towa, 1971	83709
Le Samouraï	Herald, 1968	84220
Le Testament d'Orphee	Cinedis, 1960	83616
Leather Burners	United Artists, 1943	84280
Leave Her to Heaven	20th Century Fox, 1945	83107
Leopard Man	RKO, 1943	83732
Let It Be	United Artists, 1970	83597
Let It Be	United Artists, 1970	83596
Let It Be	United Artists, 1970	84215
Let's Make Love	20th Century Fox, 1960	84259
Letter	Warner Brothers, 1940	83426
Letter to Three Wives	20th Century Fox, 1949	84172
Life of Buffalo Bill	Pawnee Bill Film Co., 1912	83218
Light of Western Stars	Paramount, 1930	83217
Little Giant	First National, 1933	84110
Little Women	RKO, R-1938	83804
Lola	Unidex, 1961	83603
Lolita	Dear Film, 1962	83612
Lolita	MGM, 1962	83611
Lolita	MGM, 1962	83613
Lone Hand Saunders	FBO, 1926	84287
Lone Ranger	Warner Brothers, 1956	83242
Lone Ranger and the Lost City of Gold	United Artists, 1958	83243
Long, Long Trailer	MGM, 1954	83810
Long, Long Trailer	MGM, 1954	84254
Looney Tune Cartoon Stock Poster	Warner Brothers, 1940	83039
Lord of the Rings	United Artists, 1978	84083
Loretta Young by Elmer Fryer	First National, Early 1930s	83975
Loretta Young by Elmer Fryer	Warner Brothers/ First National, 1930s	84359

TITLE	STUDIO	LOT
Loretta Young by Elmer Fryer	Warner Brothers-First National, Early 1930s	83974
Loretta Young by Fred R. Archer	First National, 1929	83973
Loretta Young by Melbourne Spurr	1933	83972
Lost Horizon	Columbia, 1937	83793
Lost Patrol	RKO, 1934	83924
Lost Planet	Columbia, 1953	83405
Louise Brooks	Paramount, 1920s	83986
Louise Brooks and Richard Arlen in "Beggars of Life"	Paramount, 1928	83987
Louise Brooks by Eugene Robert Richee	Paramount, 1920s	83985
Love Finds Andy Hardy	MGM, 1938	84248
Love Finds Andy Hardy	MGM, 1938	83859
Love in the Afternoon	Allied Artists, 1957	84194
Love in the Rough	MGM, 1930	83513
Love Mart	First National, 1927	83697
Love Me Forever	Columbia, 1935	83835
Loves of Carmen	Columbia, 1948	83818
Loving You	Paramount, 1957	83585
Lucille Ball	RKO, 1941	84358
Lucille Ball in "Stage Door" by Ernest A. Bachrach	RKO, 1937	84360
Mae West and Randolph Scott in "Go West Young Man" by Eugene Robert Richee	Paramount, 1936	84375
Mae West in "Every Day's a Holiday" by Eugene Robert Richee	Paramount, 1937	84377
Magnificent Obsession	Universal International, 1954	84184
Magnificent Seven	Art Krebs Screen Studio, 1960	83576
Magnificent Stranger	Unidas, 1966	83419
Man from Planet X	United Artists, 1951	83154
Man from Planet X	United Artists, 1951	83632
Man from Planet X	United Artists, 1951	83631
Man of the Forest	Paramount, 1933	83224
Man Trouble	Fox, 1930	83509
Man Who Shot Liberty Valance	Paramount, 1962	83387
Man Who Shot Liberty Valance	Paramount, 1962	83386
Man With the Golden Arm	United Artists, 1955	83570
Man With the Golden Arm	United Artists, 1955	83569
Man With the Golden Gun	United Artists, 1974	83142
Man With the Golden Gun	United Artists, 1974	84100
Man With the Golden Gun	United Artists, 1974	83143
Man With the Golden Gun	United Artists, 1974	84101
Manchurian Candidate	United Artists, 1962	84221
Mannequin	MGM, 1937	84162
Man's Castle	Columbia, 1933	83538
Many Happy Returns	Paramount, 1934	84238
Many Happy Returns	Paramount, 1934	84237
Marilyn Monroe	20th Century Fox, 1950s	83939
Marilyn Monroe	1950s	83940
Marilyn Monroe in "The Asphalt Jungle"	MGM, 1950	83941
Marion Davies by Elmer Fryer	Warner Brothers, Late 1930s	83979
Marion Davies by James Manatt	MGM, 1930s	83978
Mark of the Vampire	MGM, 1935	83255
Marlene Dietrich in "The Devil is a Woman" by Don English	Paramount, 1935	84337

TITLE	STUDIO	LOT
Mary Pickford by Melbourne Spurr	1920s	84350
Mayor of Hell	Warner Brothers, 1933	84128
Mean Streets	Warner Brothers, 1973	83123
Meet Me in St. Louis	MGM, 1944	83854
Melody	RKO, 1953	83014
Melody Cruise	RKO, 1933	83511
Men In White	MGM, 1934	83338
Merrily We Go to Hell	Paramount, 1932	83506
Mexicali Rose	Columbia, 1929	83820
MGM Animation Stock Poster	MGM, 1953	84086
Mickey Rooney and Judy Garland in "Babes on Broadway" by Clarence Sinclair Bull	MGM, 1941	84373
Mildred Pierce	Warner Brothers, 1945	83106
Miracle on 34th Street	20th Century Fox, 1947	83792
Misfits	United Artists, 1961	84178
Misleading Widow	Paramount-Artcraft, 1919	83700
Mockery	MGM, 1927	83723
Mole People	Universal International, 1956	83677
Mole People	Universal International, 1956	83676
Mondo Topless	Eve Productions, 1966	83207
Monkey Business	20th Century Fox, 1952	84258
Monogram Exhibitor Book	Monogram, 1932	84311
Monster that Challenged the World	United Artists, 1957	84035
Monster that Challenged the World	Atlantis Films, 1958	83187
Monster Zero	Toho, 1965	83661
Moon Over Miami	20th Century Fox, 1941	83826
Moonraker	United Artists, 1979	84102
Moulin Rouge	United Artists, 1934	83829
Mr. Deeds Goes to Town	Columbia, 1936	83794
Mr. Smith Goes to Washington	Columbia, 1939	83796
Mrs. Wiggs of the Cabbage Patch	Paramount, 1934	84240
Mummy	Universal International, 1959	83279
Mummy's Curse	Universal, 1944	83277
Mummy's Curse	Universal, 1944	83276
Mummy's Curse	Realart, R-1951	83278
Mummy's Ghost	Universal, 1944	83275
Mummy's Hand	Universal, 1940	83274
Murder, My Sweet	RKO, 1944	83085
Murders in the Rue Morgue	Universal, 1932	83254
My Darling Clementine	20th Century Fox, 1946	83235
My Darling Clementine	20th Century Fox, 1946	83234
My Fair Lady	Warner Brothers, 1964	83875
My Fair Lady	Warner Brothers, 1964	83876
My Son	First National, 1925	84153
Myrna Loy	MGM, 1930s	84324
Myrna Loy by Clarence Sinclair Bull	MGM, 1933	84325
Myrna Loy by Preston Duncan	Warner Brothers, 1920s	83958
Myrna Loy in "Bride of the Regiment" by Elmer Fryer	First National, 1930	83960
Myrna Loy in "Bride of the Regiment" by Elmer Fryer	First National, 1930	83961
Myrna Loy in "Emma" by George Hurrell	MGM, 1932	83959
Myrna Loy in "Parnell" by Clarence Sinclair Bull	MGM, 1937	84323

TITLE	STUDIO	LOT
Mysterious Dr. Fu Manchu	Paramount, 1929	83047
Mysterious Dr. Fu Manchu	Paramount, 1929	83048
Mysterious Dr. Fu Manchu	Paramount, 1929	83049
Nancy Carroll by Eugene Robert Richee	Paramount, Late 1920s	83957
Nancy Carroll by Eugene Robert Richee	Paramount, 1929	83956
Narrow Margin	RKO, 1952	84131
Neath the Arizona Skies	Monogram, 1934	83918
New Adventures of Batman and Robin	Columbia, 1949	83395
New Adventures of Tarzan	Burroughs-Tarzan-Enterprise, 1935	84227
New Frontier	Republic, 1939	84270
New Frontier	Republic, 1935	83372
Niagara	20th Century Fox, 1953	83883
Niagara	20th Century Fox, 1953	84137
Nicholas Nickleby	Eagle Lion, 1947	83606
Night After Night	Paramount, 1932	84158
Night and the City	20th Century Fox, 1950	83096
Night at the Opera	MGM, 1935	83770
Night Club Queen	Olympic, 1934	83057
Night in Casablanca	United Artists, 1946	83776
Night Monster	Realart, R-1949	84064
Night of the Hunter	United Artists, 1955	83103
Night of the Living Dead	Continental, 1968	83749
Night Tide	American International, 1961	83738
Night to Remember	Rank, 1959	83607
Nightmare Alley	20th Century Fox, 1947	83105
Ninotchka	MGM, 1939	83529
No Man's Gold	Fox, 1926	84277
No Time for Comedy	Warner Brothers, 1940	84244
Norma Shearer and Johnny Mack Brown in "A Lady of Chance"	MGM, 1928	84347
Norma Shearer by George Hurrell	MGM, 1930s	83988
Norma Shearer by George Hurrell	MGM, 1936	83990
Norma Shearer in "Romeo and Juliet" by George Hurrell	MGM, 1936	83989
Norma Shearer Personality Poster	MGM, 1930s	83522
North by Northwest	MGM, 1959	83349
North by Northwest	MGM, 1959	83359
North by Northwest	MGM, 1959	83369
North by Northwest	MGM, 1959	83358
North by Northwest	MGM, R-1976	83370
Not of this Earth	Allied Artists, 1957	83652
Not Quite Decent	Fox, 1929	83535
Notorious	RKO, 1946	83351
Notorious	Columbia, R-1954	83366
Notorious	Cei Incom, R-1960	83353
Now and Forever	Paramount, 1934	83862
Now, Voyager	Warner Brothers, 1942	83427
Nude on the Moon	J.E.R. Pictures, 1961	83193
Nude Vampire	Les Distributeurs Associes, 1970	83292
O. Henry's Full House	20th Century Fox, 1952	84255
Ocean's 11	Warner Brothers, 1960	83568
Ocean's 11	Warner Brothers, 1960	83567
Octopussy	MGM/UA, 1983	84103
Octopussy	MGM/UA, 1983	83144
Of Human Bondage	RKO, 1934	83422

TITLE	STUDIO	LOT
Old Maid	Warner Brothers, 1939	83423
Old Man Rhythm	RKO, 1935	83836
On Any Sunday	Fida Cinematografica, 1972	83710
On Her Majesty's Secret Service	United Artists, 1970	83140
On Her Majesty's Secret Service	United Artists, 1970	84097
On Her Majesty's Secret Service	United Artists, 1970	84099
On Her Majesty's Secret Service	United Artists, 1970	84098
Once Upon a Time in the West	Paramount, 1969	84292
One Flew Over the Cuckoo's Nest	United Artists, 1975	84190
One Man Law	Columbia, 1932	83233
One Million Years B.C.	20th Century Fox, 1966	84051
Out of the Past	RKO, R-1953	83083
Out of the Past	RKO, 1947	83084
Outlaw	United Artists, 1946	83208
Outlaw	United Artists, 1946	83209
Outlaw Josey Wales	Warner Brothers, 1976	83418
Painted People	First National, 1924	84234
Paradine Case	Selznick, 1948	83365
Paramount Exhibitor Book	Paramount, 1933	83933
Paris Bound	Pathé, 1929	83507
Paul Robeson in "Show Boat" by Freulich	Universal, 1936	83983
Penny Serenade	Columbia, 1941	83803
Pepe le Moko	DisCina, R-1940s	84111
Peter Pan	RKO, 1953	83025
Phantom From 10,000 Leagues	American Releasing Corp., 1955	84037
Phantom of the Opera	Universal, 1925	83725
Philadelphia Story	MGM, 1940	83807
Philadelphia Story	MGM, 1940	83806
Philadelphia Story	MGM, 1940	83805
Pickup	Columbia, 1951	83194
Pillow Talk	Universal International, 1959	84262
Pillow Talk	Universal International, 1959	84261
Pillow Talk	Universal International, 1959	83811
Pinocchio	RKO, 1940	83018
Plainsman	Paramount, 1936	83241
Planet of the Apes	20th Century Fox, 1968	84054
Planet of the Apes	20th Century Fox, 1968	84053
Playgirl	Universal International, 1954	84185
Pluto's Dream House	RKO, 1940	83004
Point Blank	MGM, 1967	84142
Poor Little Rich Girl	20th Century Fox, 1936	84199
Popeye in "King of the Mardi Gras"	Paramount, 1935	83037
Postman Always Rings Twice	MGM, 1946	83087
Postman Always Rings Twice	MGM, 1946	83086
Postman Always Rings Twice	MGM, 1946	83088
Practical Pig	RKO, 1939	83009
Pride of St. Louis	20th Century Fox, 1952	84306
Prince and the Showgirl	Warner Brothers, 1957	83892
Princess Comes Across	Paramount, 1936	83519
Princess Comes Across	Paramount, 1936	84242
Prisoner of Zenda	United Artists, 1937	84216
Prisoner of Zenda	United Artists, 1937	83491

TITLE	STUDIO	LOT
Private Detective 62	Warner Brothers, 1933	83060
Private Lives of Elizabeth and Essex	Warner Brothers, 1939	83479
Private Number	20th Century Fox, 1936	83537
Psycho	Paramount, 1960	83360
Psycho	Universal, R-1965	84026
Psycho	Paramount, 1960	83361
Psycho	Paramount, 1960	83362
Psycho	Paramount, 1960	83363
Psycho/ War of the Worlds Combo	Paramount, R-1965	84029
Puttin' On The Dog	MGM, R-1951	83030
Queen of Outer Space	Allied Artists, 1958	83189
Queen of Outer Space	Allied Artists, 1958	83681
Queen of Outer Space	Allied Artists, 1958	83682
Racketeers in Exile	Columbia, 1937	84107
Raiders of the Lost Ark	Paramount, 1981	84232
Range Feud	Columbia, 1931	83371
Reach for the Sky	Rank, 1956	83930
Rear Window	Paramount, 1954	84093
Rear Window	Paramount, R-1962	84092
Rear Window	Paramount, 1954	83355
Rear Window	Paramount, 1954	83354
Rebecca	United Artists, 1940	83342
Rebel Without a Cause	Warner Brothers, 1955	83579
Rebel Without a Cause	Warner Brothers, 1955	83580
Rebel Without a Cause	Warner Brothers, 1955	83578
Rebel Without a Cause	Warner Brothers, 1955	83577
Reckless	MGM, 1935	83531
Red Dragon	Monogram, 1945	84115
Red River	United Artists, 1948	84271
Red River	United Artists, 1948	83382
Redemption	Triumph, 1917	83695
Reform School Girl	American International, 1957	83200
Rembrandt	United Artists, 1936	83557
Reptilicus	American International, 1961	84046
Repulsion	Towa, 1965	84193
Rescue	United Artists, 1929	83474
Return of the Jedi	20th Century Fox/ Polfilm, 1984	83182
Revenge of the Creature	Universal International, 1955	83306
Revenge of the Creature	Universal International, 1955	83304
Revenge of the Creature	Universal International, 1955	83305
Revenge of the Creature/The Creature Walks Among Us Lot	Universal International, 1955-1956	83307
Revenge of the Jedi	20th Century Fox, 1982	83181
Revenge Rider	Columbia, 1935	84286
Rhythm of the Saddle	Republic, 1938	84281
Ride Him, Cowboy	Warner Brothers, 1932	83904
Ride, Ranger, Ride	Republic, 1936	83225
Riffraff	MGM, 1936	84161
Rio Bravo	Warner Brothers, 1959	83388
Rio Grande	Republic, 1950	83383
Rita Hayworth	Columbia, 1941	84333
Rita Hayworth in "Gilda" by Robert Coburn	Columbia, 1946	83967
Rita Hayworth in "My Gal Sal"	20th Century Fox, 1942	83968
Rita Hayworth in "Susan and God" by Laszlo Willinger	MGM, 1940	83969

TITLE	STUDIO	LOT
Rita Hayworth Royal Crown Cola Advertisement	1943	83819
RKO Exhibitor Book	RKO, 1934	84310
Road to Perdition	DreamWorks, 2002	84145
Roaring Twenties	Warner Brothers, 1939	83437
Robert Taylor by George Hurrell	MGM, 1930s	84014
Robot Monster	Astor Pictures, 1953	83687
Rocketship X-M	Lippert, 1950	83638
Rocketship X-M	Lippert, 1950	84028
Rocky	United Artists, 1977	84309
Rocky	United Artists, 1977	83715
Rodan! The Flying Monster	Toho/ DCA, 1957	84070
Rollerball	United Artists, 1975	83149
Roman Holiday	Paramount, 1953	83871
Roman Holiday	Paramount, 1953	83870
Romeo and Juliet	Rank, 1954	83610
Rope	Warner Brothers, 1948	83352
Rose of Washington Square	20th Century Fox, 1939	84201
Rough House Rosie	Paramount, 1927	83556
Ruling Passion	United Artists, 1922	84150
Rumpus in the Harem	Columbia, 1956	83790
Running Wild	Universal International, 1955	83197
Ruth Roland by Edwin Bower Hesser	1920s	84328
Ruth Roland by Lansing Brown	1920s	84327
Ruth Roland by Strauss Peyton	1922	84326
Saboteur	Universal, Late 1940s	84089
Saboteur	Universal, 1942	83344
Saboteur	Universal, late 1940s	84090
Saboteur	Universal,1958	83345
Sahara	Columbia, late 1940's	83452
Saigon	Paramount, 1948	84117
Salty O'Rourke	Paramount, 1945	84173
Samson and Delilah	Paramount, 1949	84167
San Fernando Valley	Republic, 1944	83230
Sands of Iwo Jima	Republic, 1950	83390
Sands of Iwo Jima	Republic, 1950	83929
Santa Fe Trail	Paramount, 1930	83231
Saul Bass Poster Lot	Art Krebs Screen Gallery, 1958-84	83574
Scarface	United Artists, R-1954	83435
Screaming Skull	American International, 1958	83742
Screen Snapshots	Screen Snapshots, Inc., 1920s	84147
Sea Hawk	Warner Brothers, 1940	84218
Sea Hawk	Warner Brothers, 1940	83481
Sea Hawk	Warner Brothers, 1940	83480
Sea Hawk	Warner Brothers, late 1940s	83482
Searchers	Warner Brothers, 1956	83385
Searchers	Warner Brothers, 1956	83384
Searchers	Warner Brothers, 1956	83919
Seven Year Itch	20th Century Fox, 1955	84256
Seven Year Itch	20th Century Fox, 1955	83888
Seven Year Itch	20th Century Fox, 1955	83890
Seven Year Itch	20th Century Fox, 1955	83889
Seven Year Itch	20th Century Fox, 1955	84257
Seventh Seal	Globe Films International, 1959	83615
Sex and the Single Sailor	William Mishkin Motion Pictures Inc., 1967	84269

TITLE	STUDIO	LOT
Shadow of the Eagle	Mascot, 1932	83392
Shadow of the Thin Man	MGM, 1941	83062
Shadow Strikes	Grand National, 1937	83052
Shall We Dance	RKO, 1937	83845
Shane	Paramount, 1953	83236
Shane	Paramount, 1953	83237
Shane	Paramount, 1953	83245
She	RKO, 1935	83718
She Married Her Boss	Columbia, 1935	83545
She-Creature	American International, 1956	83650
She-Creature	American International, 1956	83186
She-Creature	American International, 1956	83651
She's Dangerous!	Universal, 1937	84108
Shine On Harvest Moon	Republic, 1938	83229
Shipmates Forever	Warner Brothers - First National, 1935	84197
Shoot the Piano Player	Cocinor, 1960	83619
Show Boat	Universal, 1936	84200
Sign of the Cross	Paramount, 1932	84166
Sign of the Cross	Paramount, 1932	84165
Silent Men	Columbia, 1933	83216
Silent Men	Columbia, 1933	83221
Silly Symphony	United Artists, 1934	83005
Silly Symphony "Bugs in Love"	United Artists, 1932	83002
Silver Streak	RKO, 1934	83542
Singing Fool	Warner Brothers, 1927	83849
Sisters	Warner Brothers, 1938	83487
Sky Dragon	Monogram, 1949	84114
Slap Happy Sleuths	Columbia, 1950	83788
Sleeping Beauty	Buena Vista, 1959	84088
Slicked-Up Pup	MGM, 1950	83028
Smart Money	Warner Brothers, 1931	83431
Smartest Girl in Town	RKO, 1936	83548
Smilin' Through	MGM, R-1935	83508
Snow White and the Seven Dwarfs	RKO, 1937	83016
Snow White and the Seven Dwarfs	RKO, 1937	83015
Snow White and the Seven Dwarfs	RKO, 1937	84084
Snow White and the Seven Dwarfs	RKO, 1937	83017
Some Like It Hot	United Artists, 1959	83893
Some Like It Hot	United Artists, 1959	83894
Some Like It Hot	United Artists, 1959	83895
Some Like It Hot	United Artists, 1959	83896
Somewhere in Sonora	Warner Brothers - First National, 1933	83917
Somewhere in Sonora	Warner Brothers - First National, 1933	83916
Son of a Sailor	Warner Brothers - First National, 1933	84239
Son of Frankenstein	Universal, 1939	83261
Son of the Sheik	United Artists, 1926	83694
Song of Nevada	Republic, 1944	84283
Song of the South	RKO, 1946	83022
Sorry, Wrong Number	Paramount, 1948	84126
Spartacus	Universal International, R-1964	83925
Spider/ The Brain Eaters Combo	American International, 1958	83688
Splendor	United Artists, 1935	83550

TITLE	STUDIO	LOT
Spoilers	Paramount, 1930	83232
Spooks Run Wild	Monogram, 1941	83283
Sport Parade	RKO, 1932	83711
St. Louis Kid	Warner Brothers, 1934	84127
Stagecoach	United Artists, 1939	83906
Stagecoach	United Artists, 1939	83908
Stagecoach	United Artists, 1939	83907
Stagecoach	United Artists, 1939	83909
Stagecoach	United Artists, 1939	83910
Stagecoach	United Artists, 1939	83905
Stagecoach	R-1960	83911
Stagecoach War	Paramount, 1940	84279
Star Is Born	Warner Brothers, 1954	83857
Star Is Born	Warner Brothers, 1954	84207
Star of Midnight	RKO, 1935	83063
Star Wars	20th Century Fox, 1977	84057
Star Wars	20th Century Fox, 1977	83179
Star Wars	20th Century Fox, 1978	84058
Star Wars	20th Century Fox, 1977	84056
State Fair	Fox, 1933	83541
Stepin Fetchit	1930	84363
Stowaway	20th Century Fox, 1936	83867
Stowaway	20th Century Fox, 1936	83866
Strange Cargo	MGM, 1940	83339
Stranger	RKO, 1946	83104
Strangers May Kiss	MGM, 1931	83514
Strangers on a Train	Warner Brothers, 1951	83364
Strangers on a Train	Warner Brothers, 1951	84091
Strawberry Roan	Universal, 1933	83226
Streetcar Named Desire	Warner Brothers, 1951	84179
Sullivan's Travels	Paramount, 1941	83064
Sullivan's Travels	Paramount, 1941	83065
Sundown	United Artists, 1941	84299
Sunset Boulevard	Paramount, 1950	83092
Sunset Boulevard	Paramount, 1950	83091
Superman and the Mole Men	Lippert, 1951	83402
Superman and the Mole Men	Lippert, 1951	83401
Superman and the Mole Men	Lippert, 1951	83400
Superman in Exile	20th Century Fox, 1954	83403
Susannah of the Mounties	20th Century Fox, 1939	83863
Susannah of the Mounties	20th Century Fox, 1939	83864
Sylvia Sidney by Eugene Robert Richee	Paramount, 1930s	83976
Sylvia Sidney by Eugene Robert Richee	Paramount, 1937	83977
Sympathy for the Devil	New Line, 1970	83590
Tale of Two Cities	MGM, 1935	84169
Tales of Manhattan	20th Century Fox, 1942	83815
Tallulah Bankhead by George Maillard Kesslere	1930s	84374
Tarantula	Universal International, 1955	83666
Tarantula	Universal International, 1955	83665
Tarantula	Universal International, 1955	83158
Tarantula	Universal International, 1955	83664
Tarantula	Universal International, 1955	83159
Target Earth	Allied Artists, 1954	83647
Tarzan Finds a Son	MGM, 1939	83931
Teaserama	Beautiful Productions Inc., 1955	83192

TITLE	STUDIO	LOT
Teenage Caveman	American International, 1958	84040
Telegraph Trail	Warner Brothers, 1933	83380
Temptress	MGM, 1926	83528
Terror from the Year 5000	American International, 1958	83190
Terror from the Year 5000	American International, 1958	83680
Terry-Toons Stock Lobby Card	20th Century Fox, 1946	84085
Texas Terror	Monogram, 1935	83913
Texas Terror	Monogram, 1935	83912
That Hamilton Woman	Minerva Film, 1946	83558
Them!	Warner Brothers, 1954	83184
Them!	Warner Brothers, 1954	83669
Them!	Warner Brothers, 1954	83668
Theodora Goes Wild	Columbia, 1936	83802
There's No Business Like Show Business	20th Century Fox, 1954	83897
They Died With Their Boots On	Warner Brothers, 1947	84275
They Live by Night	RKO, 1948	83097
Thing From Another World	RKO, 1951	83654
Thing From Another World	RKO, 1951	83161
Things to Come	Film Classics, R-1947	84027
Things to Come	United Artists, 1936	83146
Third Man	Selznick, 1949	83118
This Gun for Hire	Paramount, 1947	83072
This Gun for Hire	Paramount, 1942	83073
This Gun for Hire	Paramount, 1942	83071
This Island Earth	Universal International, 1955	83645
Thomas Crown Affair	United Artists, 1968	84140
Three Caballeros	RKO, 1945	83011
Three Godfathers	MGM, 1936	84272
Three Little Pigs	RKO, R-1947	83010
Three Musketeers	Mascot, 1933	83393
Throne of Blood	Toho, 1957	83623
Thunderball	United Artists, 1965	83136
Thunderball	United Artists, 1965	83137
Thunderball	United Artists, 1965	83134
Thunderball	United Artists, 1965	83135
Tiger Shark	First National, 1932	83429
Time Machine	MGM, 1960	83659
Time Machine	MGM, 1960	83658
Titfield Thunderbolt	Universal, 1953	84260
T-Men	CID, 1950	83117
To Be or Not to Be	Metropole, 1947	83520
To Catch a Thief	Paramount, 1955	83346
To Catch a Thief	Paramount, 1955	83348
To Catch a Thief	Paramount, 1955	83347
To Kill a Mockingbird	Universal, 1963	84186
To Kill a Mockingbird	Universal, 1963	83564
To Kill a Mockingbird	Universal, 1963	83563
Tobor the Great	Republic, 1954	83167
Tobor the Great	Republic, 1954	83640
Tobor the Great	Republic, 1954	83639
Tombstone	Buena Vista, 1993	84295
Tooth Will Out	Columbia, 1951	83789
Top Hat	RKO, 1935	83844
Topper	Film Classics, R-1944	84250
Touch Of Evil	Universal International, 1958	83115
Touch Of Evil	Universal International, 1958	83116
Trail Beyond	Monogram, 1934	83915

TITLE	STUDIO	LOT
Trail Beyond	Monogram, 1934	83914
Trail of '98	MGM, 1928	83220
Transatlantic Merry-Go-Round	United Artists, 1934	83512
Tread Softly Stranger	Renown Pictures, 1958	83608
Treasure Island	MGM, 1934	84222
Treasure of the Sierra Madre	Warner Brothers, R-1952	83462
Treasure of the Sierra Madre	Warner Brothers, 1948	83461
Trespasser	United Artists, 1929	83704
Trespasser	United Artists, 1929	83703
Tumbleweeds	United Artists, 1925	83219
Two Girls on Broadway	MGM, 1940	84202
Two Mrs. Carrolls	Warner Brothers, 1947	84125
Two Women	Titanus, 1960	83605
Two Years Before the Mast	Paramount, 1946	84228
Undead	American International, 1957	83750
Unearthly	Republic, 1957	84033
Unholy Three	MGM, 1930	83724
Uninvited	Paramount, 1944	83288
Uninvited	Paramount, 1944	83289
United Artists Exhibitor Book	United Artists, 1930	83935
Unseen	Paramount, 1944	84066
Up the River	Fox, 1930	83445
Uptown New York	World Wide, 1932	84159
Vampire Bat	Majestic, 1933	83722
Van Johnson and Gloria DeHaven in "Scene of the Crime"	MGM, 1949	84365
Veronica Lake	Paramount, 1940s	83954
Veronica Lake	Paramount, 1940s	83953
Veronica Lake	Paramount, 1940s	84331
Veronica Lake	Paramount, 1940	84330
Veronica Lake	Paramount, 1940	84329
Veronica Lake	Paramount, 1941	83952
Veronica Lake by A.L. Whitey Schafer	Paramount, 1942	83955
Veronica Lake by A.L. Whitey Schafer	Paramount, 1944	84332
Vertigo	Paramount, 1958	84094
Vertigo	Paramount, R-1963	84095
Vertigo	Paramount, 1958	83350
Vigil in the Night	RKO, 1940	83518
Virginia City	Warner Brothers, Late 1940s	83490
Virginia City	Warner Brothers, 1940	83488
Virginia City	Warner Brothers, 1940	83489
Viva Las Vegas	MGM, 1964	83588

TITLE	STUDIO	LOT
Viva Las Vegas	MGM, 1964	84213
Voice of the City	MGM, 1929	83432
Wagons Roll at Night	Warner Brothers, 1941	84123
Wake of the Red Witch	Republic, 1949	84229
Wall Street	Columbia, 1929	83500
Walt Disney's Academy Award Revue	United Artists, 1937	83001
War of the Colossal Beast	American International, 1958	83183
War of the Colossal Beast	American International, 1958	83674
War of the Worlds	Paramount, 1953	83155
War of the Worlds	Paramount, R-1965	83628
War of the Worlds	Paramount, 1953	83629
War of the Worlds	Paramount, 1953	83156
Warner Brothers Cartoon Stock	Warner Brothers, 1946	83040
Warner Brothers Cartoon Stock	Warner Brothers, 1948	83041
Warner Brothers Stars of 1949 Promotional Poster	Warner Brothers, 1949	83443
Wasp Woman	Film Group, 1959	83662
Wasp Woman	Film Group, 1959	83663
Waterloo Bridge	Universal, 1931	83420
Way Out West	MGM, 1937	83786
We Went to College	MGM, 1936	83540
Weary River	First National, 1929	84156
Wee Willie Winkie	20th Century Fox, 1937	84224
Wee Willie Winkie	20th Century Fox, 1937	83865
Welcome Danger	Paramount, 1929	83778
West Side Story	United Artists, 1961	83327
Westfront 1918	Cine-Studio, 1930	83921
What a Widow!	United Artists, 1930	83705
What Wives Want	Universal, 1923	84157
Whatever Happened to Baby Jane?	Warner Brothers, 1962	84075
When Worlds Collide	Paramount, 1951	83630
While the City Sleeps	RKO, 1956	84133
Whispering Devils	Equity, 1920	84148
White Cargo	MGM, 1942	84171
White Christmas	Paramount, 1954	83838
White Christmas	Paramount, 1954	84209
White Heat	Warner Brothers, 1949	84129
White Heat	Warner Brothers, 1949	83442
White Hell of Pitz Palu	Universal, 1929	83716
White Hell of Pitz Palu	Universal, 1930	83717
White Zombie	United Artists, 1932	83256
Whoopee!	United Artists, 1930	84196

TITLE	STUDIO	LOT
Why Bring That Up?	Paramount, 1929	83769
Why Girls Leave Home	PRC, 1945	84267
Wicker Man	Lion International, 1973	83743
Widow's Might	Paramount, 1918	83696
Wild Horse Mesa	Paramount, 1932	83223
Wild One	Columbia, 1953	84180
Wild One	Columbia, 1953	84181
Wild Party	Paramount, 1929	83553
William Powell and Myrna Loy in "The Great Ziegfeld" by Clarence Sinclair Bull	MGM, 1936	84322
Willy Wonka & the Chocolate Factory	Paramount, 1971	84082
Winchester '73	Universal International, 1950	83239
Winchester '73	Universal International, 1950	83238
Wizard of Oz	MGM, 1939	83852
Wizard of Oz	MGM, 1939	83851
Wolf Man	Universal, 1941	83272
Wolf Man	Universal, 1941	83273
Woman in Green	Universal, 1945	83056
Words and Music	Fox, 1929	83534
Written on the Wind/ All That Heaven Allows Lot	Universal International, 1955-1956	84183
Wrong Man	Warner Brothers, 1957	83357
Wuthering Heights	United Artists, 1939	83559
X - The Man With the X-Ray Eyes	American International, 1963	84045
Yankee Doodle Dandy	Warner Brothers, 1942	84204
Yellow Submarine	United Artists, 1968	83598
Yellow Submarine	United Artists, 1968	83591
Yodelin' Kid from Pine Ridge	Republic, 1937	83227
Yojimbo	Toho, 1961	83622
Yojimbo	Toho, 1961	83621
You Only Live Twice	United Artists, 1967	83139
You Only Live Twice	United Artists, 1967	83138
You Were Never Lovelier	Columbia, 1942	83817
You Were Never Lovelier	Columbia, 1942	83816
You'll Never Get Rich	Columbia, 1941	84203
Young America	Fox, 1932	83539
Young Eagles	Paramount, 1930	83499
Youth Runs Wild	RKO, 1944	83094
Ziegfeld Follies	MGM, 1945	83847
Ziegfeld Follies	MGM, 1945	83846